STUDIES IN THE EARLY ENGLISH PERIODICAL

STUDIES
IN THE
EARLY ENGLISH
PERIODICAL

EDITED BY

RICHMOND P. BOND

GREENWOOD PRESS, PUBLISHERS
WESTPORT, CONNECTICUT

Library of Congress Cataloging in Publication Data

Bond, Richmond Pugh, 1899-   ed.
  Studies in the early English periodical.

  Reprint of the 1957 ed. published by the University of
North Carolina Press, Chapel Hill.
  Includes bibliographical references and index.
  1. English periodicals--History--Addresses, essays,
lectures. I. Title.
[PN5116.B6 1977]   052   77-8233
ISBN 0-8371-9683-3

To

ROBERT BURTON HOUSE

Chancellor of the University of North Carolina

Chapel Hill

1945-1957

However, the *Variety* of Matters, and *Brevity* of each *Essay*, I hope, will please those Gentlemen for whose sake I publish it; for, as mean as my Performance is, I may without Vanity call this GENTLEMAN'S LIBRARY, *A Large BOTANICK GARDEN;* wherein there are *Fruits* for the *Palate*, *Simples* for the *Health*, *Flowers* for the *Eye*, *Rarities* for the *Curious*, *Walks* for *Recreation*, *Arbors* for *Refreshment*, and something or other to entertain every Gentleman that walks in it.

The Post-Angel, January, 1702

Contents

INTRODUCTION

INTRODUCTION

RICHMOND P. BOND

THE PERIODICAL is usually a series of numbered and dated issues produced under a continuing title on a definite frequency for an indefinite period. It differs from a collection of related pamphlets or allied books in its very periodicity, and from its older, often mercurial, brother-in-print the newspaper in that the latter is more concerned with momentary matters and proceeds on a less leisurely course. The periodical is a publishing enterprise with editorial problems of contents and methods and deadlines, with business problems of production and circulation and solvency. Every issue of a periodical is a unit in serialization subject to the limitations and challenges of date, length, format, audience, purpose, material, techniques, editorship, authorship, and temper of the time; each number is a part of a whole.

I

It is the purpose of this essay to provide an introduction to the early periodic press in England, more specifically for the years from 1700 to 1760, by way of, first, an illustration of its great growth and a brief summary of the contemporary forces responsible for this enlargement, second, a condensed account of the several major and minor types of periodicals in production, and, third, a short view of scholarship past and potential in this domain of the early press. Such a general prologue to a symposium of individual studies will, it is hoped, help to guide the junior specialist in Augustan England and its journalism as well as to reinforce his senior in the true doctrine.

The seventeenth century was in the history of the periodic press a time of many beginnings, a few conclusions, and much fruitful evolution. During the period 1620-1700 seven hundred titles—newspapers and periodicals—were offered to the public, but the very great majority soon collapsed from exhaustion or starvation. The following century possessed its own origins and a remarkable extension in journalism literary and non-literary. Close to nine hundred papers were in press during the first six decades of the eighteenth century, and the number grew with the century. As to the rate of increase, in the years 1671-75 only five papers appeared in print, and in 1684-87 only thirteen; during 1701, the first year of the new century, a good two dozen journals were in operation, and the number more than doubled by the end of Anne's reign; by the accession of the third George one hundred papers were issued in a year; and the periodic productions of the final year of the century were ten times the number of those in the first year. In sum, during the one hundred eighty years preceding the nineteenth century, periodicals and newspapers in the British Isles steadily increased to a total of approximately twenty-five hundred different publications.

The titles and subtitles show a flagrant duplication and imitativeness. The lustiest vogue in titles was the use of the word *Mercurius* in the seventeenth century, when eightscore papers chose the god of tidings (and of merchants and thieves) for the noun of their names and appended an individual Latin adjective, from *Academicus* to *Zeteticus*, or simply appropriated an already popular combination, like *Mercurius Anglicus, Aulicus, Britannicus, Civicus,* or *Democritus.* Inevitably in such heavy conforming to custom a casual wit would mock the style or affect the unorthodox— thus *Mercurius Fumigosus, Infernus, Somniosus, Insanus Insanissimus,* and *Mercuriorum Stultissimus.* From time to time other fashions in titles were generated from the strength of a powerful paper, as witness the Restoration *Pacquet of Advice, Heraclitus Ridens,* and *Observator.* In the eighteenth century, newspapers favored titles containing the commonplace *Advertiser, Chronicle, Courant, Gazette, Intelligence(r), Journal, Mercury, News,* and *Post;* magazines and reviews usually elected so to be titled; and numerous *Tatlers* and *Spectators* proclaimed their titular heritage. In several cases—the *Free-Thinker, Plain Dealer, Female Spectator,* and *Rambler*—a celebrated journal adopted, perhaps unawares, the title of an obscure elder. The frequency of a paper often was stated in the title, as was its place of origin.

But all was not tiresome mimicry and prosaic propriety. There were efforts to be unique or engaging, for example, the *Busy-Body*, *Conjurer*, *Comedian*, *Con-Test*, *Crab-Tree*, *Devil*, *Elixir*, *Grouler*, *Hue and Cry*, *Inquisitor*, *Knight-Errant*, *Midwife*, *Orphan*, *Parrot*, *Tell-Tale*, and *Titt for Tatt*. In general, however, the formula for a title included brevity, indication of type or time or town, and convention, but not startling originality. The multiplication of identical titles, it should be added, brings less confusion than does the not infrequent mutation of title or subtitle or both within the conduct of a single journal. These turns in title resulted from publishing mergers, from a desire to widen the audience or change the purpose or gain variety, from the flux of affairs, from editorial whim or boredom. To give a major instance of alteration, Defoe used four variations upon *Review* during its thirteen years; to cite a minor, the *Weekly Remembrancer* of 1702 appeared under four different full names in its first six issues.

These early periodicals and newspapers had the largest possible range of continuance. Many journals started and ended with the same number. But the full course of the official *London Gazette*, initiated as the *Oxford Gazette* in 1665, and of the majestic *Philosophical Transactions of the Royal Society*, begun the same year, is not yet run. Before 1700 a life of ten years was unusual, but during the years from 1700 to 1760 the twelve most successful newspapers accumulated a total of some four hundred annual volumes.

The ruling place of publication remained London, the same for journal and pamphlet and book. But the provinces grew active, in news journals and then in magazines, partly as the result of improved postal service; during the first twenty-five years of the eighteenth century newspapers were instituted in as many provincial towns, and during the first sixty years six country centers (Bath, Bristol, Exeter, Manchester, Newcastle, and York) averaged eight journals, most of them papers of news.

An ample portion of this impressive development of British newspapers and periodicals occurred during the reigns of Anne and Georges I and II, and this growth was encouraged, of course, by the conditions of those years, conditions intellectual, social, religious, political, literary, cultural, military, and economic, conditions which strongly affected papers of news, or pertained more directly to periodicals, or related to the whole of periodic publication. All of these large and friendly circumstances were certainly not confined to the three reigns which are the specific zone of this volume, and each circumstance, general and special, is known in some degree to the experienced student of the age. These major influences are here assembled only as a body of reminders or suggestions for a closer understanding of the rise of the early English press.

The general condition which affected most deeply the Augustan decades in England was the state of mind, or point of view, then clearly characteristic of European civilization—the Enlightenment. And this intellectual awakening, enlargement, and change can be estimated as the most powerful force in the augmentation of the serial press, which itself assisted in the activities of Reason. Drawing its ideas and its conduct from the words of such philosophers as Bacon, Descartes, and even Hobbes and later from the works of the capacious John Locke and Berkeley and Hume, from the advances in science so definitely represented by the Royal Society and its longtime president, Sir Isaac Newton, and from other sources less renowned, the Enlightenment promulgated a strong emphasis on rational processes, tolerance, universality, progress, scientific search, individual freedom, and practical enterprise. These attitudes and procedures quickened the philosophical, scientific, economic, social, religious, and political issues of Britain during the years between the accession of Anne and the death of the second George, a period stable but not inactive, and indeed gave later generations of Englishmen and their kinsmen over the globe an armament for man's mastery of his world.

All of these areas of rationalistic action were in varying degrees entered by the press. In philosophy the nature of mind and knowledge, of man as self and social being; in science the empirical exploration of the universe and the application of mathematical principles to physical phenomena and the development of new techniques and instruments; in economics the improvements in agriculture and industry, the projects of specific trade, and the theories of international commerce—these matters underlay serious reading. In the arena of manners and morals endless opportunities arose for the periodical use of a reasonable and urbane persuasion:

gambling, duelling, masquerades, immorality, profaneness and profanation of God's Day, extreme fashions in dress, poor manners, and many more were the follies of life to be lashed and laughed at, with or without effect, in the periodic press. Religion and the Church furnished doctrines and traditions and ceremonies for hebdomadal debate: such themes as Latitudinarianism, the Newtonian physico-theology, Evangelicalism, the Bangorian Controversy, ecclesiastical preferments, Conformity Occasional and constant, and the fast alliance of State and Church endowed strong-minded and strong-willed contention; Quaker, Roman, Jew, Wesleyan, Deist, and Non-Juror each held in fealty his private problems and his public relations, and Big- and Little-Endians made their wars with phrases to be read as well as heard. In politics and statecraft the new age of the Glorious Revolution and the primacy of Parliament brought many topics, major and minor and medium in significance, into the papers of report and opinion—the idea of a patriot king, the Succession at home and abroad, the rights and duties of Lords and Commons, the counsel and performances of the leading ministers from "Volpone" Godolphin to the elder Pitt, the principles and practices of the parties and their cliques, control and free expression, foreign policy and colonial management, national finance, and such a spectacle as the trial of the plutonic Dr. Sacheverell. In literature and the criticism of literature the Enlightenment offered a strengthening of central sanity, a heightening of formal decorum, a reinforcement of judicious methods, and a profusion of propositions for artistic solution. The Battle of the Books was not won for good and all, and could never be: the force of critical authority and the competitive veneration of the ancients could quarrel with and compromise with a rule of reason and independent analysis, and many battles of books could break quills over standards of literary and dramatic success. Periodicals and newspapers were available as convenient media for the publication of creative and critical works if of moderate length. Science bestowed new subjects and attitudes on the poet and the proseman, but it demanded that prose style exchange the complex, leisurely, or cadenced period for a more precise composition of the clearest words in their logical places—a simplification of word and syntax which had a ready agent in the periodic press.

Moreover, in the Augustan age scientific rationalism found a hearty complement, of course, in the responses of emotion and the deep resources of spiritual belief; this accessory supply of sentiment produced or participated in desires toward reform, benevolism, egalitarianism, and philosophic optimism, most of which gained later fulfillment. The period of the energetic growth of the press contained its due amount of normal human passions often controlled by the effort to enlighten or be enlightened but also often directed into the fevers of sentimentalism or the bitter fires of bigotry. Whether mind or heart guided the idea of the season, the periodical publication made it manifest.

The chronicle of the liberty of the early press, a topic as tender as perplexed, is the history of printing interests, democratic desires, confident idealism, and the relationships of King and Parliament and people; it is, however, plainly writ that the increased political freedom of the eighteenth century gave no small momentum to the increase of the newspaper and periodical. During the Puritan Revolution, Parliament won control of the printing trade, exercised with the assistance of the Company of Stationers; the official newspaper made its beginning as a means of regulation; and the courts of law supplanted the Star Chamber and the Court of High Commission. Under the restored monarchy Printing Acts to regulate and license the press succeeded and failed according to a complex of conditions, and Sir Roger L'Estrange as Surveyor of the Press is remembered for strongly wielding his authority. Parliament kept and used its power by prosecuting "libels" against it and by a steadfast prohibition of reporting its proceedings, relenting only to permit publication of its votes. The *London Gazette* became the permanent organ of the government, and most of the years from the arrival of Charles to the departure of his brother were lean for the publisher of news or comment. With the Revolution of 1688 the prerogative of the King became the right of Parliament; in 1695 the Regulation of Printing Act was refused renewal, and licensing was proscribed as incompetent. The press did not by any means win full freedom under the last of the Stuarts and the first two Hanoverians, but the control became more indirect and less arbitrary. The "taxes on knowledge," first levied in 1712 on copies of newspapers and pamphlets, on advertisements, and on paper, and increased by the Stamp Acts of 1724 and 1757, brought revenue and an economic control. Various papers received tangible encouragement, and writers of front rank and of the craft of Grub accepted money or office. Taxation and subsidization were supplemented by criminal prosecutions for seditious libel, and Parliament could be zealous in its own cause. But strong control was better than strenuous suppression, and the conditions of serial publication were freer under Walpole than under Cromwell and Charles. The party system required an active press, and the Whigs and Tories severely criticized each other; and many were the issues of papers published in the eighteenth century which could not have been printed in the seventeenth. Parliament in time lost its long war to keep its deliberations secret, and in more time the British periodic press itself debated its liberty in terms of public responsibility and general welfare.

The entire scene of publication expanded in the eighteenth century with the growth of the reading public, which increased as the population itself grew, in England from about five and a half millions in 1700 to seven in 1760. The charity, grammar, and public schools and the private academies, though often suffering fluctuating fortunes generally or individually, taught thousands of boys and girls (the latter more genteelly) and were the principal contribution of the age to educational progress. And the press affected its own extension and power. Newspapers gathered new and more readers, who proceeded to incite more and new papers, and journalistic contest begot fresh titles. Success such as that of the *Spectator* and the *Gentleman's Magazine* provoked a large effort to share in the prestige and profits of recognition. Energetic booksellers were sensitive to their own triumphs and to any potential enlargement of audience, women included. The booksellerpublishers often had the initiative and capital to set up a new journal, given a likely editor and a fruitful old field or a promising new one; distribution was not a great problem in the tight metropolis, and a sale of five hundred copies of a half-sheet paper would pay its way if the author were not too dear, with advertisements extra. A complex rivalry in the trade stimulated a healthy competition for readers and writers. Pamphlets occasional or connected remained a staple of fugitive publication, but the periodic press was increasingly preferred by writer, publisher, and public for its frequency and reliability of operation and its constancy of title, format, price, and policy.

In the interval between 1700 and 1760 the growth of the periodical press was enhanced in its merit and prestige by the participation of writers of the first and the second order—lords of letters like Defoe, Steele, Addison, Swift, Fielding, Johnson, Goldsmith, and Smollett, and such gentry as Hughes, Budgell, Ambrose Philips, Aaron Hill, Theobald, Bolingbroke, Lady Mary Wortley Montagu, Akenside, Chesterfield, Joseph Warton, Murphy, Colman, and Thornton. The noble patronage of the seventeenth century had not fully passed into party subvention, but the status of the professional writer and the monetary advantages of editing and contributing to periodicals had ascended to the point where a talented man of letters could without great loss of dignity sell his sentences to a serial publication. The diversion of creative writers into party service can be in part explained by political conviction and in larger part by economic conditions, these men being mortal and wishing so to remain. And the amateur writer could gain a bright renown in the periodical press. The ideas and the skill of the accomplished author, with or without price, gave a fame and a worth essential to the literary, learned development of the press, which in its expansion was able to attract his cooperation—a correlative good fortune.

During half of the first sixty years of the eighteenth century England was at foreign war, with France the favorite enemy on the European Continent and the American. In Anne's reign the famous victories of Marlborough were both cause and signal of England's emergence as a great force in the Western world, and this major motion into power clearly encouraged the rise of journalism. The progress of a campaign in foreign lands and seas always provides the best material for news and comment; reports of Englishmen marching on the fields of Austria or of men-of-war sailing to engage the enemy promote national pride and glory. The business of the English Succession, the strong roots of Stuart faith, the importation of a German-minded prince never to become a fully naturalized king—these matters made news and polemics, but they did not disrupt the island as did the fratricide of Puritan and Cava-

lier in the past century.   Peace too had its uses, such as the calcula-
tion of the spoils of victory, the prospects of future alliances, the
resumption of moderate pursuits, and the recovery of more normal
commercial conditions, all suitable subjects for periodic report and
rumination.

The increased prosperity of the period furnished economic support for a growing press.   The productivity of "England's green
and pleasant land" was being enlarged through better farming
methods; many manufactures multiplied; both imports and ex-
ports grew, as well as inland trade.   From sea to sea British bot-
toms were carrying cloth, rum, tobacco, tea and coffee, naval stores,
metal ware, peltry, black men and women, and many another
article of profitable exchange.   The East India Company and the
traffic to the West Indies and North American colonies contributed
to the mercantile welfare of a fatherland more concerned with
imperialistic exploitation than judicious paternalism.   The problem
of the poor, to be sure, and that of the debtor were not squarely
faced, and the lot of the working classes was a restricted one; there
were occasional strikes and riots, a few corn shortages and corresponding years of inflation, and such a major financial crisis as the
deflation of the South Sea Bubble.   But in the final balance the
conditions of commerce were such as to build the thriving public
that would cause more newspapers and periodicals to live longer
and larger lives.

The middle class, elastic in its limits, by the eighteenth century
had achieved a strength and a consciousness of strength which would
remain a groundwork for the power of the Isles of Britain.   Given
to trade, diligence, thrift, moral rectitude, Godliness, sentiment,
humanitarianism, curiosity, the glorious principles of the Revolution, social and cultural ambitions, and a belief in the useful and
material, the citizen of the middle class had the ability first to buy
and then to read the papers which informed him of what he wished
or needed to know and the journals which could promote his
several aspirations.   The lower class had insufficient resources,
financial and literate, to sustain a large periodic press, and the
upper class was too small.   The middle class found a journalism to
serve its interest whether physical or mental or emotional or spiritual, and Daniel Defoe was its major prophet and master of the

flying sheet; this strong group inevitably strengthened the development of the press, which in turn gave the benefits of public expression. To the man of the middle place the journalistic press has remained not uncongenial—the newspaper and the periodical are not forbidding to him as reading matter, but appeal to his desire for current information and the easy occupation of an odd or tired hour.

The gregarious character of the Augustan period has become one of its clearest marks, with the club and the coffee-house as exceptionally fortunate institutions in the evolution of English society. When and where men of a feather could meet with frequency, stretch their legs, find comfort in a long pipe and stimulation in a dish of coffee or chocolate, and have their talk out, they sought and found the news of the hour, the speculations of the week. In these "penny universities" the papers lay at hand for common reading, silent and oral too, and the observations of one's neighbor across the table could be answered or not. What of the rivalry 'twixt the Tatling Esquire and his female competitor Mrs. Crackenthorpe? What were the simultaneous findings of the *Review*, *Examiner*, and *Medley*? Had the *Gentleman's Magazine* withstood the newer *London Magazine*, and was the young *Critical Review* superior to the established *Monthly*? The individual exchange of the smoking, drinking, talking, reading assembly —a school for news and views—was the best alliance between the social habit and the periodic press; but there is also a sociality in the private reading of journals being read by many other people, a kind of consociation in receiving printed words, perhaps preparatory to spoken analysis the next evening or an argumentative retort the next encounter.

Thus the spacious growth and development of the periodic press from 1700 to 1760 derived from a number of conditions in society, forming a constitution of affairs suggested here as both simple and interrelated, physical and abstract. Several of these causes for the increase of the press acted also as results because the press in turn affected its age. But in one respect the press did not advance—the concrete means of production adding nothing to the general expansion. The method of manufacturing the printed word stayed basically the same as in the years of Caxton, Shakespeare, and Dryden.

The handpress had a limited capacity in a working day, so for speedy production the use of multiple presses was necessary unless a special arrangement with a printing colleague relieved the urgency on man and machine in the shop of origin. The productive facilities for manifolding copies of journals (and books) remained constant until the next century, and so the mechanical situation in Augustan England demanded additional composition and presswork to bring forth more and larger newspapers and periodicals. The periodic press grew because the amount of printing activity grew with and for it, not because the procedures of operation improved in the printshop.

The British press did not by any means at any time exist or thrive as an isolated, parochial institution. The circumstances of the rise of the various types of English journals often had similarities to the conditions affecting French, German, Dutch, Scandinavian, Italian, Spanish, and even Russian journalism; and direct influences, through models and translations, often crossed the Channel in both directions. The newspaper itself was not an English invention, and, indeed, some of the first English corantos were published in Amsterdam; and later the review consistently drew upon its foreign contemporaries. The best example of English influence on Continental serials is the contribution of the informal journal of morals and manners, with the *Tatler* and *Spectator* as the original documents in this comparative journalism. And scholarship and science being international, the learned journal and the scientific periodical benefited from the exchange of influence to become the most European sort of serial. Equally manifest is the westward course of the periodic press from England to her American colonies, which learned the advantages and arts and crafts of serial production and used the papers from home for convenient extraction and imitation. The early American press was naturally late in its importations and for a term remained meager and derivative, but by the time of George the Third it had well begun its endless journalistic rivalry.

It may bravely be presumed that our current generation has few points of union with the period two centuries earlier because of the interposing Revolutions—the Industrial, American, French, Communist, and Nuclear Revolutions. But, despite these massive movements and the plain or subtle mutations in life, this living age obviously has many roots in the Augustan, and one of them is that of the press. Exclusive of the modern scientific processes in communication and manufacture, major portions of the techniques, types, and purposes of newspapers and periodicals today have forebears in the reigns of Anne and the first two Georges. There has been more temperate continuity than radical change, and be it granted that the essay journal by Steele and Addison has not been surpassed in the whirligig of journalistic progress.

II

No system of classification by type of the twenty-five hundred journals prior to the nineteenth century can be comprehensive and consistent; chance and change, initiative and rivalry, and the differences among publishers, editors, writers, and readers saw to it that the press, from daily to annual, held to no firm limits of kind. Even the major distinction between newspaper and periodical—that of emphasis upon current affairs—became obscured when each printed material logically the component of the other. The journal of news very frequently contained an essay or essay-letter, as today a newspaper may include an editorial suitable to any season and embrace such features as a bridge column, a department of domestic or tender counsel, and a section of something called "comics." Conversely, a periodical often published records of happenings for the convenience of its clientele. Likewise, journals with or without news made at times a mixture of literary forms: the *Spectator* included forms other than the essay, and the *British Apollo* regularly gave questions and answers in verse as well as prose.

The newspaper, bearing the current archives of events in the great city, the provinces, and the lands beyond the oceans, became an industry in eighteenth century England and a necessity to the English in their view of the world. What was new, what was recent, what was imminent gathered a greater interest as the times changed and men and manners with them. And the advertisements themselves offered news of services and commodities—instruction, books and pamphlets and journals, plays and operas and assorted entertainments, prints and pictures, auctions and lotteries and financial opportunities, notices of strayed persons and animals, rewards for things lost or stolen, houses and furniture, horses and coaches, potables of any power, tobacco and fruit, cosmetics and jewelry, clothes and fabrics, medical devices for each disease and distress, and a nest of miscellanea. These "Accounts of News from the little World" were consumed by thousands for their mercantile purposes as well as for entertainment, and these advertisements, in periodicals as in newspapers, now remain rivals to the columns of dispatches as the glass of fashion of their day and a museum of antique goods with prices attached.

The eighteenth century inherited from the very late seventeenth century the *Post Boy, Post-Man,* and *Flying-Post;* the *Daily Courant,* the first successful daily paper, began its reign with Queen Anne; later the *Evening Post, Weekly Journals* by Read and by Mist (who became Fog for safety), *Applebee's Original Weekly Journal, St. James's Evening Post, Whitehall Evening-Post, London Journal, Daily Post, Craftsman, London Evening-Post, Daily Advertiser, General Evening Post,* and *London Daily Post and General Advertiser* had long careers before the third George began his; and, of course, the *London Gazette* continued as the organ of the nation, officially written and officially read. The paper of news in the eighteenth century increased in number of titles and pages, in size, in power, and in variety of contents; it did not multiply appreciably in circulation, probably because of strong competition and taxes. As the century moved, the newspaper was itself a competitor of the periodical by embracing its more general type of article and department.

Setting aside the newspaper, we find that in the periodical the most satisfactory process of division is one founded on literary form and reinforced by a consideration of subject matter. In the eighteenth century the essay journal, the miscellany-magazine, and the review became the principal types of periodicals, and the journals of learned articles, historical summary, dialogue, questions and answers, poetry, fiction, and letters acted the lesser parts. Journals of specialized subjects and vocations can be included in these several types but for convenience can also be denominated according to their content. Another criterion for grouping is that of intention, such as the will to instruct and the effort to please, a difference often suffering from uncertainty or oversimplification.

Periodicals may also be marshalled, for particular purposes, by title, date, frequency, place of issue, and format. And there is always the test of inherent excellence, which can range from the highest grade of worth to the lowest. The conspectus of the greater and smaller types of periodicals which follows will consider them on the footing of form as they made their appearance in the special period of this volume, 1700-60, with some note of their antecedents.

The essay journal, headed by the incomparable *Tatler* and *Spectator*, was the type of early periodical which gathered the highest literary renown and became one of England's Augustan ornaments. In the seventeenth century excellent essays had appeared by Bacon, Felltham, Cowley, Dryden, and others, but they were not periodical essays nor did they constitute an essay periodical. Essays published as single works of expository prose or collections of pieces by the same hand were quite another thing from essays subject to journalistic conditions, such as space and frequency, audience and style, and the purpose and concord of the periodical in hand. The first essays serially published may be found in the mid-century *Mercuriuses* which had no news to retail or which chose merely to debate the cause of King or Parliament. Such papers of comment, grave here, jocular there, and positive almost everywhere, were at best a hard and hasty school for writers—the experienced Milton considered "it were a folly to commit any thing elaborately compos'd to the carelesse and interrupted listening of these tumultuous times." Even when no civil war compromised men's minds a licensed press provided little proper circumstance for the writing, printing, and receiving of an essay sheet cast "in the cool element of prose." Late in the century a few papers attempted the serialization of sectarian commentary. Such was the *Weekly Pacquet of Advice from Rome: or, The History of Popery,* 1678-83 and briefly revived in 1689, composed of a sizable, serious, learned essay and a final leaf much lighter called "The Popish Courant." *Pacquets* followed from Germany, Geneva (twice), and Ireland.

During the final years of William's reign and the first of Anne's there came into short life a number of journals thrown into essay form, or something similar, with little skill and often a flavor of bawdry. Some of these titles have been represented as predecessors of the *Tatler* and *Spectator:* the *Momus Ridens*, 1690, and *English Lucian*, 1698, for the dating of advices from different places in the manner of Bickerstaff's departments; the *Mercurius Eruditorum*, 1691, for the club device; the *Weekly Comedy* of 1699 and *Humours of a Coffee-House* of 1707 for the use of the dramatis personae; the *Infallible* and the *Jesting Astrologer*, both of 1700, for satire on Partridge the quack. Other periodicals of better fame have likewise been suggested as possible influences on Steele's reforming motive, essay-letters, inclusion of verse and literary criticism, and development of the single essay. The *Weekly Entertainment* of 1700 and *Mercurius Theologicus* of 1700-1 have been cited as anticipations of Steele in style and purpose; they were, to be sure, upright essay journals, but they had little to offer Mr. Bickerstaff. No proving of such sources or influences is possible, and no disproof. Steele did not require suggestion in the journalistic habit of dating dispatches or in the anti-Partridgean business; the Club in the *Spectator* did not closely resemble any earlier group, and there was no governing board in the *Tatler;* verses and reviews and essays had, of course, appeared in large plenty. Steele may have selected from any or all of these various periodicals some of the devices, procedures, and kinds of content he wished to put in operation; he may have chosen among them unknowingly as one employs a forgotten sight or something once read; and he may have been but slightly affected by certain minor periodical publications prior to the *Tatler*. At any rate, the total effective influences come not to the sum of the *Tatler* itself, not by a long chalk; say all the parts were old, the union of them was new. To go beyond the dredging of sources, the reasons behind the magnificence of merit in the *Tatler* and *Spectator* would seem to lie less in periodical precedents or even in the circumstances of the age than in the keen enterprise of Steele and the elegant brilliance of Addison and their complementary collaboration.

The most considerable monument of essay journalism was made by the never idle Daniel Defoe—his *Review* of events and policies in the spheres of statecraft, economics, and morality. For eleven years Defoe wrote his journal of opinion in a mood of moderation: nine volumes of the regular issues from 1704 to 1713, augmented by prefaces, five long monthly supplements, and twenty-three numbers of the separate but related *Little Review*. The weekly, then semi-weekly, then tri-weekly papers were given to an essay or two and, for a season, a concluding section called "Advice from the Scandalous Club," proposed as "a little Diversion, as any thing occurs to make the World Merry." It was in this appended account of "Nonsense, Impertinence, Vice and Debauchery" that Defoe printed and answered letters and thrust at a variety of socio-moral evils. The letters he received and felt an obligation to answer flowed over into the supplementary papers. Defoe wrote with point and spirit, and his view of affairs comprehended such a mass of deed and theory for so long that his performance stands as the most remarkable single achievement in the history of professional journalism. The *Review* was certainly the most important essay sheet to precede the *Tatler*, and Defoe as predecessor and contemporary may well have indirectly encouraged Steele in the general adoption of editorial seriousness and in the special pursuit of reform, and also stimulated him in the employment of eidolon, correspondence, single essay, and minor serial techniques. And Mr. Review from his close reading of Mr. Bickerstaff very likely drew elements to emulate. Such a mutual though unequal debt is a happy source of the prosperity accomplished by the early English journal of essays.

On the day in April of 1709 that Isaac Bickerstaff, Esq., produced his first *Tatler*, Defoe had entered his fourth volume; ten weeks later he was naming Bickerstaff "that excellent Anatomist of the Ages Follies" and calling on him to add to his anatomy of the Pretty Fellow one of the Idle Fellow. The *Review* remained friendly to the *Tatler* and *Spectator*, which though cousins-german lived different lives as essay periodicals. Indeed, the *Tatler* and *Spectator*, so often associated as if brothers of one birth, were different from each other in frequency, use of the eidolon and club device and departmentalization, division of authorship, and some sorts of content. They were similar, certainly, in other important ways—format, editorship, principal authorship, literary forms and style, general substance, and dominant purpose. Whatever editorial devices and traits Steele received from antecedents, the *Spectator* had need of only one predecessor, the *Tatler*. These two journals, publishing 906 half-sheets during most of 1709-12 and half of

1714, brought something vernal to the reign of good Queen Anne, "Culture's palmiest day." They united the desires to amend morals, improve manners, and elevate taste, and they proceeded, the first on a tri-weekly schedule and the other on a diurnal and later tri-weekly frequency, to present in the public interest their ideas and ideals "in such a manner, as even pleased" the Town. The ironical sallies, the turns of wit, the easy imagery, the learning fairly worn, and the wisdom of gentility animated essays on social life, man- and womankind, belles lettres, daily philosophy, and high religion. The *Tatler* and *Spectator* laced rather than diluted their essays with correspondence both genuine and minted for the issue, studies of people single and assembled, fictions apposite and true, and a taste of old and new poetry. All these elements of form and substance Steele and Addison wove into the continuity of a serial publication to be read at home and coffee-house. The immediate success of Messrs. Bickerstaff and Spectator, as well as their long dominion in the literary press, came from their very real proficiency in periodical procedures, their direction of diversity into unity, and, perhaps best, their mastery of the middle style, where graceful urbanity joined with vigorous simplicity.

The tremendous reputation of the *Tatler* and *Spectator* has endured as one of the verities of literary history. Immediately they were read and quoted and discussed and imitated. Volumes of reprinted essays began to appear before all the folio numbers had been printed, and for the remainder of the century editions of one or the other of the two journals were issued on an average of once a year and continued as a favorite publisher's project well into the nineteenth century. Mr. Spectator had said that "Imitation is a kind of artless Flattery," and imitations of the *Tatler* and *Spectator* indeed flattered them abundantly. When the writer approached the manner of the originals and had something to say, the imitation won its way, but when he preferred the accidentals to the substantives, his imitation mustered with its colleagues in oblivion. It is a good history, and a poor one.

The essay journal, derivative or independent, served the purpose of politics, religion, popular philosophy, and literature and the theater as well as morals and manners. With competent editors and talented contributors the papers most worthy of note were the

Female Tatler, 1709-10, by Bickerstaff's distaff rival, Mrs. Cracken-thorpe, "a Lady that knows every thing"; the *Examiner*, 1710-14, aided by Swift himself; Steele's own *Guardian*, 1713, in the political shadow of his earlier work; Theobald's *Censor*, 1715 and 1717; Philips' *Free-Thinker*, 1718-21; Hill's *Plain Dealer*, 1724-25; the general and dramatic *Prompter*, 1734-36, by Hill and Popple; the *Female Spectator*, by Mrs. Haywood in 1744-46. In the fifties appeared the second efflorescence—Johnson's *Rambler*, Hawkesworth's *Adventurer*, Moore's *World*, and the *Connoisseur* by Colman and Thornton. These dozen periodicals would have borne distinction to the press of any era. There were also the four papers by Fielding from 1739 to 1752, the *Champion, True Patriot, Jacobite's Journal*, and *Covent-Garden Journal*, which mingled essays with news, as did also the able *Bee* by Budgell in 1733-35, the *Grub-street Journal*, 1730-37, and the valuable *Gray's Inn Journal* of 1753-54. Two illustrious series of essays outran the fame of the newspapers containing them—Johnson's "Idler" in the weekly *Universal Chronicle*, 1758-60, and Goldsmith's "Chinese Letters" in the *Public Ledger*, 1760-61, renamed in a separate publication *The Citizen of the World*, now a phrase for the device of the foreign observer-correspondent. Other newspapers plentifully gave their subscribers an essay, perhaps disguised as a letter, to lead the issue and consume space not readily filled with news. By the end of our period the essay journal had in fact lost much of its franchise to the newspaper and the magazine, each of which often relied on the essay as an integral portion of its fare. As an illustration, Oliver Goldsmith had no current superior in the writing of the periodic essay, but most of his finest pieces were not published in essay journals.

The early miscellany journal has value both for its own substance and for its part in the making of the "magazine." The first such serial medley was the *Gentleman's Journal*, a monthly of thirty-three issues in 1692-94, conducted by Peter Motteux, who would later translate Rabelais and Cervantes and request a puff from Mr. Spectator for his new vocation as importer of rich silks and fine laces. The whole of each number took the form of a letter to a gentleman in the country, which imposed a kind of unity on an olio of prose and verse—odes, songs with music, fables, allegories, fiction, dialogues, enigmas, questions, letters, translations, scientific articles, literary notes, essays on scattered themes, news, and even a few illustrations. Such a packet of reading matter can hardly be excelled as an *index elegantiarum* in its generation, a companion in time and revelation to the heavier and quite dissimilar question-answer *Athenian Mercury*. The *Gentleman's Journal* enjoyed many contributors and sought the reading support of women, who were even honored with the title for one issue, the *Lady's Journal*. This periodical secured recognition as the prototype of the literary miscellany and was by the criterion of diverse constituents actually the first English "magazine."

The next notable miscellany, and one not so well known, was the substantial *Post-Angel* by John Dunton, a journalistic entre-preneur of large part in the history of the periodical. This new Duntonian venture appeared monthly from January of 1701 to September of 1702 as a shilling quarto. In his lengthy preface the undertaker admitted his title to be new and surprising, and set forth his design

to shew *how we should enquire after News, not as* Athenians *but as Christian, or* (in other words) a Divine Emprovement of *every Remarkable Occurrence* that happens under the Sun, (for I'll endeavour to make a *Universal Entertainment* upon all Subjects;) and I have settled such a Correspondence, that I hope to insert several things worth reading out of the *common Road of News;* for sure a *Post-Angel* is able to *out-flie a Post-Master, Post-Man, and Post-Boy;* and those lesser *Fliers,* the *English* and *London Post.*

The journal had at its beginning five parts: "the *Remarkable Providences* of Judgment and Mercy, that hapned in" the month of issue; biographies of eminent persons that died in that month; "A new *Athenian Mercury,*" containing questions and answers from Dunton's defunct *Athenian Mercury,* with promise of additions, alterations, and corrections; the public news at home and abroad; and an account of books recently published or imminent. The first three of these departments were each to occupy three sheets, and news and books were to have the tenth and last sheet. Later were added three sections—"The Poetical Project," one of challenges and responses, and "The Gentleman's Library; Or, Essays on all manner of Diverting Subjects." The particularity of this paper is the "Spiritual Observator" under each head, a short or longish essay on the preceding matter, a dilated comment usually moralistic or pietistic, to promote the reformation of English life. Moreover, Dunton was not one to save words; his editorial statements here are long and frequent, and are thereby peculiarly rewarding to the historian of early periodicals. The *Post-Angel* is not a masterwork of style, but it spoke for one temper of its day, and Dunton saw that the essay, poem, summary of news, letter, and question were major forms for public interest, and by combining them in a single serial he advanced the evolution of the journal of miscellaneous contents and containers.

Shortly after the first communication of the Post-Angel reached London, Mrs. Ann Baldwin published the *Memoirs for the Curious*, with care to "Advertise the Publick, Least Any might Apprehend, that the Authors of this Undertaking, did take the Model of their Design, from the *Post-Angel*," with which there was "no Co-incidence of Matter." Dunton's paper would have been a difficult model, and, apparently, the *Memoirs* had a greater desire for similarity to the periodicals of summary and review. Through letters, relations, narrations, a dialogue and a fable, and a final section of news, books, and manuscripts this singular journal strove to give an "Account of What Occurrs that's *Rare*, *Secret*, *Extraordinary*, *Prodigious* or *Miraculous*, through the World; whether in *Nature*, *Art*, *Learning*, *Policy* or *Religion*," in order to correct vulgar errors and manifest universal truth. As an earnest record of wonders and unaccountable things the *Memoirs* deserved a career beyond its two known numbers. The following year the *Pacquet from Parnassus* sought and attained a larger variety in form, tone, and content. Many poems were included, one of them sometimes ascribed to Addison, and a letter to a minister who had used several hard words in his sermon, entitled "To the most Deuteronomatical, Polidoxolagist, Pantaphilogical, Linguist Mr. *A. B.* Archi-Rabbi-Sophi, Phenodand, Diotrephes de Huntsby." The printer of the *Pacquet* informed the reader, "I hope to Breed, like Tame Pidgeons, every Month"; there followed, apparently, only one issue.

The *Muses Mercury* properly described itself on the title page as a "Monthly Miscellany. Consisting of Poems, Prologues, Songs, Sonnets, Translations, and other Curious Pieces, Never before Printed." Claiming to be "very near a kin" to the *Gentleman's Journal*, this *Mercury* invited transmission of non-partisan, non-scandalous material in the various forms, prose or verse, "ev'ry Thing that has any relation to the Studies of *Humanity*," in the belief "that nothing is more Profitable to Mankind, than that which delights them." A considerable amount of poetry was accepted to accompany reports of books, plays, and operas. The essay "Of Old English Poets and Poetry," followed by "The Nut-brown Maid," is the foremost fraction of prose. John Oldmixon, miscellaneous writer, fashioned the wares of the *Muses Mercury* for the literary gentry from January of 1707 until the next January, and collected a company of contributors who were or would become names well known. Begun the same month as the *Mercury*, the *Monthly Miscellany; or, Memoirs for the Curious* lived a longer but less interesting life, 1707-9. It started as a solid miscellany for a serious public, including matters of divinity, law, philosophy, mathematics, science, history, travel, husbandry, trade, biography, poetry, and news. Its first issues furnished lists of problems to engage the minds of its readers ("Is Nature preferable to Art?"), and it enclosed such standard forms of presentation as the essay, letter, and abstract. But the *Monthly Miscellany* changed by its second year and grew less miscellaneous and more learned, with an emphasis on natural philosophy as the subject and the abstract, often translated from the French, as the vehicle. In November of 1708 the memoirs of Captain Avery, pirate, appeared as a relief from the surrounding dullness. During 1711 the *Delights for the Ingenious*, as monthly and then as quarterly, proposed to entertain both sexes with a great variety of enigmas, mathematical questions, stories, epigrams, adventures, paradoxes, songs, anagrams, emblems, dialogues, elegies, epitaphs, and other diversions in prose and rhyme. John Tipper, the almanac maker for ladies, included astronomical observations and a few essays, and he received an ample number of postpaid verses and solutions to the printed problems from his cooperative readers, many of whom certainly read also the concurrent columns of the *Spectator*. The literary monthly declined in favor as the age altered and other kinds of periodicals advanced.

The type of periodical that acted as a compendium of recent history differed greatly from the much more literary miscellany journal. The historical collection or summary made a strong beginning prior to the eighteenth century, in fact, before the newspaper press, on which it had a large dependence, had gained a striking proliferation. As early as 1645 the *Monthly Account*, apparently the first English journal of that popular frequency, called itself a "Collection of all the most speciall and observable Passages" of the whole of the preceding month, "briefly rallyed together, and brought into small compasse; not filled with flatteries, forgeries, and contradictions." In March the *Generall Account* gave a survey of the kingdom by counties and may have been a sequel to the other *Account* by the same bookseller, Richard Harper. In 1660 the *Monethly Intelligencer* expanded the communication of occurrences from Great Britain to the "most principal Places of the World," and furnished a prospectus embracing most of the reasons for existence claimed by later historical registers.

This *Monethly News* is intended to be printed and published the first day of every Moneth in the Year, being judged of Excellent Use to this Commonwealth. First, for its Truth and Brevity, fit to be kept to posterity. Secondly, for the benefit of the Countrey, who cannot enjoy the publique News every three days. Thirdly, that the common people may enjoy it in all places, being of a small Price, and but once a moneth. Fourthly, it contains some useful Observations for the ensuing Moneth.

The writer—whoever it was the publisher Cossinet had secured—relished his opportunity and went on with a sprightliness not common to historical journals.

Since the commencement of Intelligence by Printing, Pamphlets of that kinde have as numerously invaded and infested the World, as Flyes a great mans Kitchin, or a Butchers Shambles in the Summer season; All of them consisting of more words and iterations, than either worth or weighty matter. The design of this Book is not to furnish the Reader with Bumbast Effutitious Expressions, nor yet with vain Tautologies or idle repetitions; but onely to present him with a Brief (yet perfect) Compendium of all the Transactions of the Affairs of most habitable parts of the world; as also of such as are Domestick, and of particular concernment to all English men, for the preceding Moneth; with other things of most signal and remarkable consequence; as, the various Diseases reigning therein, with the number that each killeth: of great use to modern Speculators, principally Physicians. And (that there may not be one link of Homers Golden Chain wanting) the Celestial causes of all Mundane affairs in general, are observed, as they lye imbodied in the Writings of the best Annual Prognosticators or Astrologers. In fine, it is intended to take cognizance of all things that may be useful for Statesmen, Divines, Lawyers, Gentlemen of all sorts, Souldiers, Seamen, Merchants, and all persons of private Condition, either in City or Countrey. And it is desired, that each Reader would (not onely buy, but) keep this *Monethly Intelligencer* by him, it being resolved (by the Author hereof) a Continued Collection of the most clear and certain account of all things useful, that can possibly be obtained: And this impartially and truly, without flattery or insinuations of doubtful matters, to please the humour of any Interest, as is the common guise of Newsbooks.

The *Monethly Intelligencer* evidently lost its energy in one number. The *Monthly Recorder* printed five issues in 1682, and in a statement of intentions emphasized the haste, inaccuracy, and uncertainty of the ordinary newspaper, all of which were to be amended in this journal for a penny a month. *Modern History* in 1687-89 offered to provide an account not merely of civil, ecclesiastical, and military occurrences (grouped by countries) but also "all Natural, and Philosophical Productions and Transactions" only once a month for caution's sake and "without *Wracking* Peoples Expectations by any Longer Intervalls." The *Present State of Europe: or, the Historical and Political Monthly Mercury* continued from 1690 to 1736 as a translation of the *Mercure historique et politique*. The *Monthly Register*, 1703-7, which was printed for Samuel Buckley, later the Gazetteer, declared that its business was "not to foretel, amuse, or divert, but to record," promised to admit "Original Papers" of public interest, and added the legend "Without any Reflections" to its title page. The *Monthly Journal, of the Affairs of Europe* of 1704 put forward a "*History* of the *Times*, with Proper and Entertaining *Reflections*, but free from *Partiality*" in a connected account of each country, alleged to contain matters "Not extant in other Accounts." The *Political State of Great Britain*, by Abel Boyer, became an authoritative monthly summary for three decades, 1711-40; often it included vital statistics, passages from newspapers, and such documents as addresses, memorials, and letters. The *Monthly Chronicle*, 1728-32, supplied more than accounts of home and alien affairs by adding important papers of state, lists of books, honors, preferments, promotions, births, marriages, and deaths, and prices of goods and stocks as well as helpful indices. In his preface the writer answered the objection that taking notice of current prices is needless by prophesying truly—"but if we carry our Views to distant Times, for which this Work is designed, as well as the present, it will certainly, not be displeasing, to see how these from Time to Time vary and change." Economy of time and money, convenience, wide coverage, authenticity, and respect for posterity answered as reasons for the making and buying of monthly journals of historical digest. Thus did the periodical recording current events become established on a monthly basis for people who could not or would not read all the gazettes but who were inclined to have a memoir of their public yesterdays.

A few weekly sheets also claimed the special advantage of survey—the *Epitome of the Weekly News*, 1682; Whitlock's *Weekly News-Letter*, 1695; J. Wilkins' *Weekly Survey of the World*, 1696, promising to let the gentleman know how the world stands and "the great Wheels move"; and the *Weekly Medley*, 1718, which would act as historian, critic, and busybody, and which introduced its effort with a dissertation on the state of the press and public curiosity. But the weekly review was actually little more than a weekly newspaper and thus inferior to the monthly because the latter could better verify and select and dispose its reports. The *Historical Journal* in 1697 attempted to register "the most considerable Occurrences in Europe" once a fortnight and succeeded for at least four weeks. The *Historical Register*, on the other hand, found the monthly rate of issue too fast and proved its preference for the quarterly by continuing from 1717 to 1739. Meanwhile the annual conspectus, with one volume to the year, had taken its stand with a longer view. There were the *History of the Reign of Queen Anne*, by Boyer, *Compleat History of Europe* from the beginning of the century to the end of Anne's reign, *Annals of King George*, first of that name, *Annals of Europe*, 1739-44, and finally the *Annual Register*, in which Burke wrote the survey of events for many years. This last book of annals, which was begun in 1758, is still a standard compilation in an active age when the Yearbook is a solid necessity and the monthly abstract has yielded much of its way to the weekly "news magazine."

The publication of the *Gentleman's Magazine* for January, 1731, was an event paramount in the progression of English journalism, an occasion comparable to the commencement of the *Gazette* and *Philosophical Transactions* in 1665 and to the establishment of the *Tatler* and its resplendent successor in another orbit of the same firmament. Founded by Edward Cave, journalist come from Coventry, who for editorial ubiquity called himself Sylvanus Urban, Gent., the *Gentleman's Magazine: or, Monthly Intelligencer* at once asserted it contained "more in Quantity, and greater Variety, than any Book of the Kind and Price," which was sixpence. After a lengthy "View of the Weekly Disputes and Essays in this Month" the first issue ceded four pages to poems and six to a "Monthly Intelligencer" and comprehended sections of such current data as extraordinary accidents, casualties, ships lost and taken, deaths, marriages, promotions civil and military, ecclesiastical preferments, sheriffs, stocks, bills of mortality, goods, foreign advices, bankrupts, books, and fairs for the following month, together with a narrative from Edinburgh, an essay on credulity in witchcraft from Pennsylvania, and observations on February gardening. Certainly this was a periodical dedicated to assembling the miscellaneous for the general reader, and thus a descendant of the miscellany journal. In this respect the *Gentleman's* included nothing novel—all of these heads of information, and more, had been collected in previous journals though not under one cover. But the first half of the issue presented the striking feature—the abridgment of the papers of news and comment during the month, or at least up to the final week needed for editing and printing. Ten papers, such as the *Craftsman* and *London Journal*, provided thirty-five condensed essays, chronologically grouped under title, which was plainly acknowledged with date and issue specified. These epitomes show a skillful telescoping of the originals in a process closer to extracting than abstracting; indeed, the *Gentleman's* became quite adept in the practice of condensation—a union of truncation, paraphrase, and quotation.

Sylvanus Urban well understood that his monthly view of the weekly sheets constituted his first point of appeal, and so he explained in an introduction the reasonableness of his undertaking. Assuming that a "nice *Model* is as entertaining as the Original, and a true *Specimen* as satisfactory as the whole Parcel," and finding that two hundred half-sheets were being printed each month in London and as many elsewhere, and supposing that in such loose papers many things deserving attention "are only seen by Accident, and others not sufficiently publish'd or preserved for universal Benefit and Information," Cave reached his conclusion: "This Consideration has induced several GENTLEMEN to promote a Monthly Collection, to treasure up, as in a *Magazine*, the most remarkable Pieces on the Subjects above-mention'd, or at least impartial Abridgments thereof, as a Method much better calculated to preserve those Things that are curious, than that of transcribing." And here was the word "magazine" in a new application, a term for a serial which abridged the essays of its weekly contemporaries for the reader who did not make it his business to consult all the transient sheets for pieces of wit and intelligence, with such pieces of value stored safely and reinforced by "some other matters of Use or Amusement."

The new *Magazine* stood in clear line of succession to the miscellany periodical (often a monthly), and also inherited conspicuously from the historical summary, though the *Gentleman's* made its survey by means of condensations rather than compilations. It is fair to place this journal—"the first magazine" so called—as a product of both types of periodical, as an expansion of the miscellany (especially in the direction of the general reader) and a modification of the serial compendium (particularly in favor of the excerpt). In one respect the scheme for appropriating material had been anticipated by the *Grub-street Journal*, initiated one year earlier, but the *Grub-street* had taken only items of news from the other papers, with acknowledgments, and not made abridgments of essays from the weekly press. Cave's accomplishment lay in the modification of the historical survey by presenting a close view of the current controversies in the papers, augmented by other monthly intelligence and miscellaneous departments of interest to a wide and practical public. He developed the techniques of the miscellany journal and the historical review, and joined them in a new composition; and when he named his work a *Magazine* he bestowed on the world of serials a term to be used, and misused, in astronomical quantities.

The *Gentleman's*, of course, did not remain as it began, but admitted more and more original matter. It employed the young Sam Johnson and assisted in the movement of free reporting with accounts of Parliamentary sessions lightly concealed behind "Debates in the Senate of Magna Lilliputia." It had a heavy sale and remained for a century what it wished to be—a treasure room of valuable information. Not merely did readers discover that this magazine gave them a very good assortment of desiderata, but other publishers discovered that the new formula could be adopted to their own profit. In 1732, the next year, the first formidable rival appeared—the *London Magazine: or, Gentleman's Monthly Intelligencer*, prefixing "London" to the rearranged title of its progenitor and using the motto "Multum in parvo" instead of "E Pluribus Unum." The *London* appropriated the departments of the *Gentleman's* but gave longer condensations and anticipated its model with a version of the transactions of Parliament; and it had its own long success. Budgell's *Bee* attempted to suck the quintessence of the weeklies each week, 1733-35, but the next major competition came from the *Scots Magazine* in 1739, which from Edinburgh named its two famous predecessors, admitting that "it is much easier to improve the plan of another, than to form one," and adding that the distance from the place of their publication rendered "their contents stale before they came to hand."

In the seventeen forties the original practice of the "magazine" —the abridgment of the current press—sharply declined, but the magazine continued as a popular periodical, generally a monthly, of miscellaneous and usually original content. The name survived the occasion of its first agency. Concisely, "magazine" began as a new term for a repository of extractive summary with motley additions and embellishments, but in a short time left its first idea of preserving pieces liable of loss, and went over to the other part of Cave's project, that of collecting divers pieces of information and entertainment. The word "magazine" nowadays is often loosely applied to any publication not obviously a book in hard covers or a daily newspaper.

But the practice of extracting and compiling was well enough known in 1750 to breed the ultimate in dependency—the *Magazine of Magazines*, which was set up to reprint matter from books and other periodicals. Such a preying upon the preyers actually came to little beyond the forcing into print of Gray's *Elegy*, a manuscript copy of which had fallen into the hands of the new despoiler. Gray refused to cooperate with the pirate and got Walpole's aid in rushing the poem into print; the poet barely won the race of defeating the best idea the *Magazine of Magazines* had ever had, which was not to reprint at all but rather to print a poem the English-reading public has since caused to be reprinted uncountable times.

In 1741 the fortnightly *History of Our Own Times* in four numbers by a "Society of Gentlemen" summarized the history of Europe and "the Great World," digested the essays in the current press, and included a long review and a list of new books and pamphlets (sometimes with short comment), a department of poetry, and military, mercantile, maritime news. Also in 1741 the eminent publisher Dodsley essayed a weekly magazine predominantly literary, the *Publick Register*, but soon forsook it; five years later he sponsored the *Museum*, a semi-monthly, Mark Akenside editing, with no more success. A *British Magazine*, edited by John Hill from 1748 to 1750, was ornamented by a copper plate at the head of each issue; another in Edinburgh, 1747-48, carried, as did the *Scots*, the "Journal of the Proceedings and Debates in the Political Club," meaning Parliament, from the *London Magazine*. The *Universal Magazine of Knowledge and Pleasure* in 1747 opened its store of popular varieties—science, cookery, husbandry, sport, and other fresh features—and kept its public into the next century. The *Student* of Oxford, a 1750-51 monthly, set out occasionally to "comprehend all the branches of *polite* Literature" under the hand of Christopher Smart, and sustained an attitude not oppressively Oxonian. Samuel Johnson's *Literary Magazine, or, Universal Review*, 1756-58, showed its double nature in its full title. And there were others before 1760. Magazines maintained their growth throughout the Georgian years: some enlarged the range of format, tone, material, and mode for the general reader, and others grew specialized for select or professional groups of subscribers. The magazine adapted and absorbed earlier types of periodicals and by 1800 had gained a mighty seat in the British council of publications, and it has come to this present time as a truly major force in commerce, culture, education, and public persuasion.

The early review journal and the learned journal were associated because the purpose of each was to promulgate special knowledge for the professional scholar or the erudite amateur; the learned journal, commonly scientific or medical, gave reports at first hand of advanced investigations, and the reviewing journal presented at second hand summaries of research, though this latter type of periodical usually went beyond the natural sciences to embrace such important fields as theological and classical scholarship. The alliance within an individual journal of direct recording and convenient reporting was natural enough, and has lived on into the present scholarly journal, where specialized articles often are amiably attended by reviews of specialized volumes in the same territory of human knowledge. The Royal Society began the publication of its work in 1665 with the *Philosophical Transactions* under the editorship of Henry Oldenburg, a serial still regnant in the kingdom of science and the oldest English periodical of continuous issue. The second learned journal was the *Philosophical Collections*, 1679, 1681-82, gathered by Robert Hooke, secretary of the Society, and likewise carrying abstracts of scholastic books. Among the serials of science were the *Medicina Curiosa*, 1684, *Medical Essays and Observations*, 1733-44, and *Miscellanea Curiosa Mathematica*, 1745-53.

The *Bibliotheca Literaria*, a very learned "Collection of Inscriptions, Medals, Dissertations, &c.," appeared in ten numbers from 1722 to 1724, to each of which was appended a department of "The Labours of the Learned," arranged in order by the city of scholarly activity. The *Phœnix Britannicus* for six issues in 1731 reprinted scarce and choice pieces of great variety, most of them from the late sixteenth century and early seventeenth. John Jortin's *Miscellaneous Observations upon Authors, Ancient and*

Modern, 1731-32, emphasized classical scholarship and conceded itself to be "relatively dry" but not "absolutely dry." Jortin indulged in some criticism, and in his preface defined the critic in terms of his own deficiency—"an extensive knowledge, a thorough skill in learned languages, a happy sagacity, a sound judgment, an obstinate application to study." Learned articles occasionally showed up in more popular journals, and semi-learned essays not infrequently found their way into essay sheets, miscellanies, and magazines. And periodical lore even had its jester—the *Useful Transactions in Philosophy,* 1709, satirized learning with such papers as "An Essay on the Invention of Samplers," "Some Natural Observations Made in the School of Llandwwfwrhwy," and "A New Method to Teach Learned Men How to Write Unintelligibly," often with marginal references to the *Philosophical Transactions.*

The periodical of books began as a mere list, the *Mercurius Librarius,* 1668-70, the quarterly "Term Catalogue" valued so highly as a record of the publishing trade. A successor appeared with the same title in 1680, a sort of *Publisher's Weekly,* which was a compilation planned "not to make any large Harangue, either in the Praise, or Dispraise, of any Book, but barely to give an Account of the Title, and Design of it," with the book to be returned to the publisher on demand and a fee of sixpence to be paid for insertion. But the bare titles of books given in the common catalogues being "somewhat dry things, scarce able to raise in men that gust and appetite to Learning," the *Weekly Memorials for the Ingenious* in January of 1682 offered accounts of scientific works, drawing much material from the *Journal des Sçavans,* which was the way, the preface proclaimed, of Oldenburg and Hooke. A quarrel between the writer and his publisher soon bred a rival *Memorials* by the original author. In 1688 another *Weekly Memorials* abstracted only one book in each of its two half-sheet numbers.

Then began the English career of Jean de la Crose, an energetic Huguenot. His *Universal Historical Bibliotheque* for the first three months of 1687 proposed to be an "Account of Most of the Considerable Books Printed in All Languages ... Wherein a Short Description is Given of the Design and Scope of Almost Every

Book: and of the Quality of the Author, if Known." These accounts were in the main translations (cut to fit England) of articles in Continental journals. "But as to the Books Printed in *England,*" said the conductor, "I have not yet had that Assistance all Foreigners have from time to time, which is to have Abstracts ready drawn, sent them by the Publishers, or Authors, without which it is not possible for any one Man to go through with such a Task as this is." The next year one number of the *Bibliotheca Universalis* came from Edinburgh as an "Historical Accompt of Books and Transactions of the Learned World," by John Cockburn, but then lost its license. In 1691 de la Crose resumed his work with the *History of Learning,* in which he announced the exchange of the translation of foreign journals for the abstract of works both domestic and foreign, where he would "mark out the most considerable Passages, and the Places best writ of every Author," but would omit "giving a Judgment upon the Style and Language of Authors." De la Crose excused himself from abstracting treatises in certain areas, "any thing too particular in one Faculty," but did not deny the natural sciences, where he invited the communication of discoveries, the *Philosophical Transactions* being presently interrupted. The *History of Learning* at once prompted the weekly *Mercurius Eruditorum,* offered as the dialogue of three friends who agreed to give each other their comments on what they have been reading and to "sift not only the Authors of Books, but their Journalists themselves"—an interesting critical procedure rather well executed. De la Crose soon founded his third review periodical, the *Works of the Learned,* 1691-92; it also emphasized science at the expense of "Plays, Satyrs, Romances and the like, which are fitter to corrupt men's morals, and to shake the grounds of Natural Religion, than to promote Learning and Piety," and it added a section of book news. More than any other man this French editor receives the credit for establishing the English reviewing or abstracting journal.

John Dunton, journalist extraordinary, as a publisher of books saw the utility of publishing a periodical on books. He had issued the *Works of the Learned* during part of its life, and from May of 1692 brought forth the *Compleat Library* for two years, a monthly journal to contain "News for the Learned" and accounts of the choicest books, including those printed for John Dunton. And before the age of Anne there began and ended several other periodicals on books—a second *History of Learning*, 1694, in a sole number, which suggested its value in service "to the best Libraries, as a direction for the Choice of Books; and in some measure to the meanest, by supplying, in part, the defects thereof"; the *Miscellaneous Letters*, 1694-96, with the avowal "to keep a Medium betwixt a meer Catalogue and a real Abridgment, Abridgments having a natural Tendency to destroy good Books"; a scarce *Weekly Advertisement of Books* in 1696; the *Occasional Paper*, by Richard Willis, which gave each of its ten epistolary numbers in 1697-98 to a religious book or topic, thinking it a good service to good manners and doctrine to have books considered calmly by men of moderation, who will "set the Publick right in it" without loss of charity; and two journals in 1701 called the *New State of Europe*, which combined learning with public transactions. Meanwhile de la Crose had undertaken his last serial, a *History of the Works of the Learned*, 1699-1711, the principal organ of reviewing during most of the Queen's reign; he repeated the resolve to "keep a Medium betwixt tedious Extracts, and superficial Catalogues, made up only of Title and Preface; the former being tiresom to the Reader, as well as injurious to the sale of Books, and the latter being a meer Imposition on the Publick," but remembered "our Province is that of *Historians* and not of *Criticks*."

The *Censura Temporum*, 1708, affected the dialogue form to enliven the discussion of current works and was fairly successful considering the weight of the material, mainly theological. Two years later Michel de la Roche, another Gallic Protestant, undertook his *Memoirs of Literature*, 1710-14, 1717, in a weekly folio sheet of summaries (some translated) and news from the capitals of learning. Bernard Lintot issued a *Monthly Catalogue* in 1714-15, and J. Wilford another listing of books under the same title, 1723-29. De la Roche's *New Memoirs of Literature*, a monthly of 1725-27, had long reviews, little criticism, and news of bookish activity, and upon its discontinuance Andrew Reid "ventured to supply" its place with the similar *Present State of the Republick of Letters*, which lasted from 1728 to 1736. However, in 1730 de la Roche himself made a "Continuation" of his *New Memoirs* in the *Literary Journal,* a quarterly equipped with an index to each of its two semi-annual volumes. And in 1730-34 Bower's *Historia Litteraria* preserved the habit of summary reviewing with slight evaluation, though it promised "As to our *Criticism,* the most arduous as well as important Province of a Journalist, we shall lay it down with the greatest Modesty, Caution, and Impartiality, and shall make every Consideration subservient to Merit." For the first six months of 1735 the *Literary Magazine, or Select British Library* and in 1735-36 Chambers' *Literary Magazine: or, the History of the Works of the Learned* increased the quantity of reviews without affecting the quality. This latter monthly combined with the *Present State* to form a new periodical, the *History of the Works of the Learned,* 1737-43, which took the cumbrous second name of its younger parent and prolonged the tradition of the abstracting journal. The *British Librarian,* by the historian William Oldys, in only six monthly issues of 1737 reviewed books and manuscripts, mostly of an antique age. The *Literary Journal,* by Jean Pierre Droz, gave Ireland a review from 1744 to 1749; Droz planted in his abstracts more analytical comment than suited the worn habit of the type.

The history of the review journal prior to the *Monthly Review* and the *Critical Review* constitutes a slow and somewhat dreary tale because the reviewing periodical did not for the most part review books in the sense now accepted but rather gave its pages to "accounts" of them, meaning original or translated abstracts with or without excerpts. Moreover, the books thus presented were not usually the belletristic works which have concerned later generations; the science summarized is gone, and the scholarship on ancient figures and theological problems has lost much of its interest. The books were dull, most of them, and the accounts of them were concentrated dullness. Too little estimate of merit and demerit, too little criticism theoretic and applied, accompanied the heavy epitomes, whatever the stated design of the editor. Inclusiveness often was claimed, but the realm of the survey was overlong limited to the works of the learned; honesty of appraisal likewise became an empty promise when few books were critically analyzed at all and the editor's chief choice lay in the selection of fruitful titles. These journals took themselves quite seriously as depositories of an erudition prepared by the learned summarizer or translator for the learned student, who thus could satisfy his curiosity with short, royal roads to learning, or for the less expert, who could patch his mind for conversational gambits and epistolary pretense. The early review journals have value, assuredly, as bibliographical instruments; they indicate certain tastes of the time though commonly they do not treat of the works we now revere or propose judicial opinions of the books which they presented; they have a better value as forerunners of the later reviews than as sufficient organs of critical principles directing critical practices. During almost each year of the half century preceding the appearance of the *Monthly Review* the English reader could buy a review journal, but the reader in the middle group—the person not occupied with organized lore or with the letterpress of the street—remained badly served. Whatsoever desire he had for guidance in the winding ways of humanistic letters was not answered. For appreciative or derogatory critiques of the books of the season, for aesthetic flavored to his wholesome taste, he could find no impressive organ of reviewing, and so he turned to the current pamphlet or to the essay journal of literary station, or he sought no printed counsel at all but resorted to the booksellers themselves and their stock in trade.

The inauguration of the *Monthly Review* and the *Critical Review* wrought no sharp revolution in the reviewing periodical. The former started in 1749 and was long edited by Ralph Griffiths and son under liberal auspices; the *Critical* began seven years later under the supervision of Smollett and continued as a conservative rival for two generations. Both journals carried a number of articles by Goldsmith and a sample of Johnson's ability; each presented long reviews and brief accounts, and relied on a small coterie of frequent reviewers and an extended circle of occasional contributors. These the two foremost reviews of the second half of the century did not abandon the firm fashion of quoting and abstracting (and a tolerable amount of summary is ever a proper element in a review) with a modicum of evaluation, but threw aside the tradition of selecting bookish books written for the benefit of savants. They chose the more popular highway and attempted a prompt, comprehensive coverage of literary, general, and occasionally specialized works for the accommodation of the average intelligent reader; it was in this change of purpose affecting a larger land of books and audience rather than in a radical change of the constitution of the review that the *Monthly* and the *Critical* made a difference in the history of this type of journal. Their sensible initiative attracted followers to their camp (usually entitled *Review*) by popularizing the medium, and their reviews of books of continuing interest give us today some notion of their first reception. These two journals were not full grown review periodicals in the later mode, but they were in the course of development toward the critical journal of books which consolidates literary history and literary criticism and literary journalism.

The dialogue journal became popular late in the seventeenth century and sustained its vogue into the eighteenth as a vehicle of partisanship. A few papers, to be sure, employed dialogue for variety's sweet sake or as an attempt at dramatic interplay; the *Wandring Whore* soon after the King's restoration in 1660 was cast into an exchange between four characters of very low life, and appropriately appended a list of the names (some with addresses) of the "Crafty Bawds, Common Whores, Wanderers, Pick-pockets, Night-walkers, Decoys, Hectors, Pimps and Trappanners"; a *Weekly Comedy* was presented in 1699 and another in 1707; Novel and Scandal in the *General Postscript* and Bess o' Bedlam and her brother Tom in the *Tatling Harlot* commented in passing on the contemporary *Tatler;* and even the highly dignified *Censura Temporum*, 1708-10, chose dialogue to inspirit its discussion of theological books.

But the periodical to introduce the dialogue method as a polemical device seems to have been *Heraclitus Ridens,* which for some eighty weeks in 1681-82 included an anti-Whig discourse between Jest and Earnest, an occasional poem, and a frequent series of self-answering queries, to give "a true Information of the state of things, and advance your understandings above the common rate of Coffee-House Statesmen who think themselves wiser than the Privy-Council, or the Sages of the Law, when in truth they are only fit to make Senators in *Goatham,* to hedge in a Cuckow, or drown an Eel." *Democritus Ridens* very soon attacked *Heraclitus* in a weekly anti-Popish dialogue and added satiric advertisements.

In 1686 *Hippocrates Ridens* adopted the dialogue form for "Joco-serious Reflections on the Impudence and Mischiefs of Quacks, and Illiterate Pretenders to Physick." A *New Heraclitus Ridens* appeared briefly in 1689. The increase of the Dissenting faction bred another *Heraclitus* in 1703 of more numbers than its original, and in 1718 a discourse "concerning the Times" again appropriated the title.

Six weeks after Jest and Earnest entered the weekly stage Sir Roger L'Estrange, energetic in his power as licenser of the press, borrowed the dialogue and fastened it on English journalism for a generation as a factional procedure. His *Observator. In Question and Answer*, sometimes *Observator in Dialogue*, for six years vindicated the Government, exposed the Jesuits, and disagreed with Dissenters. Here the colloquy had two voices of a single mind; one speaker supplied occasion for the other's argument, of which no Whig dog would have the better. Promptly there was rebuttal from the *Observator Observ'd*, and a long parade began of *Observators*, meaning journals in dialogue on affairs temporal and spiritual. Late in 1681 a *Protestant Observator* included dialogue and rhetorical questions, and a *New Dialogue* again "Observed" the *Observator*. In 1693 the *English Spy: or, the Critical Observator* ridiculed the *Athenian Mercury*. The misnamed *Poetical Observator* appeared in 1702-3, and in 1702 Tutchin's *Observator* turned the one-sided dialogue to favor the Whigs for a decade, and two years later Charles Leslie's *Observator* (later *Rehearsal* and usually so called) gave the Tory view of life. In the same year there appeared the *Observator Reformed*, the *Observator's Tryal and Defence*, and the *Comical Observator*, this last containing a good paper on coffee-house company, "the impatient News-Hounds of the Age," who must have included Mr. Bickerstaff's Political Upholsterer. In 1705 a minor *Observator* combatted the Union with Scotland; in 1707 there was an *Observator Reviv'd* in defense of Dissent and opposition to the *Rehearsal*; in 1708 the *Scots Observator* remarked strongly against Defoe's *Review* and the "News-Cobblers, who when they have no News make some, and when they have bad News patch it up, and Tinker-like, make two Holes to mend one." In 1716 appeared a *Weekly Observator*, and the habit was spent. "Observator" had been a common term to cover controversial unilateral dialogue. A few other journals followed the fashion by using the word for non-dialogue sheets in order to indicate opposition toward papers of that name or to entitle periodicals of commentary, that is, of observation in its true sense and not in the journalistically derived usage. Dialogue declined, but the weeping-laughing philosopher and Authority himself had for a time made a mode to arm the warfare in political practice and ecclesiastical polity.

More valuable to the historian of ideas than the dialogue journal was another type of popular publication—the periodical of categorical questions and their answers. This class of journal was related to the work of Heraclitus and L'Estrange in that those worthies had proposed queries (though for their own answering) and in that a sequence of questions and answers gave a semblance of dialogue. Whatever the origin of the idea, John Dunton, industrious projector, initiated in 1691 the *Athenian Mercury* to resolve "all the Nice and Curious Questions Propos'd by the Ingenious" with the aid of several expert colleagues in his Athenian Society. Queries were received in great plenty, queries of theology, moral philosophy, natural philosophy, folklore, and criticism, queries for fact and opinion, queries to be met only with common sense, salt, or evasion, and queries never to be solved then or now. For five years the Society twice a week matched minds and wits with their fellow citizens, and the result is a storeroom of data on English interests in William's reign. The bulk and variation of topic preserved in this "Casuistical Mercury" is exceeded by no other spy o' the time.

"Mercury" was no longer merely a proper-common noun for a newspaper; Dunton's journal of questions and answers sober and flippant gave the word a new turn. In less than a year Tom Brown's *London Mercury* (later *Lacedemonian*) became a brief rival more satirical than competitive. In 1693 the *Ladies Mercury* proposed not to encroach on the Athenians and bounded its province "to only that little Sublunary, *Woman*." Dunton himself had set aside issues for the service of the Fair; his new rival lasted four weeks. The *Jovial Mercury* enjoyed the same length in the same year. Charles Povey in 1707-8 used questions as a minor section of his *General Remark on Trade*.

After the death of the *Mercury* Dunton sought to revive his Athenianism. His monthly *Post-Angel* of 1701-2 included "A new *Athenian Mercury*" again to satisfy the ingenious of either sex; the *Athenian News: or, Dunton's Oracle*, 1710, likewise included a "Casuistical-Post, or Athenian Mercury" among its numerous departments and scourged its new rival, the *British Apollo*, as a "*dull, ignorant, false and impertinent Scribler*," even promising to re-answer his questions. But Dunton perforce gave way to this interloper, which held for three years the public appointment of resolving the doubts of Anne's England and still holds high interest as a true copy of its intellectual faculties. The printing of universal questions and the answers thereto in a journal established for that purpose disappeared save for an occasional revival like the *Daily Oracle*, 1715, and the *Weekly Oracle*, 1734-37, half newspaper, half question-answer paper. No Mercury or Apollo or Oracle could reply with confidence and merit to the toilsome inquiries of a public waxing wider and deeper in its mental relations; the satisfaction of the curious gradually was assumed by journalistic Question Boxes and specialized organs of Notes and Queries.

Poetry entered the periodic press in the *Mercuries* of the Commonwealth, where wretched verses supplemented the pointed prose. For example, the first issue of *Mercurius Medicus*, 1647, medical only as a "Soveraigne Salve for these sick Times," offered an epitaph for its fellow *Mercuries*, calling them firebrands and "ink-squitterers."

> A Miscellanie here doth lie,
> An heap of Prose and Poesie:
> The curs'd disease that reft from us
> The Devills deare *Britanicus*,
> Hath in a mad mood a better slaine,
> *He that had a loftier vaine.   * *Melanchol.*
> Nor could he passe from us alone,
> *Pragmaticus* is also gone:
> And *Clericus* that should have staid
> Over the dead for to have praid,
> Was snatcht away, the Fates would thus,
> They're gone with *Diabolicus*.

And *Mercurius Nullus*, dated "From tomorrow morning, till yesterday at Noon, 1654," gave a motto for journeymen journalists of any date:

> Here's Newes that's false, and Newes that's true,
> Here's Newes that's old, and Newes that's new,
> Here's Newes that's good, and Newes that's bad,
> Here's merry News, and News that's sad:
> And here's presented to your view
> Newes lawful, and unlawful too:
> What shall I say? I've here in store,
> Such Newes as ne're was heard before.

The first number of the *Parliaments Scrich-Owle* in 1648, "the first year of the decease of King *Oliver*," was entirely in verse, but the later issues were only partly versified. In the same year the first English journal completely (though sadly) metrical was properly called *Mercurius Poeticus*, a title used in 1654 for a prose newsbook and in 1660 a paper with scattered bits of verse. The scarce *Al a Mode de Paris* for one issue in 1659 turned the news into doggerel no civil plight could condone. Rarely did any paper printing poems occasionally or exclusively equal the ingenuity of *A Weekly Pacquet of Advice from Rome* in 1680 with its imbedded "Jesuits Double-fac'd Creed, In Three Languages," English and Latin and Greek. Each version is to be read three ways—across the full line and down each half.

> Where th' Altar's drest - - - The Worship's scarce divine,
> The People's blest - - - Whose Table's Bread and Wine.
> He's but an Ass - - - Who their Communion flies,
> Who shuns the Mass - - - Is Catholic and wise.

Momus Ridens, 1689-90, made most of its "Comical Remarks on the Weekly Reports" in couplets. *Miscellanies over Claret*, 1697, the first monthly periodical of verse, sought to justify its subtitle of "the Friends to the Tavern the best Friends to Poetry." The *English Martial* of 1699 was a poetical, epigrammatical monthly; the *Diverting Post*, 1704-5, sloughed off its modicum of prose and outlived its small poetic merit; the not too serious *Poetical Courant* of 1706 included a short poem "On the Death of an Infant. By

Mr. *Addison*" but is not otherwise notable; in 1707 the *Diverting Muse* ran one lengthy tedious issue of five poems. Ned Ward's *Poetical Entertainer,* 1712-13, promised to digest tales, satires, dialogues, and intrigues into verse, "To be publish'd as often as occasion shall offer"; there were only five occasions for this "harmless Draught of cooling *Helicon*" to refresh the minds of men under the divisions of the day, "over-run with a News-Leprosie." In 1713 the *Monitor* for two months was poetically "Perform'd by Mr. Tate, Poet Laureat to Her Majesty, Mr. Smith, and Others." After this pale commencement the journal of verse was virtually laid aside for half a century, and its failure cost Mercury little and the Muses less. Poetry became a regular department in many a literary miscellany and magazine, and often was admitted into essay sheets and newspapers; thus the periodical poem long remained an ingredient more casual than considerable.

The function of fiction resembled that of poetry in the history of early periodical literature. Only a few journals gave themselves entirely, or almost so, to imaginative narrative: for instance, the *News, From the Land of Chivalry,* 1681, retailing the adventures of Don Rugero de Strangemento, Kt., commonly called Sir Roger L'Estrange; the *Monthly Amusement,* 1709, publishing a novel or play or sometimes both in each issue, from French, Spanish, or Italian writers, every piece to "be an intire Work of it self"; the *Records of Love,* also a contemporary of the *Tatler,* a series of Saturday romances for the sentimental Fair; and in 1715-16 *News from the Dead: or, the Monthly Packet of True Intelligence from the Other World,* "Written by Mercury" and printed and sold by John Morphew "in the Year 5663." Novels, to be sure, got serialized, before and after separate appearance, like *Launcelot Greaves* and *Robinson Crusoe,* respectively, and the essay sheet, including the *Spectator* itself, used a story, tale, fable, apologue, or dream vision as an exemplum, and the miscellany frequently made the short fiction one of its offerings. But the place of fiction, like that of verse, in general became that of component, a fraction of an issue rather than the whole number.

The letter was on occasion utilized as the basic form to envelop the substance of a periodical. Manuscript news letters, of course, circulated freely in the seventeenth century; as a result, from 1696 well into the next century *Dawks's News-Letter,* printed in special scriptorial type and begun "S^r," catered to the conservative reader who preferred to have his news in what at least looked like a handwritten letter. Letters of current news long remained a principal source for many papers; in a few instances the title of a journal claimed such an origin, for example, the *Packet of Letters,* 1646, and *Packets of Letters,* 1648. In time the letter became a device to gain variety or an informal approach to the recipient, like the reviewing *Miscellaneous Letters* of 1694-96, the important *Gentleman's Journal,* and the Edinburgh *Letters of the Critical Club,* 1738. However, the periodical in epistolary dress, as a single letter or as a collection, did not thrive. The main place of the letter in the Augustan press was as a communication to a newspaper or periodical, whether a genuine message from a reader or a fabrication by the conductor of the journal. The correspondence column in a thousand current papers continues to prove the high position in the public mind of the Letter to the Editor, and the adroit employment of the letter form in the *Tatler* and *Spectator* endures as a superb confederacy of unity and variety.

The method of classifying serials by content rather than form can be useful and accurate on occasion. A number of early journals of politics, religion, criticism, and science had an integrity of content; two minor types of periodicals sorted by subject—commerce and music—will here offer diverse illustration. The commercial papers separated into three classes: the journal, usually a giveaway, devoted to advertisements largely or entirely, such as the several *City Mercuries* of the Restoration period, the *General Remark on Trade* in 1705 (with welcome data on advertising), and the *Generous Advertiser,* 1707; second, the journal providing information of a mercantile, maritime, or agricultural character, like the *Merchants Remembrancer,* giving prices current in 1681, John Houghton's important *Collection of Letters for the Improvement of Husbandry and Trade,* 1681-83, and a decade later his *Collection* for the same purpose, the *Tusser Redivivus,* 1710, consisting of quatrains from Thomas Tusser's *Hundreth Good Pointes of Husbandrie* with observations thereon, and the *Marine Intelligencer* of 1711; and, third, the journal of commentary on trade, its theory and problems, for example, the *General History of*

Trade, 1713, *Mercator,* 1713-14, and *Manufacturer,* 1719-20, all by the diligent Defoe, who had written much in his huge *Review* on matters economic. All of these papers, and more, carry a manifest value for the historian of England's growing life on Exchange. At the other end of subject matter from the journal of commerce stands the less numerous musical monthly, represented by Playford's *Mercurius Musicus,* 1699-1702, and the *Monthly Masks of Vocal Musick,* advertised in the *Tatler.*

In its great abundance the periodical press of 1700-60 admitted various titles of more interest for their singularities than as members of a class. Tom Brown's *Infallible Astrologer,* of unstable title, in 1701-2 made merry predictions for each day of its week, and the *Monthly Weather-Paper* made serious meteorologic predictions in 1711. The *History of Cradle-Convulsions, Vulgarly called Black and White Fits,* 1701, was a monthly reflection on the rise of that disease in the bills of mortality. The *Whipping Post* put to use in 1705 the tribunal device on contemporary papers and handed down satirical sentences, wherein Defoe's *Review* was found guilty "of Coyning *New Nonsence,* and Murdering *old sence."* *Mercurius Romanus,* a penny weekly paper of substantial run in 1706-7, was written in Latin except for proper names and occasional words hard to render in Roman terms, and a *News Journal* of 1723 and *Flying Post* of 1728 reported in both French and English. And a serial of many languages appeared in 1719-22 —the *Compleat Linguist,* a "Universal Grammar Of all the Considerable Tongues in Being," to be published monthly, "One Distinct Grammar each Month, till the whole is perfected," starting with Spanish.

III

A great many—indeed, a distressing number—of the journals of the seventeenth and eighteenth centuries are extant only in unique copies or unfinished files. The zeal of such men as Thomason, Nichols, Burney, Hope, and Aitken is honored in their collections, but it was impossible for them to counteract entirely the results of small press runs, lack of historical insight and foresight, and general carelessness. The holdings of the British Museum and the Bodleian Library are the most complete. The *Census* by

Crane and Kaye in 1929 showed that only about half of the papers issued from 1620 to 1800 could then be located, in part at least, in American libraries; however, the files at Yale, Harvard, Texas, and the Huntington Library are numerous. A microfilm project annually makes available the texts of many rare journals. At best the student of the early British periodic press will encounter the basic problem of accessibility and occasionally even of existence. Further to pique the curious, some journals have left no remains at all save in casual references and advertisements, such as the *Bill of Entry*, 1683, apparently the first daily commercial paper, commended by John Houghton in his *Collection of Letters,* and the *Rehearsal Reviv'd,* which angered Defoe into comment in his *Review,* and *Queen Anne's Weekly Journal,* 1735-39, recently discovered and soon lost at sea. And there are the titles that were only a gallant hope or satirical device, like the Dissenting *Free-thinker* suggested by Dudley Ryder and the jocular *News-Letter of Whispers* and *Account of the Works of the Unlearned* proposed by Pope to the *Spectator.*

The great usefulness of the periodic press in proper historiography can nowadays be safely assumed; the vast quantity of fact, theory, and emotion in the early newspapers and periodicals offers a truly comprehensive spectacle of British civilization during one of its most influential eras and illustrates the maxim that yesterday's news is today's memory and tomorrow's history. Historians of political, military, economic, and social life, historians of ideas and ideals, historians of the arts, letters, and sciences—all can confidently discover in the journalistic records what the Augustans were doing and hoping, were saying and thinking. The problem of the faithful investigator lies not so much in whether the item of particular interest exists as in where it rests within the archives of the press.

The newspapers and periodicals of these two centuries have become during the last several decades a domain of advanced study increasingly prominent. As is natural enough in a new, wide, and fruitful field of research, the current condition of scholarship here is mixed—superior accomplishments, indifferent efforts, shoddy performances, broad intervals, excellent opportunities. The bibliographical contributions have fortunately taken the lead. The

Union List of Serials, the *Union Catalogue of the Periodical Publications in the University Libraries of the British Isles*, the *British Union-Catalogue of Periodicals* in process of publication, and the *Tercentenary Handlist* of the *Times* have registered collectively the journals in this period and beyond, and the *Census of British Newspapers and Periodicals, 1620-1800*, by Crane and Kaye, though not compiled with uniform care, has been of considerable use, especially to American students. The bibliography of corantos and early newsbooks by Dahl, the catalogue of the fine Thomason Collection, the chapter on the press in Morgan's detailed bibliography of the Queen Anne period, the catalogue of scientific and medical journals of the seventeenth and eighteenth centuries by Garrison, the hand-list of English provincial newspapers and periodicals from 1700 to 1760 by Cranfield, and the index and finding-list by Ward of serials from 1789 to 1832—these more specialized bibliographies have given their distinctive aid for the decades from the beginning of newspapers through the Romantic period. The catalogues of the collections of seventeenth and eighteenth century journals at the University of Texas, the Huntington Library, and the Bodleian Library, by Stewart, by Gabler, and by Milford and Sutherland, have earned a citation of merit, and the old catalogue of periodical publications in the British Museum has well served the hands of uncountable readers. The complementary, or secondary, bibliography by Weed and Bond enumerates the many studies of these early British journals. And a huge subject index of all eighteenth century newspapers and periodicals is now under way.

The format of the English newspaper has been described and bountifully illustrated by Stanley Morison. Careful editions of Steele's *Englishman* by Blanchard and Fielding's *Covent-Garden Journal* by Jensen and of the *Spectator* by Donald Bond (now in press) provide valuable texts, and the facsimile edition of Defoe's broad *Review* by Secord is an appropriate benefit. Historico-critical works on the *Gentleman's Magazine* by Carlson, the *Grub-street Journal* by Hillhouse, and the famous-infamous *North Briton* by Nobbe, as well as biographies of the leading literary men concerned with periodicals and of journalistic figures like Motteux and Icabod Dawks, by Cunningham and Morison, respectively, have made their individual contributions. The acute analysis of a special topic, such as that by Watson of the relationship of the magazine serial and the essay tradition, is a critical advance; another recent and interesting volume is *The Newsmen of Queen Anne*, edited by Ewald, a collection of varied, readable excerpts from the press of 1702-14, mostly newspapers. Notes and articles on men and titles in early journalism are far too many for comment in a summary survey. Various studies of subjects related to journalistic activity have been successfully pursued, for example, the monograph by Stevens on party politics and journalism, the book by Hoover on Johnson's Parliamentary reporting, and the volumes by Siebert and by Hanson on the freedom of the press and the relation of the law to the press. As to general histories, the works by Madden on Irish periodical literature, by Couper on the Edinburgh periodical press, and by Craig on the Scottish press of 1750-89 are competent chronicles, and J. B. Williams has prepared the way for a more thorough study of English journalism down to the foundation of the *Gazette*. But the history of English journalism by Fox Bourne is diffuse and obsolete, and the history of the English literary periodical by Graham wants the accuracy and acumen required of a standard work. The recent *March of Journalism* by Herd is too superficial to satisfy even its own purpose. Thus neither the English newspaper nor the English periodical has yet had an adequate comprehensive account.

The desiderata in this richly rewarding area of research are, therefore, numerous and various. Short studies and sizable would be welcome of many individual periodicals and of editors, writers, and publishers of periodicals. Careful editions of the most meritorious and important journals would prove quite helpful, especially one of the *Tatler*. The major and the minor types of periodicals, considered by form or by content, would repay thoughtful and scrupulous investigation, for instance, the trade paper, the dialogue periodical, and "ladies' home journalism." Inquiries into influences from within and without the press can clarify its progression. Particular devices would prove appropriate for critical scrutiny, such as the eidolon, the club, correspondence, the motto, and serialization. Bibliographical explorations could make a collaboration of the history of the periodic press and the history of printing. The economic basis of journalistic society also would become clearer from specific investigations of circulation, the "taxes on knowledge," the profits of periodical publication, the wages of editor- and authorship, and especially (in the absence of a creditable history of advertising) the finances of advertisements. After further research down these broad avenues and narrow ways can come the general union of particular conclusions; a series of vigilant analyses will induce authentic syntheses.

For the present volume the editor invited the six contributors to prepare essays, based upon their graduate researches at the University of North Carolina and later study, on six prominent English journals—the *Tatler, British Apollo, Free-Thinker, Prompter, Female Spectator,* and *World*—whose years of publication met each of the first six decades of the eighteenth century. The subjects of these essays illustrate the diversity of studies in the early periodic press—influence, business operation, authorship, literary form, special content, and bibliography. In an attempt to enclose such a variety of topic within a valid unity of time and medium, the editor has served as general counsel to the project and has introduced the volume and the subject with a brief view of the republic of periodical letters in the Augustan era. He desires to acknowledge gratefully the essential assistance, as ever, of Marjorie N. Bond and the grants by the Research Council of the University of North Carolina to aid publication.

RICHARD STEELE, GAZETTEER
AND BICKERSTAFF

THE LONDON GAZETTE

Nos. 1-23, [November 16] 1665-February 1, 1666, as *Oxford Gazette*; No. 24, February 5, 1666, to the present.

Semi-weekly to June 25, 1709; tri-weekly.

Folio half-sheet or sheet.

Editor: Richard Steele, May, 1707-October, 1710.

Colophon: "Printed by *J. Tonson* at *Grays-Inn* Gate. 1710."

THE TATLER

Nos. 1-271, April 12, 1709-January 2, 1711.

Tri-weekly.

Folio half-sheet.

Editor: Richard Steele.

Colophon: "Sold by *John Morphew* near *Stationers-Hall;* where Advertisements are taken in."

RICHARD STEELE, GAZETTEER AND BICKERSTAFF

ROBERT WALLER ACHURCH

WHEN Steele in the spring of 1709 elected to set up as Censor of Great Britain and act the gamesome Isaac Bickerstaff, he had achieved military and social experience, had written some verses, a devotional tract, and three plays, and for almost two years had held the office of the writer of the *London Gazette*, official newspaper of the nation. Thus his knowledge of life and letters, together with his industry and amiability and native talent, provided promising equipment for the undertaking of a new journal of comment on affairs literary, dramatic, social, and moral in a style vigorous but urbane. As the Gazetteer he had at hand the budgets of dispatches which he could utilize for authoritative columns in the *Gazette* and also for his other paper as a section of current intelligence welcome to his readers, who felt the normal itch for news of the day.

At the outset of the *Tatler*, combining the novelty of literary experiment with the security of journalistic convenience, Steele announced he would divide his Lucubrations into five departments, each "under such Dates of Places" as would properly prepare his audience for the paragraphs which would follow—accounts of pleasure and gallantry under the heading of White's Chocolate-House, poetry under that of the famous Will's Coffee-House, learning under the title of the Grecian, foreign and domestic news from St. James's Coffee-House, and other subjects from his own apartment. These four places of public resort, catering as they did to men who sought to drink, talk, and read with citizens of like interest, were known as centers of particular fraternity. The special clientele of St. James's Coffee-House included the gentry given to public affairs. So it was that Richard Steele set in motion his editorial enterprise—he could continue as Gazetteer, and as

Gazetteer he could pass along to Bickerstaff such tidings as would fit neatly into the St. James's department of the new journal, a comfortable arrangement important to the launching of the *Tatler*. But the Gazetteer-Bickerstaff partnership was not long to last, and its alteration proved momentous to the career of that great periodical.

The purpose of the present essay is to examine this marked change in the conduct of the *Tatler* as the frequency and quantity of foreign and home news diminished. But first it is necessary to correct by means of factual evidence certain ill-grounded conjectures and inadequate explanations of the reasons why Steele, writer of the *London Gazette*, with the definite advantages he had over his rival "news-mongers," first neglected, then abandoned this popular portion of the *Tatler*. Indeed, scholarly reasoning has been so confused that his dropping of the department of news from the *Tatler* has sometimes been improperly identified with the larger problem of why he abandoned the *Tatler* itself.

This false identification of two separate problems has been accompanied too often by variously modified repetitions of two explanations of Steele's change in editorial practice. One assigned reason is that the loss of the Gazetteership in 1710 prompted him to withdraw the news department from the *Tatler*, and the other is that his good friend and mentor Joseph Addison persuaded him to discontinue the publishing of news in that journal. It apparently was the brilliant Macaulay who first declared that when Steele lost the *Gazette* he dropped the articles of news from the *Tatler* and resolved to bring the paper to a close. A generation later Alexandre Beljame erroneously stated that news disappeared from the *Tatler* after its eighty-third number and attributed the disappearance to Addison's collaboration with Steele after August of 1709. Later biographers of Addison and Steele and historians of the periodic press have, with one notable exception, been sufficiently satisfied with received doctrine to spare themselves an examination of the pertinent data and a strict reappraisal of the subject.[1]

The exception is C. N. Greenough, who published a significant study of this problem, in which he systematically compiled factual data concerning the frequency and length of the various departments of the *Tatler* and showed graphically the progressive elimi-

nation of all of them except that dated "From my own Apartment."[2] Greenough suggested as Steele's reasons for dropping the
news department, first, the traditional view that Addison disapproved the practice; second, Steele's own indifference toward the
news department; third, the increased volume of advertisements,
which took up the space formerly given over to news items; and,
fourth, the gradual change in the character of the *Tatler* from a
miscellany of some five departments into a single, unified essay
which "naturally crowded out not merely the news from St.
James's, but all other headings except the one—usually 'From My
Own Apartment'—appropriate to the kind of paper which the
Tatler in its later and more typical days found most effective,—the
lay sermon on taste."[3]

An examination of available evidence for the first of these
reasons—Addison's influence in persuading Steele to discontinue
the news department—does not reveal any substantiating testimony;
on the contrary, it makes this conjecture quite unlikely. The first
negative evidence is found in the fact that not until late in September, or more likely in October of 1709, can Addison's influence as
coadjutor in the editorial policies of the *Tatler* even be assumed.[4]
For after his arrival in England from Ireland, September 19, 1709,
Addison proceeded with Wharton to the latter's country place in
Buckinghamshire.[5] Even when he returned to London somewhat
later, he was preoccupied with efforts to retain his seat in Parliament and, failing that, in getting his salary as Keeper of the Irish
Records increased.[6] Apparently whatever collaboration with
Steele he may have undertaken began about the middle of October.
In fact, his first contribution to the *Tatler* after his return from
Ireland did not appear until October 1, 1709 (No. 75), and not
until November 19 (No. 96) was he the sole author of an entire
number.[7] Yet the decline of news in the *Tatler*, a tendency notice-
able as early as July, had by September 8 (No. 65) reached the
point after which the St. James's department became very rare.[8]
The exact time at which Steele settled upon a fairly consistent
editorial policy is likewise uncertain. Dobson believed that after
October 13, 1709 (No. 80), the *Tatler* "had already found its
raison d'être,"[9] but Greenough thought that the editorial policies
had not become fixed before November 19 (No. 96).[10] As a matter

of fact, news items in the *Tatler* from September 13 (No. 67) through November 19 occur only six times, and range in length from a half-inch to three inches, in contrast to the earlier news columns ranging up to eighteen inches and occurring in practically every number.[11] Therefore, the approximate and perhaps fortuitous coincidence of Addison's arrival in England from Ireland with the decline of news in the *Tatler*, a decline which had begun months before his return, appears to be very slight evidence for the traditional assumption that Addison was responsible for Steele's abandonment of this department.

Nor do the indications that Steele cared little more than Addison for the news department "seem to justify us in regarding Steele and Addison as essentially at one in this matter of news in the *Tatler*."[12] Even though, as Greenough pointed out in reaching his conclusion, Steele from the beginning of the *Tatler* reminded his readers several times that "Politic News is not the Principal Subject on which we treat" and that lacking news "from Courts and Camps, we hope still to give you somewhat new and curious from our selves," the intent is clearly not to minimize the importance or interest of the St. James's department, but merely to boast of the variety of kinds of "news" which was the province of the *Tatler* and to point out that a dearth of foreign intelligence would not subject the reader to a "dressing up a second Time . . . the same dish which they [the news-writers] gave you the Day before. . . ."[13] On the contrary, there is positive evidence from Steele himself that he regarded the news department as quite an important component of the *Tatler* in attracting readers to his money-making project. In his dedication of the first volume of the *Tatler* to Arthur Maynwaring, Steele declared that "the Addition of the ordinary Occurrences of common Journals of News brought in a Multitude of other Readers" than those attracted by the name of Bickerstaff.[14] Furthermore, some years later Joseph Spence made the following note: "I have heard Sir Richard Steele say, that though he had a greater share in the *Tatlers*, than in the *Spectators*; he thought the news article, in the first of these, was what contributed much to their success."[15]

A partial explanation of Steele's apparent animadversions against news is to be found in the contemporary passion of Londoners for news, a passion which Steele not infrequently made the subject of satire in the *Tatler* after the news department had been dropped;[16] for, as Ned Ward picturesquely phrased the public appetite, "*News* is the very Oracle of *Government; the Life of Trade; and the Delight of the People.*"[17] Thus there ought to have been some more conclusive and demonstrable reason for Steele's dropping the St. James's department than those traditionally offered.

Greenough was obviously not wholly satisfied with the reasons he gave for the disappearance of the news department. He suggested, on the basis of editorial statements in two papers,[18] that Steele was being "scooped" by some of his "Brethren of the Quill" in the matter of providing the day's news. In fact, Greenough declared, "One suspects this, next to the development of the single essay, to have been the most potent cause of the change."[19]

The plan of this study is to examine the *London Gazette* during the period of Steele's editorship, especially during the period which coincided with his writing the *Tatler,* to determine precisely what were his policies in editing the news of the two papers and what reasons more probably prompted Steele's discontinuing the news in the *Tatler* than those formerly advanced. As a point of orientation and comparison between the news and the date of its appearance in the *Tatler* and in the *London Gazette,* the *Daily Courant* will be employed. This, the first daily newspaper, from its inception March 11, 1702, had maintained a high record of accuracy and promptness in reporting foreign and domestic affairs.[20] Steele in an extremely censorious essay on contemporary newspapers had only praise for the *Courant,* especially for its clarity and accuracy, "this Paper differing from the rest as an History from a Romance."[21] The best that Defoe could do to find fault with the dispatches of the *Courant* was to quibble over the accuracy of the editor's translations or humorously to censure the editor's immodesty in coming out every day.[22]

When Steele became Gazetteer May 1, 1707,[23] with the stipend of three hundred pounds annually, less a tax of forty-five pounds,[24] the *London Gazette* was a semi-weekly paper appearing on Mondays and Thursdays, bearing the imprimatur "Published by

Authority" and edited under the supervision of the Secretary of State for the Southern Department. Although the *Gazette* was usually first with important news and at the same time more reliable than the privately owned newspapers,[25] evidence indicates that not infrequently such thrice-weekly competitors as the *Post-Man*, the *Post Boy*, the *Flying-Post*, and the *Daily Courant* obtained and published important news before it appeared in the *Gazette*.[26] Information may have been obtained, for a fee, from the scribes and lower clerks in governmental administrative offices, where confusion and carelessness were apparent.[27]

Steele, as Gazetteer, sought to change this situation by proposing reforms designed, as he wrote, "to raise the Value of the paper written by Authority, and Lessen the esteem of the rest among the Generality of the People," to which purpose he added the more pecuniary one: "For the advancement of the Credit and Income of the Gazette. . . ."[28] Specifically, he requested that all ministers in each province be instructed to send "a circular Letter every Post of what passes in their respective stations directed to the Gazetteer" and that the letters to the Gazetteer be allowed "to come in the Flying Packet," that "he may in the name of the Secretaries of State prevent Packets passing thro' the Offices to Writers of News," and that "the Gazette be published three times a Week vizt on Tuesday Thursday and Saturday." Steele especially urged this last proposal, that of altering the days of publication "to Post days," a change which would "furnish the readers with a Series of occurrences without interruption of other Papers and most neccessarily Diminish their reputation and Sale." However, to have given the Gazetteer such control over the news coming into the Secretaries' offices would, indeed, have raised the "lowest Minister of State" to a position not contemplated in the creation of the office. Steele's proposals were not at the time accepted,[29] but he did apparently receive permission to urge governmental agents to send him the local news of their areas.[30] Such news he sadly needed when the packet boats from Holland failed to arrive with fresh dispatches of the war abroad.

Annoyed by the experience of editing a paper which was often largely anticipated by others, Steele must readily have decided when he initiated the *Tatler* to make it a thrice-weekly appearing on the post days. For with this schedule he could utilize the first-hand, authoritative dispatches and letters to which he had even freer access than did the paid agents, located in the Secretaries' offices, of the other newspapers. Certainly he must have seen that publication on the post days had a double advantage to the *Tatler*—prompt distribution of his paper and effective use of news available to him. Moreover, in his *Tatler* he would not be restrained, as he was in the *Gazette,* to the editing of the news in such a way as not to transgress "the Rule observed by all Ministries, to keep that Paper very innocent and very insipid."[31] Interesting variations appear in his editing the same news for the two papers.[32]

When the *Tatler* first appeared, as it did on the post days, Tuesdays, Thursdays, and Saturdays, the *Gazette* was appearing on Mondays and Thursdays, so that Steele through his access to the official dispatches, bulletins, and foreign gazettes brought in by the packet boats[33] had the advantage for his own paper of anticipating the news in the *Gazette* on two days of each week, that is, on Tuesdays and Saturdays.[34]

Steele in the first number of the *Tatler,* speaking in the role of Isaac Bickerstaff the astrologer, declared he had the power of divination, so that *"by casting a Figure"* he could tell *"all that will happen before it comes to pass,"* but he promised to use this last faculty *"very sparingly."* Though the public did not know it at the time, this magic derived from his position as Gazetteer. Later, this astrologer's aerial sprite Pacolet is the eye-witness conveyor of supernaturally fresh news,[35] but generally Bickerstaff pretended to no other news correspondent than Humphrey Kidney, the waiter at St. James's Coffee-House, "who has the Ear of the greatest Politicians who come hither."[36] Humphrey Kidney was as much a disguise for the Gazetteer editing the St. James's department of the *Tatler* as Isaac Bickerstaff was for the jovial sinner playing the role of Censor of Great Britain.

From the initial number of the *Tatler* Steele "scooped" the *Gazette* whenever the differing dates of publication permitted. For example, in the St. James's department of the first *Tatler* (April 12, 1909) there are three news dispatches cited and narrated, two from The Hague, one of the 16th of April and the other of the 19th, and a third from Ghent dated the 17th of April.[37] None of these items is in the *Gazette* of the preceding date, Monday, April 11, but all are in *Gazette* No. 4531, published the following Thursday, April 14. Steele also "scooped" the *Daily Courant* (No. 2329) for this day. Not until the following day, Wednesday, did the *Courant* (No. 2330) publish these items. *Tatler* No. 2, of course, appeared on the same day, Thursday, April 14, that the *Gazette* made its second and last appearance for the week. Half the news in this *Gazette* had already been anticipated by the Tuesday *Tatler*, but fresh news had arrived (or been held over!) from Venice, Berlin, and Vienna. In this simultaneous appearance of the two papers he was editing, Steele impartially divided the latest news, so that no one reading only the *Gazette* or the *Tatler* for that day had all the news. The *Daily Courant* for that day had been generally "scooped"; in only one particular did it have any of the news in either of Steele's papers.

There is, however, a great deal more objectivity in the style of the news items as Steele reported them in the *Gazette* than in the *Tatler*. Characteristic of the more colorful style he used in the *Tatler* in contrast to the baldness with which he reported the same fact in the *Gazette* are the following extracts from each paper for April 14th:

Letters from *Venice* say, the Disappointment of seeing his *Danish* Majesty has very much disquieted the Court of *Rome*. [*Tatler*]
The King [of Denmark] does not design to proceed to Rome, as was expected. [*Gazette*]

Apparently a newspaper "Published by Authority" could not afford the luxury of mentioning disappointment and disquietude about a court with which the government was not at war, or attribute the cause of such disappointment to his Danish Majesty Frederick IV.

Steele's third *Tatler*, Saturday, April 16, not only anticipated the news in the *Gazette* for the following Monday (No. 4532), but also presented the facts of the Emperor Joseph's preparations of his army for the ensuing campaign against the French in greater detail and in more picturesque diction.[38] The *Daily Courants* (Nos. 2332, 2333) for Friday and Saturday contain none of the news items in the Saturday *Tatler* except the bare fact of the Marshal de Thesse's arrival in Genoa, without the additional information of the Marshal's activities since his arrival and his purposes in being there. All these lively details which Steele gave in his *Tatler* he characteristically omitted from the more staid account in the *Gazette* for the following Monday.

An examination of the remaining numbers of the *Tatler* which contain news shows that this editorial pattern adopted by Steele in the initial issues was maintained throughout, but that the appearance of news in the *Tatler* became more and more sporadic. Two facts account for this decrease of news in the *Tatler*, neither of which coincides with the suppositions hitherto advanced. These facts are the decrease of sustained newsworthy events abroad from the middle of May, 1709, through the winter of 1710 and a change in the periodicity of the *London Gazette*.

A newspaper's dependence for its sales or even its existence upon newsworthy events is, of course, fully understood by news editors. Steele recognized the fact and so informed his readers in the St. James's department of the eleventh *Tatler* (May 3, 1709):

As Politic News is not the Principal Subject on which we treat, we are so happy as to have no Occasion for that Art of Cookery, which our Brother Newsmongers so much excel in; as appears by their excellent and inimitable Manner of dressing up a second Time for your Tast the same Dish which they gave you the Day before, in case there come over no new Pickles from *Holland*. Therefore, when we have nothing to say to you from Courts or Camps, we hope still to give you somewhat new and curious from our selves. . . .

And about five inches of inconsequential news follow.

Though this passage has been cited by Greenough and others to show that Steele did not care for news as a feature of the *Tatler*, neither this conclusion nor the guess that Addison had advised him to discontinue the department of news is needed to explain the passage. The explanation of Steele's editorial statement is simpler than either of these hypothetical reasons. Steele was simply warning his readers not to expect news in each *Tatler*, as they had come to expect, and assuring them that his paper had other resources than news for its popular appeal. He did so because packet boats bearing the packets of news—or "Pickles" as Steele called them—for one reason or another, especially because of contrary winds, frequently did not make England on schedule and were sometimes a week late. Moreover, when they did arrive on schedule the dispatches they brought were often no more than repetitions of old matter. This condition was especially true of the dispatches and foreign gazettes arriving in the spring, summer, and fall of 1709. They were largely filled with reiterations of positions of the allied forces, which for long periods of time were completely inactive pending projected peace negotiations.[39] Since domestic news, except for ship sailings, proclamations, addresses, and advertisements for felons, was practically an undeveloped and apparently unpopular kind of reporting, unless it could be used for political polemics by such papers as the *Review, Observator, Rehearsal,* or later the *Examiner,* the absence of military or diplomatic achievements abroad starved the papers subsisting on news.

In the next *Tatler* (No. 12) under the rubric of his "Own Apartment" Steele briefly announced: "There has a Mail this Day arriv'd from *Holland;* but the Matter of the Advices importing rather what gives us great Expectations, than any positive Assurances, I shall, for this Time, decline giving you what I know. . . ." There was no *Gazette* for this day (May 7), but the *Courant* (No. 2351) indicates how dull the news was that Steele decided to withhold from his readers while leading them to look forward to something good in his next *Tatler*—news which apparently did not develop.

The eighteenth *Tatler* (Thursday, May 19) requires special attention because in this number is Addison's essay on the decline of news and the fall of the news-writers, an essay, like Steele's editorial comment in the eleventh *Tatler,* illogically but generally cited to show Addison's distaste for news; yet there is not a statement in it which deprecates the publishing of bona fide news. Indeed, following the essay are six and a half inches of dispatches concerning the progress of the Peace preliminaries. The essay is simply a bit of heartless levity at the expense of editors suffering from a dearth of salable news. Steele had already initiated the theme in the eleventh *Tatler.*

The prospects of the news-writers brightened when the advice from Brussels of June 6, N.S., was that Louis XIV "had absolutely refused to sign the Preliminaries to the Treaty which he had, in his Majesty's Behalf, consented to at the *Hague*."[40] Such an announcement meant renewed activities of the allied and French armies. Editorials on the perfidy of the French monarch and the marchings of armies form the matter of the next several *Tatlers*, *Courants*, and other papers publishing news.

Then on June 20th of 1709 a change was announced in the periodicity of the *London Gazette* which very materially affected the special advantage which Steele had enjoyed in editing the news department of the *Tatler*. Prominently placed under the heading of the *Gazette* for this day (No. 4550) appeared the following notice:

Whereas there are many Acts of State, as well as Notices which regard the private Interest of the Subject, the Promulgation of which is often retarded longer than the Nature of them will admit: It is thought fit, that the *Gazette* shall, for the future, be Publish'd three times in the Week, *viz*. on *Tuesday*, *Thursday*, and *Saturday;* beginning on Saturday next.[41]

Were there other reasons for this change in the publication dates of the *Gazette?* Had complaints been registered with the Secretaries of State against what might be regarded as Steele's misuse of his Gazetteership to the detriment of the reputation and possibly the sale of the *Gazette* and certainly to the distress of other editors of newspapers? Or, because of the declining value of the foreign news and the apparent absence of any prospects of much activity on the Continent, did Steele decide to make the St. James's department of his paper less important and therefore urge again with more success his proposal of 1707 that the *Gazette* be made a thrice-weekly appearing on the post days? Whatever the explanation, the significant facts are that from June 25, 1709, until the end of the *Tatler* the publication dates of the *Tatler* and the *Gazette* coincided and that Steele could no longer "scoop" the news in the *Gazette* in two out of three of his *Tatlers*. It is noteworthy that of the sixty-three *Tatlers* containing news seriously presented thirty-one occur in the first thirty-three numbers, that is, through June

25, and that the remaining thirty-two are scattered through the two hundred and thirty-eight numbers of the *Tatler* thereafter.

However, after the *Gazette* became a thrice-weekly, Steele for a time continued his St. James's department, but tended steadily to reduce the length and frequency of it. His policy in editing this department now became of necessity what his policy previously had been in editing the St. James's department on the one day (Thursday) each week which coincided with the *Gazette*, that is, when he did not omit the department altogether, to use the department for specious news,[42] to condense considerably the more interesting news items in the *Gazette*,[43] to publish in the *Tatler* items which for one or another reason never appeared in the *Gazette* at all,[44] or to combine the last two procedures.[45]

The absence or irregularity of fresh and significant news from abroad continued to plague Steele and the other news-writers. Despite London's concern over the success or failure of Marlborough's siege of Tournay, Steele had to report in the *Gazette* (No. 4561) for July 16: "*The* Holland *Mail of the 23rd of July N. S. is not yet arrived.*" Not until four days later did the news of the surrender of the town arrive.[46] By July 30 Defoe was complaining, "We have been since last *Saturday* without a Post from the Army. . . ."[47] Steele with difficulty filled the columns of the *Gazette* for that day with routine news. The *General Postscript*, which after the fifth number appeared on Mondays, Wednesdays, and Fridays, made its principal function the summarizing of news in the current papers which appeared on the post days, Tuesday, Thursday, and Saturday.[48] Not infrequently during this period the editor, after summarizing the *Gazette* for what little was in it, declared that there was little else of a material nature in the other papers.[49] On Monday, October 10, the editor of the *General Postscript* in his sixth number protested, "The Advices that came by the last Mail are so mix'd and confus'd, that without the Front of a News-Writer No-body can venture to report any thing from 'em." Steele evidently thought so too, for he largely filled the *Gazette* (No. 4597) of that date with proclamations and addresses, and omitted the news department from the *Tatler*. Indeed, in the previous *Tatler*, Thursday, October 6, he frankly declared, "I have no Manner of News," and filled this section of his paper with a parody of a letter from Marshal Boufflers to Louis XIV, which in its original form had first been published in the *Paris Gazette*, September 29, N.S., was reprinted in the *Amsterdam Gazette*, October 4, N.S., and finally appeared in the *Daily Courant* (No. 2479) for October 4, O.S. This scarcity and sameness of foreign news continued throughout October, with the exception of the unexpected surrender of Mons, October 21, N.S., news of which seems to have reached England in time for most of the newspapers to publish the event simultaneously.

This exciting flurry of news was followed by a long lull, so that the news-writers had to rewrite old stuff. The *Post-Man* included two letters which "vary only in a few useless Particulars from what has been mention'd before in the *Gazette. . . .* The *Daily Courant* is fill'd up with an old Account. . . ."[50] Steele on October 20, the day after this complaint in the *General Postscript*, announced in effect the end of his news department for that year and the reason: "All the Forces in the Field, both of the Enemy and the Confederates, are preparing to withdraw into Winter Quarters."[51] However, the public appetite for news does not seem to have diminished, and the editors of papers dependent upon news did the best they could. As Novel put the matter near the end of October when Scandal told him the people wanted news, not scandal: "What, would they have us invent and entertain the *Publick* with *Impertinencies* as they [the news-writers] do! For my part I don't find a Syllable for News, fit to be publish'd, in all the *Bundle* [of news-sheets]; and how they'll be able to oblige the *People* this Winter, I protest, *Scandal*, I can't imagine!"[52] Meanwhile, the *Gazette* allowed its advertising to run well over into a second column, though a fourth to a half column was normal, and frequently doubled the size of the type in well-spaced lines, for example, No. 4615, November 19, 1709, which is a typical *Gazette* until No. 4674, April 6, 1710.

Whatever intentions Steele may have had of reviving his St. James's department with the resurgence of the armies on the battlefields in the spring of 1710 would have been quelled by a still further increase in the frequency with which the official news organ, the *Gazette*, tended to appear at this time. This increase in frequency took the form of the special issue, appearing when news of consequence reached London between its normal publication days or even on the normal days of publication if the regular issue had already been published before the arrival of the important news. The likelihood is that Steele was himself responsible for this further effort to increase the reputation of the *Gazette* and to forestall other newspapers. Certainly by this time, April of 1710, Steele had found that his *Tatler* could prosper without a news department. Be that as it may, when the renewed activities of the allied armies brought successes in Flanders, Picardy, and Spain between April 14 and September 16, 1710, at least six such extra issues appeared.[53] These issues, two of which came just at the crucial period in April when Steele, because of the new and exciting reports from the Continent, might have revived the news department in the *Tatler* on the old basis of dividing the news with the *Gazette*, even more completely impaired the advantage the *Tatler* had enjoyed when the *Gazette* appeared only twice a week. Henceforth, any really striking news was likely to appear in a special issue from Whitehall a day before it could possibly be published in the *Tatler*.

Only four times thereafter did Steele publish news in the *Tatler*, in each instance concerned with Captain Steele's favorite topic, military maneuvers and victories. The first two appeared in successive numbers and are examples of those typically spirited and explanatory accounts, enriched with French terminology, of military maneuvering of the allied armies.[54] Three months later, near the middle of August, when he was harassed by debts, troubled by the fall of the Whigs,[55] concerned about a new paper, the *Examiner*, which seemed determined to give his *Tatler* a political dye much deeper than it had, Steele sketched for *Tatler* No. 210 a brief character of a censorious prude, threw in a letter and a reply, and filled eleven columnar inches of paper with another well written account of a military engagement, this time of General Stanhope's victory at Almenara. Although this account was, Bickerstaff said, an abstract of a letter from Milan, actually it is a considerable expansion of the more pertinent details of the item from Milan published in the *Gazette*.[56] Steele's final St. James's department, which appeared less than a month before he ended his

Gazetteership,[57] contained a brief summary of the movements of the armies in Spain, following the allied victory under Stanhope at Saragossa.[58]

Though the more probable reasons for Steele's diminishing and eventually dropping news from the *Tatler* should now be apparent, two other reasons advanced by Greenough and a somewhat related one advanced by Walter Graham remain to be evaluated. Besides his belief that the decline of news was due to the distaste of Addison and to the indifference of Steele for news and to the possibility that other newspapers were "scooping" the news in the *Tatler*, all of which reasons have been shown to be invalid, Greenough thought that the growth of the single essay "naturally crowded out not merely the news from St. James's, but all other headings except one—usually 'From My Own Apartment,' "[59] and that the growth of advertising paralleled the growth of the single essay and the elimination of the news.[60] The last part of this theory is generalized from a graph, but the substantiating value of this graph is questionable since an examination of the individual *Tatlers* in which news appeared after the frequency of the department had definitely begun to decline reveals no correlation between the presence or absence of news and the amount of advertising in the same *Tatler*.[61] However, the increase in the amount of advertising does seem to parallel the growth of the single essay. This correlation may have no other significance than that as the popularity and circulation of the *Tatler* increased so, naturally, did the advertising. Similarly, the lack of significant news may have necessitated Steele's lengthening the essay under the rubric *"From my own Apartment"* and may have contributed, among other influences, to the development of what turned out to be the more successful type of literary periodical, the single-essay journal which became the *Spectator*.[62]

Graham's explanation of the dropping of news from the *Tatler* is a kind of ex post facto theory of natural evolution and selection:

Several writers on the subject have taken unnecessary pains to explain the dropping of new [*sic*] elements from the *Tatler*. The fact that the news was dropped from the *Gentleman's Journal, Post Angel*, and

Diverting Post shows that it was not a remarkable circumstance, but rather the logical result of competition. The *Tatler* had to be one thing or the other—it chose to be a journal of entertainment rather than a newspaper. Like the contemporary *British Apollo,* it found that it could not compete with the regular newspapers without abandoning its more distinctive features, and it chose not to abandon them. The *Tatler* was not an isolated example, but was really one of four literary periodicals, within a period of ten years, which began with news elements, but gradually allowed these to be displaced by other kinds of matter.[63]

Unfortunately for this theory, the instances cited are not pertinent, except one and that one does not substantiate it.[64] The *British Apollo,* with its questions and answers in prose and verse and its department of news is the only periodical of the four which is comparable in time and kind to the *Tatler.* However, an examination of the news department in the *British Apollo* reveals the following facts: first, during that period of the *British Apollo* which coincides with the period of the *Tatler* when the St. James's department was one of its most prominent and most frequent departments,[65] the space devoted to news in the *British Apollo* is almost twice that in the *Tatler;* second, the news in the *Apollo* is nearly always twenty-four to forty-eight hours behind the same news in the *Daily Courant* and in the *Tatler,*[66] and in fact, the news in the *British Apollo* seems to be a revision of that in the *Daily Courants* preceding; third, though with the dearth of news in the late summer, autumn, and winter of 1709-1710 the news in the *British Apollo* shrinks from its former average of a full column or more to an average of half a column, the department was not abandoned until four months after the *Tatler* had come to an end, that is, until March 28, 1711; and, fourth, at that time the *British Apollo,* making its final efforts to survive, reduced its size from four folio pages to two, and in order to accommodate itself to half its former space reduced its questions and answers by at least one page and omitted its department of news. Thus the *British Apollo*—the only really analogous periodical of the four cited by Graham to show a common tendency of news to disappear from a periodical which was not primarily a newspaper—also dropped its news section for reasons other than those of competition from the regular newspapers.

Because of his ready access as Gazetteer to reliable, first-hand news dispatches Steele made the St. James's department one of the most prominent and popular components of the early numbers of the *Tatler*. The reasons for the gradual elimination of this department are to be found in circumstances connected with the *London Gazette* and Steele's editorship of it rather than in surmises about Addison's and Steele's distaste for news. As long as the *Gazette* was a twice-weekly paper appearing on Mondays and Thursdays, Steele was able to make his *Tatler*, appearing on Tuesdays, Thursdays, and Saturdays, the bearer of the earliest authoritative news for two of its three appearances each week; but when the *Gazette* became a thrice-weekly, published on the same days as the *Tatler*, and began to publish extra issues for important news, this priority was lost, and the importance of the news department in the *Tatler* diminished. The effect of this increase in the periodicity of the *Gazette* is immediately perceptible in the decreased space and frequency with which the department of news appeared in the *Tatler*. The scarcity of news of interest during the summer, fall, and winter of 1709-1710 further discouraged Steele's use of the news department. Thus did the Gazetteer assist Mr. Bickerstaff and then resign to him the sheets of the *Tatler*. A consequent lengthening of the essay or essays in each paper became a necessity which materially contributed to the development of the *Tatler* into the single-essay literary periodical.

NOTES

1. Macaulay's declaration appeared in his review of Lucy Aikin's *Life of Joseph Addison, Edinburgh Review*, LXXVIII (1843), 235, and Beljame's ideas in his *Le public et les hommes de lettres en Angleterre au dix-huitième siècle*, 2d ed. (Paris, 1897), p. 277. Meanwhile John Forster had written a spirited defense of Steele in reply to Macaulay, but repeated the conjecture connecting Steele's loss of the *Gazette* with the cessation of the *Tatler: Quarterly Review*, XCVI (1855), 557, reprinted in *Historical and Biographical Essays*, 1858. H. R. Fox Bourne simply paraphrased the assertions of Macaulay and Beljame so as to intensify the errors of both: *English Newspapers: Chapters in the History of Journalism* (London, 1887), I, 73. W. J. Courthope in his *Addison* (New York, 1884), p. 97, and Austin Dobson in *Richard Steele* (New York, 1886), p. 123, n., corrected earlier views concerning the time at which Steele discontinued the news items in the *Tatler* and the mistaken connection of his loss of the Gazetteership

with this discontinuance. Both of these corrections George A. Aitken embodied in his *Life of Richard Steele* (London, 1889), I, 244, n. 2, but he erred in saying that No. 175 is the last *Tatler* containing news. However, the illogicality of the idea that Steele's discontinuance of the news department was connected with his loss of the Gazetteership was first pointed out by Wilhelm Ricken in his *Bemerkungen über Anlage und Erfolg der wichtigsten Zeitschriften Steele's und den Einfluss Addison's auf die Entwicklung derselben* (Elberfeld, [1885]), p. 8. The recent biographers, Willard Connely in *Sir Richard Steele* (New York, 1934) and Peter Smithers in *The Life of Joseph Addison* (Oxford, 1954), do not deal with the matter. Walter Graham in neither his *Beginnings of Early Literary Periodicals* (New York, 1926) nor his *English Literary Periodicals* (New York, 1930) makes an adequate analysis of the problem. Harold Herd's *March of Journalism* (London, 1952) is negligible.

2. "The Development of the *Tatler*, Particularly in Regard to News," *PMLA*, XXXI (1916), 633-63. The suggestion at the end of the article that a study of some of the contemporaries of the *Tatler* which also published news might give additional light upon Steele's reason for discontinuing the news department led to the present reinvestigation of the whole problem.

3. *Ibid.*, p. 655.

4. The earliest evidence of any interference by Addison in the content of the *Tatler* is found in an informal letter he wrote Joshua Dawson, Secretary to the Lords Justices of Ireland, November 29, 1709, in which he referred to a "Story about the L^{tt} Gener^l & the Irish Lucretia very archly told & designed for the Tatler, tho it never came to his hands, but I took care to put a stop to it out of my respect to the General, but this I would not have known for a thousand Reasons": *The Letters of Joseph Addison*, ed. Walter Graham (Oxford, 1941), p. 194. Though Graham does not identify either the persons concerned or the incident, he points to this letter as the only concrete evidence of the long-suspected restraining influence of Addison on the scandal-mongering tendencies of the *Tatler*. Actually, however, the letter proves only that Addison's preventing the story's reaching Steele was prompted not so much by an interest in the editorial policies of the *Tatler* as by his concern for the victim of the story.

5. Elford Chapman Morgan, "The Public Career of Joseph Addison," Ph.D. dissertation, University of North Carolina, 1941, p. 206.

6. *Ibid.*, pp. 207-10.

7. Thomas Tickell, in the preface of the first collected edition of Addison's works, 1721, pp. xii-xiii, implies very slight aid, not editorial collaboration, by Addison in the *Tatler* as opposed to the *Spectator*, an important implication which Steele seems to confirm in his Dedicatory Epistle to William Congreve for the second edition of Addison's *Drummer* in 1722: see *The Correspondence of Richard Steele*, ed. Rae Blanchard (London, 1941), pp. 510-11. See also Morgan, "Public Career," pp. 213-14.

8. Greenough, "Development of the *Tatler*," Table I.

9. *Richard Steele*, p. 105.

10. "Development of the *Tatler*," p. 655.

11. *Ibid.*, Table I.

12. *Ibid.*, p. 653.

13. *Tatler* No. 11 (May 5, 1709). See also Nos. 1 and 4. The text of the issues of the *Tatler* used in this study is that of the original half-sheets unless otherwise stated.

14. *Tatler*, octavo, I (1710), iv.

15. *Anecdotes, Observations, and Characters of Books and Men*, ed. Samuel Weller Singer (London and Edinburgh, 1820), p. 325.

16. For example, *Tatler* Nos. 155, 160, 178.

17. Double to Blunt in the *Weekly Comedy*, No. 1 (August 13, 1707).

18. *Tatler* Nos. 46, 137.

19. "Development of the *Tatler*," p. 658. Through careless dating in a comparison between a news item in the *London Gazette* and a similar one in the *Tatler*, Greenough missed a key to the real reasons: see below, note 34.

20. Bourne, *English Newspapers*, I, 65-67; Stanley Morison, *The English Newspaper: Some Account of the Physical Development of Journals Printed in London between 1622 & the Present Day* (Cambridge, 1932), pp. 73-74.

21. *Tatler* No. 178. The compliment came, however, after Steele's department of news in the *Tatler* had become rare and inconsequential.

22. *Review*, ed. Arthur Wellesley Secord (New York, 1938), Vol. I, Nos. 13, 17, 40, 78, 83, and others. All subsequent references to the *Review* are to this edition.

23. Connely, *Sir Richard Steele*, p. 103; Smithers, *Life of Joseph Addison*, p. 124.

24. Steele to Mrs. Elizabeth Scurlock, September 3, 1707, *Correspondence*, ed. Blanchard, pp. 201, 470, n. 1.

25. James Sutherland, "The Circulation of Newspapers and Literary Periodicals, 1700-1730," *Library*, 4th ser., XV (1934), 115.

26. See, for example, William Thomas' letter to Edward Harley, April 1, 1708, *Historical Manuscripts Commission, Portland MSS*, IV (1897), 485.

27. Cf. I. S. Leadam, *The History of England from the Accession of Anne to the Death of George II (1702-1760)* (New York, 1909), p. 131.

28. *Correspondence*, ed. Blanchard, p. 23. These proposals appear in two fragments, neither of which is dated or addressed; Blanchard provisionally assigns them to 1707. The document printed by Blanchard as No. 23 is also in the Blenheim Collection (C. I. 41), a location which strengthens the attribution to Lord Sunderland as recipient.

29. Laurence Hanson, *Government and the Press, 1695-1763* (Oxford, 1936), p. 89.

30. See, for example, his letters to Joshua Dawson, Secretary to the Lords Justices of Ireland: *Correspondence*, ed. Blanchard, pp. 24-25.

31. "Mr. Steele's Apology for Himself and his Writings," 1714, *Tracts and Pamphlets*, ed Rae Blanchard (Baltimore, 1944), p. 339.

32. Of the two hundred and seventy-one numbers of the *Tatler* sixty-seven contain the department of news labeled *"St. James's Coffee-house"* (Nos. 1-11, 13-25, 27-33, 35-38, 40-44, 46, 49, 51, 53, 55-59, 62-63, 66-67, 69, 74, 76-77, 80, 83, 88, 96, 136-137, 174-175, 210, 225). Usually the department is dated the day preceding the day on which the *Tatler* appeared, but occasionally the department is dated the same day as that of the paper itself (e.g. No. 88), and sometimes the day of the preceding number (e.g. No. 57). Steele's practice seems to have been to date his St. James's department according to the day of the arrival of the dispatches from which the news was written. However, three of these sixty-seven occurrences contain no other news than that no news had arrived (Nos. 42, 69, 77), and two others do not contain news in the proper sense of the word (Nos. 96, 137). But one *Tatler* which has no St. James's department contains regular news items of considerable length under the rubric *"From My Own Apartment"* (No. 64), and another under the same rubric treats current news in a humorously satirical way in an essay and in a letter from Pasquin, Bickerstaff's aerial assistant (No. 129, probably by Addison). Finally, in his essay on the Political Upholsterer, Addison reported the allied investment of Douay through the mouth of the officious Upholsterer (No. 160), but that fact was hardly news at the time. Thus the study of the correlation between Steele's editing of news in the *Gazette* and in the *Tatler* involves only sixty-three numbers of the *Tatler* in which news is given primarily as news and four others (Nos. 96,

129, 137, 160) in which the news cited or alluded to is not the primary purpose of the item.

33. J. Macky seems to have been the Master of the Packet Boats at this time (See *HMC, Portland MSS*, IV, 672). The traveling time in the first decades of the eighteenth century for news from the Continent to England was for the "Holland mail" about six or seven days (*ibid.*, III, 546; IV, 107).

34. Greenough, following the cue of the *Examiner* in the satirically humorous issue pointing out striking similarities between the news in the *Tatler* and that in the *Gazette*, also scanned some other *Gazettes* for comparable news in the St. James's department of the *Tatler* and, like the *Examiner*, printed in parallel columns an instance of the news in the *Gazette* and that in the *Tatler* to show that "Steele often used in his two papers precisely the same news and phrased it in almost the same words": "Development of the *Tatler*," pp. 658-659, 660. However, through what must have been a failure to notice the dates and certainly through an error in labeling *Tatler* No. 10 "No. 11," Greenough missed the significant fact that *Tatler* No. 10 of May 3, 1709, "scooped" the news in the *Gazette* for May 5 (No. 4537) by two days.

35. *Tatler* Nos. 15, 26, 64.

36. *Tatler* Nos. 1, 56.

37. Steele dated his St. James's department April 11, which date probably meant that these dispatches had arrived sometime Monday, the day before the publication date of the *Tatler*. Of course, all or nearly all foreign dispatches were dated eleven days ahead of the British Old Style calendar, so that these three letters had, according to Old Style dating, been written on April 5, 8, and 6, respectively.

38. William Oldisworth, the anonymous annotator of the *Tatler*, took special exception to Steele's fine writing in this account: *Annotations on the Tatler Written in French By Monsieur Bournelle*, 1710, I, 15.

39. G. M. Trevelyan, *The Peace and the Protestant Succession*, "England under Queen Anne," III (London, 1934), 1, 4, 28. There was, of course, the important interlude of Malplaquet, August 31, 1709, O. S.

40. *Tatler* No. 23 (June 2, 1709, O. S.).

41. Italics reversed in the original. This notice in briefer form is repeated in No. 4551 and in No. 4552, Saturday, June 25, with which number the *Gazette* began its new publication schedule.

42. *Tatler* Nos. 42, 46, 56, 69, 77, 96, 129, 137.

43. *Tatler* Nos. 36, 38, 40, 41, 43, 44, 51, 53, 62, 63, 64, 66, 67, 74, 83, 88: *Gazette* Nos. 4555, 4557, 4559, 4560, 4562, 4563, 4570, 4572, 4580, 4582, 4583, 4585, 4586, 4593, 4602, 4607. When Steele did include news in the *Tatler* this policy of a selected condensation of the *Gazette* was the procedure he most frequently followed.

44. *Tatler* Nos. 35, 57, 58: *Gazette* Nos. 4554, 4576, 4577.

45. *Tatler* Nos. 33, 37, 49, 59, 80: *Gazette* Nos. 4552, 4556, 4568, 4578, 4599. In three instances after June 25, items appeared in the *Tatler* which later appeared in the *Gazette*: *Tatler* No. 55 (August 16, 1709) and *Gazette* No. 4575 (August 18); *Tatler* No. 76 (October 4, 1709) and *Gazette* No. 4596 (October 6); *Tatler* No. 136 (February 21, 1710) and *Gazette* No. 4669 (March 25).

46. *Gazette* No. 4563 (July 21, 1709).

47. *Review*, Vol. VI, No. 51.

48. Greenough in suggesting the *General Postscript* as a rival of the news department in the *Tatler* and as a possible influence in determining Steele to abandon this department ("Development of the Tatler," p. 658, n. 20) could not have examined the paper; for it was from its beginning a professed "Extract," or digest, of previously published news that was in the editor's opinion significant, with remarks on the *Tatler, Review, Observator*, and other papers.

49. For example, *General Postscript* Nos. 3, 4 (October 4, 6, 1709).

50. *General Postscript* No. 10 (October 19, 1709).

51. *Tatler* No. 83. The *General Postscript* (No. 12) and the *Gazette* (No. 4602) announced the same fact, and the former reiterated the scarcity-of-news theme. Actually, two more news items appeared in the *Tatler* in 1709, each a half-inch item: one (No. 88) announced the departure of Marlborough for England, and the other (No. 96) is a humorous allusion to Louis XIV's prowess in killing pheasants.

52. *General Postscript* No. 13 (October 26, 1709). "There's no News" (No. 18) continued to be the lamentation of the *General Postscript* until it quietly expired November 11, 1709.

53. Friday, April 14; Monday, April 17; Friday, August 11; Thursday, August 17; Saturday, August 26; Saturday, September 16. These papers, though carrying the imprimatur "Published by Authority," did not bear the title of *London Gazette* but were headed simply "Whitehall," with the date of issue; nor were they numbered. Three of these extra issues, it will be observed, appeared in the afternoon or evening after the *Gazette* had been published that morning. In each case the next *Gazette* contained practically a reprint of the news from the preceding extra issue.

54. Nos. 174, 175 (May 20, 23, 1710). Both accounts are based on news to be found in the current *Gazettes*, Nos. 4593, 4594 (May 20, 23).

55. It was about this time that Steele is thought to have spent a day or two in a spunging-house: *Correspondence*, ed. Blanchard, pp. 263-64, 265, n. 1.

56. It is this St. James's department in the issue of August 12, 1710, which a writer for the *Examiner*, perhaps Dr. William King, combed for phrases and variants of language in the version published by Steele in the *Gazette*: see *Examiner*, Vol. I, No. 5, August 31, 1710. This comparison was thought by Greenough ("Development of the Tatler," pp. 660-62) to have checked any impulse by Steele to continue using in both the *Gazette* and the *Tatler* similar versions of news, a conclusion hardly justified since the department had already all but ceased to appear since the preceding autumn. In fact, the comparison was made not so much to expose Steele's editorship of the two papers, a fact which the editor of the *Examiner* seems to have taken for granted was common knowledge, as it was to bring ridicule upon the *Tatler*, hence loss of popular influence, one of the reasons for which the *Examiner* had been started. Moreover, the whole of the account from which Steele wrote his version for the *Tatler* appeared not in the current *Gazette* (No. 4729), August 12th, but in an "extra" dated from Whitehall, August 11, a full day before Steele's rewrite of the battle in the *Tatler*. This fact was not noted by Greenough or by Mr. Examiner. Finally, the comparison in the *Examiner* did not appear until nearly three weeks after the date of the *Tatler* and *Gazette* concerned and was no more than an introduction to the real purpose of the attack. The true purpose of the attack is to be found in Steele's postscript to the account of the battle, in which he very subtly tossed a barb at the Tories, or, at least, so Mr. Examiner chose to interpret the postscript. Steele later sought revenge in a comparison of passages in two *Examiners* (Vol. I, Nos. 6 and 11) and observed how very hard it is "that a Man cannot publish Ten Papers without stealing from himself," though, he protested, "Such Criticisms made a Man of Sense sick, and a Fool merry": *Tatler* No. 239.

57. The exact date of Steele's resignation as Gazetteer is uncertain. In one of his letters addressed to his wife, he may refer to his having resigned the office, but the letter is not dated. Aitken dated it May or June, 1709, but Blanchard with much better argument would date it "late August 1710": *Correspondence*, p. 268. Abel Roper applied to Harley, October 17, 1710, for the position, "Mr. Steel having resigned his place of Gazetteer": *HMC, Portland*

MSS, IV, 615. Cf. Swift's *Journal to Stella*, ed. Harold Williams (Oxford, 1948), I, 57, 67.

58. *Tatler* No. 225 (September 16, 1710).

Except for what seemed to be happy prospects for further allied victories, there is no clear reason for Steele's resuscitation of the news department in these four isolated numbers. One suspects that Steele's sporadic publishing of news in the *Tatler* after the summer of 1709 is to be accounted for by his reluctance to abandon a department which, though no longer the prominent feature it had been, would on occasion provide "filler" material when original essays ran somewhat short of the customary three columns or when "*Mr*. Bickerstaff [was] *taken extremely ill with the Tooth-ach*" (No. 175).

59. "Development of the *Tatler*," p. 655.

60. *Ibid.*, pp. 653-54.

61. *Ibid.*, Table I, especially Nos. 75 ff., in which the appearance of the St. James's department often coincides with an abnormally large amount of advertisements.

62. Greenough stresses the fact that the predominance of the single essay under "My Own Apartment" or its equivalent "Shire Lane" is established by November 29, 1709 (*Tatler*, No. 100). However, the fact is equally demonstrable that the tendency toward this development begins to evidence itself more than fifty numbers earlier and that on the basis of the average number of inches of news in the St. James's department the beginning of this tendency coincides with the thrice-weekly appearance of the *Gazette*. See "Development of the *Tatler*," Table II, p. 656.

63. Walter Graham, "Some Predecessors of the *Tatler*," JEGP, XXIV (1925), 552.

64. The *Gentleman's Journal* of 1692-94 was a literary monthly of very miscellaneous content, with news in the first two numbers and rarely thereafter. The *Post-Angel*, a long miscellany, ran for twenty-one months in 1701-2 and included an abridgement of news; contrary to Graham's statement, this section of news was not withdrawn. The *Diverting Post* started in 1704 as a weekly and became a monthly the next year; its first issues contained news of and for the polite world, but its major attention was centered on verse, often coarse. Thus none of these journals resembled the *Tatler* enough to offer a fruitful comparison or grounds for conclusions on the relationship between newspapers and periodicals with respect to the printing of news.

65. April 12-June 25, 1709: *Tatler*, Nos. 1-33; *British Apollo*, Vol. II, Nos. 5-26. The *British Apollo* during this period was a twice-weekly appearing on Wednesdays and Fridays. After December 26, 1709 (Vol. II, No. 79), it became a thrice-weekly, published Mondays, Wednesdays, and Fridays.

66. For example, the *British Apollo* for Saturday, April 23, 1709 (postponed in publication because the regular day of issue was Good Friday) announced in its news section that the "Duke of Marlborough will embark for England the first fair Wind," but the *Tatler* for the same day (No. 6) announced: "Last night between seven and eight, his Grace the Duke of Marlborough arrived at Court"! Such a lag between the news in the *Tatler* and that in the *Apollo*, while not always so ridiculous, is the rule, not the exception. Yet the latter continued to publish news for two more years.

THE SALE AND DISTRIBUTION OF THE
BRITISH APOLLO

THE BRITISH APOLLO

Subtitle: *"Curious Amusements for the INGENIOUS.* To which are added the most Material Occurrences Foreign and Domestick."

Vol. I, Nos. 1-117, Vol. II, Nos. 1-117, Vol. III, Nos. 1-156 (No. 113 omitted), Vol. IV, Nos. 1-20, February 13, 1708-May 11, 1711. Twenty-one four-page supernumerary monthly papers, April, 1708-December, 1709. Five twelve-page quarterly papers, November, 1708-November, 1709.

Semi-weekly to Vol. II, No. 79; tri-weekly.

Folio sheet; folio half-sheet.

Editors: Aaron Hill; Marshal Smith.

Colophon: "Printed for the Authors, by *J. Mayo,* at the *Printing-Press,* against *Water-Lane* in *Fleet-street.* Where Advertisements are Taken in."

THE SALE AND DISTRIBUTION OF THE
British Apollo

WILLIAM F. BELCHER

PLEASED THOUGH the public was with the appearance of a question-and-answer journal in the year 1708, the *British Apollo* was scarcely an innovation, for many readers remembered its prototype, John Dunton's *Athenian Mercury*, which had absolved them of doubts and settled their wagers from 1691 to 1697.[1] Dunton had achieved some personal prominence by his successful venture, though most of the writing had been done by a group of editorial assistants,[2] who had accepted letters containing questions on any subject and had published them along with appropriate answers in the *Mercury*. The popularity of this type of periodical was instantaneous[3]—it gave men a chance to ask anonymously without fear of disclosure questions which, because they were either dogmatic or heretical, might lead to hard fortune in that age of violent opinions. Although the *Athenian Mercury* was abandoned when in time the reading public had exhausted its interest, Dunton, proclaiming his exclusive right to Athenianism, continued vigorously in the early years of the eighteenth century to attempt to make the paper of questions and answers once more the popular type of journal it had been by publishing similar monthly periodicals and volumes of selections from the *Mercury*. Yet Dunton's projects were derivative: all of the questions answered in them were those which had been submitted years before to the Athenian Society.[4] The public was naturally apathetic toward this warmed-over fare.

By 1704 there was dramatic evidence that the curious reader wanted a question-monger for his current problems. The admission in the fiftieth number of the *Review* that Defoe would answer queries he liked was followed by receipt of so many letters that supplements had to be published to provide space for them.[5] Later the *Little Review* was established for the benefit of querists,[6] but because Defoe was impatient with frivolous letters and busy with political affairs, he deserted his device.[7]   It was this same interest that supported the new *British Apollo* from 1708 to 1711, a relatively long life, especially when one remembers that its most prominent competitor was the *Tatler*.

Problems mundane and spiritual, whimsical and sober, were sent by the hundreds to those who provided the prose and verse answers in the *British Apollo*.   All opinions found expression in its pages.   In these early years of the eighteenth century earnest and honest Englishmen were questioning more than ever before the literal truth of the Scriptures and were disturbed by apparently contradictory material in them.   In their search for "truth" they were even more interested in the new science than in bringing forward antithetical Biblical texts.   And among the inquisitive were also the young, who demanded some kind of standard for social activity, particularly in the realm of courtship and marriage. These interests in science, religion, and manners insured the success of a periodical devoted to them.   Such was the *British Apollo*.

Few would deny the superiority of this periodical as an index to intellectual curiosity in Anne's London.   But it has also a substantial and unique value for the history of journalism.   Since many questions about the manner of conducting the paper are answered in its pages, there is in it more information about the distribution of a periodical and about the financial arrangements of its publishers than can be found in any other major journal of the time.   These matters of interest to the twentieth century investigator were generally disregarded by the editors of early eighteenth century periodicals: the problem of a Steele or a Defoe was to appeal through the content of his journal to the public who bought it, not to describe the manner in which it was distributed and paid for.   Only in a paper like the *British Apollo*, where readers unacquainted with the practices of the publishers of periodicals could ask questions, were the operations of the trade treated extensively enough to give even a fragmentary picture of them.   The absence or scarcity of information on sales and distribution in early English journals clearly makes it impossible to know how typical the *British Apollo* was in these respects, but it seems plausible that some of its procedures were sufficiently representative to give us at the least a general illumination of publishing conditions. Since such matter is particularly uncommon, this information is of as much value today as the more frequent and much longer paragraphs on religion and science. Religion and science had spokesmen; printing was practiced, not preached.

Not only in answers to questions, however, do we find the abundant information about periodical publication provided by this journal. If not the first, it is clearly one of the earliest papers sold by subscription,[8] and there are numerous explanatory paragraphs directed to those unfamiliar with the details of this method of publication. Other frequent advice is given about the submission of queries, for, with letters providing at least half of the material published, it was necessary for the projectors to lessen some of the confusion they had wished upon themselves. The sum of these bits of advice, along with other pieces of evidence in answers to queries about the undertaking, gives us an interesting and reasonably accurate picture of the general conditions of periodical publication at one of the most significant periods in the history of literary journalism, from the time of Richard Steele's venturesome beginning in the *Tatler* to that of his master craftsmanship in the *Spectator*.

I

According to the first issue of the *British Apollo*, the subscription plan provided that the paper was to be "deliver'd at all Persons Houses within the Bills of Mortality" on Wednesdays and Fridays "at two Shillings a Quarter; not to be paid till the End of the Quarter." Proposals had been published and a "great many" persons had subscribed before the first number was printed,[9] but as a means of further filling the subscription rolls the conventional practice of providing introductory copies was followed for a brief period:[10] many other papers, we are told, were "given away *Gratis* the first Quarter, at least for a whole Month,"[11] so that it is clearly a token of the immediacy of the *British Apollo's* success that only the first two issues were given away.[12] In fact, the demand for copies of the first number so far exceeded the hopes

of the publisher that all were disposed of before the second number
was printed five days later.[13]

By the time the seventh issue of the periodical was published,
references to limitation of delivery to houses within the bills of
mortality were omitted from the running advertisement of the
project, and in the thirty-eighth number delivery was promised in
"the City or Suburbs." Many individuals and public houses had already been obtaining the papers at their doors.[14]   It was recommended, however, that those who lived in the country have a friend
in town or an innkeeper accept the papers for them, because the
bearers could not conveniently meet the "Carriers" sent by country
subscribers to make payment.[15]

Although delivery was usually made to subscribers on the morning of the day of publication,[16] there were unavoidable delays.
One boy was removed from his employment because he was "too
Negligent in his Business,"[17] and several others who had absconded
distributed no papers at all.[18]   Late delivery, however, was commonly a result of such an increase in the number of subscribers
that it was impossible to reach them all promptly.   The only
remedy was to employ additional paper carriers and to "divide the
Walks," an alleviation the managers of a journal increasing in
popularity found necessary a number of times.[19]   Only infrequently
was it impossible to serve patrons as a consequence of an indefinite
address, as on the occasion of a request for delivery to George
Alley, at which time the subscriber was publicly advised that he
must give a more specific address because there were "eleven Alleys
of that Name about Town."[20]

On the quarter days collections were made by the paper carriers.
During the first year and a half of publication subscribers were
reminded beforehand of the approach of the day for payment.
On March 19, 1708, one week before the first quarter day, a
request was made to subscribers to leave on Lady Day "what is due
for this piece of the Quarter, with their Servants who take in the
Paper, and that it be paid to the Men who then carry it, and to
no others."[21]   In June subscribers were reminded as early as the
18th that the quarter would end on the 24th and were also admonished by the statement that a "great Part of our Subscribers
were so Curteous last Quarter as . . . to order their Servants to pay

our Men and Boys as soon as the Quarter was up." Only with prompt subscribers did the editors care to deal, for the bearers could "spare but little time to Collect the Money."[22] By June 30 most, but not all, of the "Quarteridges"[23] had been paid.[24]

With little difficulty a third collection was made on Michaelmas (September 29), but when a collection was announced for the fourth quarter ending on St. Thomas's Day (December 21),[25] subscribers complained. For their two shillings they had received twenty-six papers during the second quarter and twenty-eight during the third. Now they were being asked to pay the same amount for twenty-three papers. Those who objected were appeased with a compromise:

Altho' the Quarter be up on St. *Thomas*'s Day, and 24 Papers now deliver'd out, yet since some reckon it not up till *Christmas* Day,[26] we shall not urge Payment of any this Week; only such as will be so kind, we shall esteem our generous Incouragers, by reason prompt Payment will be a great ease to our Servants, . . . Especially now, since the Number of our Subscribers is so greatly increased.[27]

So much greater had this increase been by the fourth quarter day that a part of the collection had to be made on a Monday, when no paper was published.[28] Still later, on March 25 and June 24, 1709, collection required more than one day and was made on days when no paper was published.[29] After June 24, 1709, subscribers were no longer reminded of the days on which payment was due. Only at Christmas of the same year was there a further note on collection. Remembering the difficulties on St. Thomas's Day in 1708, the directors of the project anticipated complaints as early as December 16: "N. B. *On* Wednesday *next, being St. Thomas's Day, the Quarter is up, we hope all those Subscribers who came in this Quarter will be as prompt of Payment as our former.* . . ."[30]

II

Although subscribers received and were obliged to pay for only the regular issues of the *British Apollo,* distributed on Wednesdays and Fridays, it was a part of the original plan of the promoters of this question-and-answer project to issue monthly supplements containing questions and answers for which there was

not room in the regular or *"Weekly"*[31] issues. It was explained
that these supplements would sell at twopence each or at sixpence
a quarter, but as "Supernumerary" papers they were optional with
subscribers.[32] Although they were the same size as the regular
issues, their price of twopence (twice the rate for the regular
papers) was justifiable. Because they carried no advertising and
were printed in a smaller type than were the regular, numbered
issues, their printing cost more than did that of the regular papers.
In addition, their greater length was evidence of the relatively
greater efforts of the writers who answered the questions.[33]

The first three monthly papers, those for April, May, and
June, 1708, were carried by the men at the time they delivered
the regular issues.[34] After this start it was decided that they would
be distributed on the first Monday of each month, because such a
practice would lighten the task of distribution by avoiding publication of two papers on the same day and would be "more acceptable"
to many readers.[35] This plan for publishing the monthly supplements was followed, even with the added expense of the paper
carriers on off days,[36] until they were discontinued.[37]

Unlike the monthly supplements, which were planned from
the first as a part of the question-and-answer project, the sixpenny
quarterly supplements were established several months after the
beginning of the project as part of an honest effort to publish answers to all the questions received. By September of the first year of
publication there were so many letters on hand that it was impossible to answer all of them in the regular issues and the monthly
papers. An attempt was made to quiet the clamor of dissatisfied
querists: *"NOTE,* that whereas we have a vast Number of
Questions more sent than can be answer'd according to our
Present Method, after Quarter Day, we shall proceed in one,
whereby we shall give Answers to all worthy of Solution."[38] Less
than a month later the second series of additional issues was
proposed: ". . . a Quarterly Book of 3 Sheets in a small Character . . . ; we have no doubt but this will be acceptable, since it
will not raise the Yearly Charge to that of the most vulgar News
Paper, altho' a whole Sheet and upon fine Paper, besides we
oblige none to take it, but such as desire it."[39]

When the first of these quarterly supplements was promised for

November 22, 1708, it was again pointed out that even with the additional sixpence for the new supplement, the total yearly cost of the periodical remained less than the price of a newspaper for the same period.[40]   Readers who may have begun to suppose that there would be no end to multiplication of issues were assured that there would be no further increase, so "that no Coffee-houses, &c. as well as private Persons" might "have any just exceptions to the Charge."[41]   It seems quite likely that only a limited supply of the first of these sizable papers was printed, for the sale of them was restricted to subscribers and those who would "become such,"[42] and to the favored ones these new supplements were sold only for cash; they were not added to the quarterly debt.   The defense of this practice, as made publicly, was that the money was needed to pay printing costs and that the bookkeeping entailed in allowing them to be subscribed for would be excessively tedious and expensive.[43]

After a time, thinking that the monthly and quarterly issues might be a distasteful obligation to subscribers who had to pay an additional shilling for them each quarter, and observing that their sales were lagging, the editors attempted to enhance their value by the addition of an attractive feature:

At the Request of several Gentlemen and Ladies, we shall insert in our *Monthly Papers* and *Quarterly Books*, for the future, some Lines set to Musick, compos'd by the best Masters, the words and Musick new every time, to give a more pleasing variety; . . . We must be excus'd from disposing of the *Monthly Papers* with the Musick to any, but those who Subscribe for the *Weekly*.[44]

This announcement was made in mid-July.   By the time of the next monthly supplement, for August, there had not been sufficient time as yet to obtain the "Characters," or type, but music was promised for the quarterly supplement later in the month.[45] When this supplement was advertised a week before its publication, readers were assured that it would contain "an Entertainment of Musick," and an appended notice offered surprising news: "*Note*, That after a little time, all our Entertainments of Musick will be perform'd in a Grand Consort, to which all our Subscribers,

who have been such a Quarter of a Year, or have taken for a
Quarter of a Year Back, will have Right to Tickets."[46]

In a period of three months, however, even those who subscribed for the supplements as well as the regular issues would have
spent only two shillings. If concert tickets, which normally cost
more than twice this amount,[47] were to be awarded for such short-
lived fidelity, the owners of the paper were being unnecessarily
free-handed. Only the most ingenuous among the new customers
could have been astonished by an immediate retraction: "*Note,*
That after a little time, all our Entertainments of Musick will be
perform'd in a Grand Consort, to which all our Subscribers, who
have been such a Half a Year, or have taken for Half a Year Back,
will have Right to Tickets. There being a Mistake in last Paper."[48]
Four shillings in subscription money was a somewhat better return
for such generous projectors.

Just one day before the publication of the first music, however,
there was a lusty attack on the feature. In the second issue of the
Female Tatler published at the shop of A. Baldwin,[49] Lady Sly,
who was one of the friends of Mrs. Crackenthorpe, the putative
authoress of the periodical, became almost hysterical with amusement over the *British Apollo*'s introduction of music into its pages.
It would be somewhat incongruous, she believed, to have crowded
together at a concert "his Grace and my Lady Duchess, *Jack Tar,*
and Mrs. *Top-gallant-Sail,* with every Coffee-Man, and his Wife,
that takes in the Papers."[50] So venomous was Lady Sly's attack
that for some time both the *British Apollo* and the Baldwin *Female Tatler* indulged in unrestrained name-calling and recrimina-
tion.[51]

After musical entertainments had been published in the fourth
quarterly supplement[52] and in the monthly issue for September,
1709, it became apparent that it was highly impractical to publish
only one voice part of a simple song, as had been done. Publication of all the voice parts would have taken the ready space in a
monthly supplement;[53] publication of only one part made it necessary for the musically inclined subscriber to buy all the parts elsewhere if he wanted to use the music. For this reason, only the words
of a song were given in the monthly paper for October, 1709,[54] and
only one other musical attraction was printed in the periodical.[55]

So also was the concert ill-contrived. After its first mention,[56] it was not alluded to again until a concert was advertised for the benefit of Mr. Turner, who set the music for the *Apollo*. Readers were told that "the Authors . . . are not the least concerned in this [concert], which is wholly at the Charge of the said Mr. *Turner*."[57] Somewhat as an afterthought an apologetic denial of any further intention to provide a concert was printed several days later:

Whereas we formerly mention'd a Consort of Musick, the number of our Subscribers now is so large, that neither the Play-house, nor any of the usual Halls for Musick, will near contain them, which renders it absolutely impracticable; yet (tho' none of our Subscribers have been at the least expence thereon) we shall more than make amends for the Disappointment, by reason after *Christmas* our Paper will come out three times a Week, on which account we shall add the Assistance of several, who are absolute Masters of what they undertake. We are likewise settling a Correspondence for the freshest News, and shall also insert Home-News of all things which happen of Consequence.[58]

Whether the cost of subsidizing a musical performance was excessive, whether the idea of encouraging subscribers from the extremes of the social scale to rub elbows in embarrassing proximity was wisely to be avoided, or whether the number of subscribers was too great to be accommodated in any of the playhouses or music halls,[59] we can only conjecture. But anyone who examines the paper knows that after these few strains were struck there were doubts, and all melodies stopped together. The lesson the projectors learned, as did many who read the papers, was that supplements to a paper are ordinarily dead weight, a source of pride only to their producers.

The faithful who supported the question-and-answer project were probably chagrined at being bilked of their concert tickets, none the less so when they discovered that the reward for their loss would be the replacement of the supplements by an equally expensive Monday paper. To most of them, even as it is to us, it was obvious that this compensation was merely an expedient of the managers of the paper. A plan to abandon the supplements had been announced weeks before with no reference at all to cancellation of the concert:

Whereas the only Material Objections we ever knew made to our Paper, were these, *viz.* That by reason it comes out but two days in a Week, the Town is the greatest part of the Week without any Entertainment from it. That the Coffee-houses are forc'd to take in another Paper, for want of it on Mondays.[60] That by reason we reserve many Questions for our *Monthly* and *Quarterly Papers,* many are forc'd to stay so long for Answers. To obviate all such Objections for the future, we design as soon as this Quarter is ended, to sink the *Monthly* and *Quarterly* into another Paper to come out every Monday, and at no higher rate, than they pay who have all now, *viz.* 3*s. per* Quarter, which is as Cheap as any Paper which comes out, tho' ours are whole Sheets, finer Paper, and at infinite more Pains, being encourag'd to this extraordinary Charge, by the great numbers continually added. But first we desire all our Subscribers at their leisure to leave their Thoughts hereon with our Servants in their Walks.[61]

Yet just as subscribers had been allowed to decide whether or not they would take the supplements, so were they permitted choice in determining whether they took the Monday papers as part of their subscription, for, as the editors explained, they "would not impose on any"[62]—a rather equivocal position for those who had at one time offered the new papers as a substitute gift. They were no different from the weekly papers in format and were numbered consecutively with them. Probably most of the customers accepted them, for only the first one was puffed.[63]

III

The income of the periodical was enlarged by sales of other items than regular and supplementary issues of the paper. There were title pages, prefaces, and indexes for the collected volumes which could be purchased separately, as well as complete sets of the periodical. Of these, the indexes probably were the most profitable and most necessary. As the number of answered questions increased, there were more and more repetitious queries submitted. But even these needed some attention, as was recognized when they were answered in the following fashion: "Q. *The Querist desires to know why a Loadstone draws Iron to it. And you will oblige Yours,* &c. *A.* See *British Apollo,* Numb. 30."[64] In time these references became so burdensome that the periodical had to cease admitting them: the number of such questions became so great that no one on the staff of the paper could find time "to look them out," nor could the references be printed because they would "too much fill up" the papers.[65]   The projectors felt that an index would give the querist a chance to determine for himself whether his question had already been answered and would thereby lessen their own work.[66]   Even the nonsubscriber was urged to provide himself an index, for he could read the answers to his queries at a friend's home or at a nearby coffee-house.[67]

An index was promised for the week after Lady Day, 1709, at which time the first volume of the *British Apollo* was completed, but with regret it was discovered that the making of an index can take much longer than is expected.[68]   When a second delay occurred, the editors were clumsily apologetic:

We are sorry we are forc'd to disappoint the Town this Day of our *Index*, the Reason is, our Printer sent us word, That it is so great a piece of work (there being between two and three Thousand Questions) that he cou'd not get Hands enough to do it by this Day, it is also to be consider'd, not one Sheet cou'd be set before *Lady-Day*, because we were forc'd to take the last Paper into that Time, but he has faithfully Promis'd it shall be out next Wednesday, but we doubt not of it's giving great Satisfaction when it comes, to make amends for the Delay.[69]

This time the index was published on the promised day, at a price of sixpence, and consisted of fourteen pages printed in three columns.   Although its chaos of jumbled entries requires a dash of clairvoyance in its users, those responsible regarded it with pride. They promised that any public house desiring a copy might have it "tack'd to a Board the better to preserve it."   Certainly, they believed, it should increase the custom in any coffee-house.[70]

Knowing from experience the difficulty of producing an index, the printer made sure of finishing that for the second volume before he advertised it, nearly six weeks after the volume had been completed.[71]   In size it is four pages smaller than the index to the first volume, and although its price was not mentioned in advertisements, it is rather unlikely that it sold for any more than did the first one.   The index for the last complete volume of the *British Apollo* was issued after the periodical had ceased publication.[72]

The smallest of the three, only four pages, its price was not given in advertisements.

A source of smaller income than the indexes was the sale of title pages and prefaces to those who wanted their bound collections to present a handsome appearance. Even before half of the first volume had been printed, its title page was sold for one penny.[73] Although at least one querist resented having to pay as much for it as for a regular issue of twice the size, the publishers defended their practice by explaining that "a Title Page of a Book, how few Words soever it contains, costs as much Printing, as if full on both sides." Moreover, limited demand increased its cost, for "in printing but a few Sheets the Charge much exceeds in proportion of printing many."[74] The preface and title page for Volume II, however, were given to subscribers as restitution for their having missed the paper which should have been the first issue of Volume III.[75] For the advertised title page and the accompanying half-sheet preface to be bound with the issues of Volume III there were no prices given.

More profitable than title pages were the back issues provided for new subscribers. Since the *British Apollo* had a cumulative value, in that questions were answered only one time, sets were supplied, along with single papers to fill gaps, for a long period after the papers had first been published. As early as the third issue of Volume I whole sets (hardly "sets" at the time) were advertised. Within a month "Impressions" of some of the issues were "quite out," but the papers were "in the Press to be Reprinted, in which their Errata's . . . [would] be corrected, so that any . . . [might] . . . be furnish'd from the Beginning."[76]

During the course of Volume I these sets were available for new readers at the regular subscription price.[77] But in the eightieth number of the paper readers were told the few sets remaining would be the last available since the papers had been twice reprinted.[78] After the fifth number of Volume II, however, single sheets of the first volume were still being offered for sale to any who desired them,[79] and there also remained a supply of sets, ranging in price from 12s. unbound to 15s. 6d. bound in calf.[80] These complete collections were advertised only until July, 1709;[81] yet not until January, 1710, did the periodical contain a statement that all the sets of the first volume of the *British Apollo* had been "dispos'd off" and a proposal to reprint the volume in octavo.[82]

Just as sets of the first volume were advertised, so were those of Volumes II and III.[83]   By the time the third volume was completed, sets were available of the "2d or 3d Vollumes in Folio, containing about 2000 Answers to Curious Questions, in most Arts and Sciences, at 12*s*. Gilt Edges and Letter'd on the Back."[84]   This amount is somewhat less than the publisher asked for similar bound copies of the first volume, but since the notice appears only in the last issues of the paper, it probably represents a price reduction for the purpose of disposing of surplus copies.[85]

IV

Because of the nature of the periodical a demand for the questions and answers of Volume I continued after the original issues were sold, and the publisher did not let requests for reprinting go unheeded.   The first mention of republication of Volume I came in reply to a querist who had heard that Bickerstaff planned to

> . . . *Publish His Wise Lucubrations,*
> *Revis'd and Amended,*
> *When the First Volumes ended,*
> *With Notes and many Additions.*[86]

He wondered whether the *British Apollo* might follow the example of the *Tatler*.   Assuring him that there had long since been intended a second edition of Volume I, a publicist explained that it had been deferred "for the Correcting several Over-sights, Mistakes and other Errata's," and that "now it will soon be in the press for a Book[87] in *Octavo*."[88]   A month later, in February, 1710, specific proposals were advanced.   The subscriber for this abridgment was to make a down payment of 2s. 6d. and pay an additional 2s. 6d. on delivery.   After subscriptions were closed, not one set of the edition was to be sold for less than 7s., "nor any Subscriptions taken after the Charge for Printing . . . [was] receiv'd."   As an incentive to quantity buying, a seventh copy was to be given free to the subscriber who purchased six copies.[89]   These proposals did not begin to be realized for several months, however, for it was late in July before the edition was in the press, promised for publication early in the fall.[90]

The publication of the second edition of Volume I in octavo, insofar as it was a more ambitious undertaking, was even more delayed than the printing of the indexes. First fixed for Michaelmas term, the date of distribution was changed several times until publication, several months late, in January, 1711.[91] Although it was asserted that there would be "but very few Printed more then what . . . [would] be subscribed for,"[92] there was either a small demand for or a plentiful supply of the edition, because it was advertised until the *British Apollo* ceased publication in May, 1711, and in 1717 was still being disposed of by the printer at a price of 4s. a set of three volumes.[93]

As was true of many papers of the period, advertisements contributed substantially to the financial support of this periodical. Half a crown was the price for an insertion of a notice in the *British Apollo*, "those from Quacks excepted."[94] Yet since charlatans were responsible for the most frequent and lengthy advertisements in early eighteenth century journals,[95] the barrier against them was removed—covertly, of course—after the twelfth issue of the *Apollo*: a moderate length was the only restrictive measure enforced after that time.[96] Accepting such notices was a financial necessity:

Whereas upon the *Gazett*'s coming out 3 times a Week, several decline putting their Advertisements into other Papers, upon Prospect of their decreasing in their Numbers, we are desir'd to give liberty for bringing into our Paper, any such Advertisements as are admitted into other Papers; . . . Our former reasons for Exceptions against some, being also now remov'd, therefore our Printer is ready to take in any such as others accept of.[97]

Readers who objected to papers filled with miraculous cures were told that the advertisements were no more related to the authors than were those in the *Gazette* related to the State:[98] they were the responsibility of the printer.[99] But accountable for them or not, the authors would have been the last to deny their importance. The 1,697 that appeared in the *British Apollo* made an average of more than four in each issue, or, in terms of income, better than two crowns, as much as was received from the sale of 100 copies of the paper itself.[100]

Only one other source of income was alluded to in the paper. This was the sale of "Books of Guards neatly bound to keep 'em [copies of the periodical] in, at two Shillings a piece."[101]   These folders, which held 150 papers,[102] were of service to collectors of the single issues who desired to protect the papers until they were bound. They were advertised throughout the life of the periodical.

Supplementary revenue was possible when money was occasionally sent in by querists desiring immediate or particularly important answers, but these fees were not accepted.   More than once querists were denied answers until the money enclosed with their questions could be returned; yet the problem was not a serious one, for offenders were cautioned at length only once:

Whereas some Persons have sent us Money inclos'd with their Questions . . . we desire such Persons to send Directions . . . how we may remit the Money to their own Hands, and we shall return it, for we think it not honourable to receive Money on such account.   And whereas we are also inform'd that divers others have sent Money to us, which never came to our Hands, we desire the Senders to inform us, who they deliver'd the Money to, and we will take care also that shall be return'd.[103]

There were apparently no other means of providing public financial support for the owners than these that have been mentioned: the sale of the regular issues at one penny (or two shillings a quarter), the monthly supplements at twopence, the quarterly supplements at sixpence, the index at sixpence, the prefaces probably at one penny, the title pages at one penny, bound and unbound collections at twelve to fifteen shillings sixpence per volume, a second edition of Volume I at five shillings, advertisements at half a crown, and books of guards at two shillings.

What the editors may have collected over a particular period of time from one subscriber may readily be estimated, but of the number of subscribers at any one time we have merely the most general notion.   Only one reference to their number suggests anything at all specific.   In answer to a question about the effect of the popularity of Steele's *Tatler* on the circulation of the *British*

Apollo it was "frankly" owned that "the universal Approbation that Gentleman's Paper has met with may have prevented us from gaining near two thousand Subscribers, we might have had more, had not that been publish'd."[104] Without firmer figures of circulation any hope to make general estimates concerning profit from such a project as this is sharply limited.[105]

V

For the early eighteenth century no better demonstration of the financial basis of periodical publication is available than is provided by the ample details scattered throughout the *British Apollo*. Nor is there a more plentiful source of information about the distribution and publication of these early papers. The parts played by the printer, the booksellers, the paper carriers, and the coffee-houses that assisted in this popular and authoritative project are profusely illustrated. Of this group, the printer, as might be suspected, was the most important. From his shop came the issues of the paper, and into his shop flowed both queries and subscriptions.

Requests for subscriptions were sent to the printer.[106] Apparently a list of subscribers was kept in his shop, for at a time when the periodical was daily increasing in popularity, new readers were asked to submit their requests for delivery only on off days, when the paper was not published, *"because we* [the projectors] *should not be so liable to make Mistakes, or miss some in entring them in our Books, as when they croud in together on those two days."*[107] Questions and advertisements were also submitted to the printer, John Mayo, and he offered for sale books of guards, sets and single issues of the paper, and supplements.[108] His shop was clearly the center of the question-and-answer project.

Considering the variety of material Mayo found it necessary to set up in publishing the *British Apollo,* he did a commendable job. Instead of a single essay from the hand of a Steele or a Defoe, with whose handwriting—no matter how difficult—a printer would soon become familiar, what he deciphered was a body of letters in hundreds of hands. For the editing of queries he took responsibility. To the complaint of a querist who charged that his question had been altered, the authors answered that such alteration was probably the "Corrector's of the Press," since letters were forwarded just as they were received; the authors did not trouble themselves with editing questions, but left "all that to the Printer and his Corrector."[109]   And it was the printer who received censure for a number of the errors which appeared in the paper,[110] although the authors generously reproached themselves for several mistakes.   Once they were careless in the delivery of copy to the printer;[111] on another occasion the press was found fault with, but only because several words interlined in some copy had been overlooked.[112]   Again, because a part of an answer on a separate piece of paper had been mislaid, an incomplete answer was published.[113] Such matters as these were not so serious as the difference "between one of the Gentlemen concern'd and the Printer" which made it impossible for Mayo to bring out the first issue of the third volume on time.[114]   Whatever the disagreement may have been, one likes to imagine that the disputants were reconciled over a remaining bottle of the "Right and Fine Irish Usquebaugh" which Mayo had sold from his shop two years before.[115]

Besides the printer, several London booksellers played necessary roles in the conduct of this question-and-answer project.   For the convenience of querists and subscribers, two places other than Mayo's press[116] were at first designated for collection of questions, of communications relating to subscriptions, and of advertisements. These were the shops of the booksellers "*W. Keble* in *Westminster-Hall*" and "*Tho. Bickerton* at the *Golden Flower-de-luce* in St. *Paul's Church Yard.*"[117]   Their job, however, unlike that of Mayo, was only to forward information about subscriptions.   One reader, for example, objected that he had spoken to Keble about delivery of the periodical, but had received nothing in three weeks. He was told that the booksellers sent "none abroad," that for service at his door it was necessary to write Mayo a letter "superscrib'd" for the *British Apollo*.[118]   Similarly they accepted advertisements and questions which were to be transmitted to Mayo,[119] and from their shops they sold both single issues and sets of the periodical.[120]

During the seventh month of publication, when Bickerton moved to a shop in Little Britain,[121] a new agent was added to minister to the needs of readers and querists, Carter at the Green

Dragon in St. Paul's Churchyard,[122] where he performed the same functions as did Bickerton and Keble.[123]   Keble, however, soon left the service of his friends.   A brief notice advised readers: "*Note*, We desire no more Letters may be sent to Mr. *Keebl* [*sic*], in *Westminster-Hall*, and that they who took Papers of him would direct their Letters to Mr. *Mayo*'s and our Servants shall bring them."[124]

Carter and Bickerton continued as the only agents for the *British Apollo* from that time until well into the third year of publication, when the proposals for printing the second edition of the first volume were first announced.   Two booksellers were then added to help circulate them: Clark, in Birchin Lane, and Harbin, in the Strand.[125]   Both of them later became agents of the paper, along with Woodward, who owned a shop in St. Christopher's Churchyard.[126]   But only Clark and Harbin, together with the printer Mayo, collected questions for the twenty issues of the failing Volume IV.[127]   They sold papers, of course, but the subscription plan had then been abandoned, the street sales being handled by "Hawkers who . . . [carried] the other News."[128]

In order to extend the *Apollo*'s services to the public, there were several attempts to enlist the assistance of public houses. Early in the project it was stated almost boastfully that "the Generality of Public-houses . . . [took] in both *Monthly* and *Quarterly* [issues],"[129] and later, as if to confirm the journal's value, that not "one Chief Coffee-house . . . [had] left the *Apollo* from the first, nor 6 in all, of such who have broke or remov'd."[130]   With such regard for places where the literate gathered it is not surprising that the index to Volume I, "tack'd to a Board the better to preserve it," was offered to public houses for the regular price.[131]   That the coffee-houses of London did not immediately take advantage of this offer is apparent, however, from a note which appeared two months later:

Whereas great numbers of Questions are continually sent us, which we have answer'd before; to prevent that trouble for the future, both to our Querists and our selves, we shall plant Indexes fix'd to Boards in several Coffee-houses in the principal parts of the Town, for such as have not Indexes to have recourse to, where also Questions, Subscriptions and Advertisements, will be taken in, of which we shall give Publick Notice.[132]

A similar proposal made again within the same year added that because many of the letters delivered at a few places had been lost, these same coffee-houses would also take in "Letters."[133] Despite these protestations the names of the auxiliary stations were not published in the periodical.

VI

The services performed for the *British Apollo* by the bookseller agents were only perfunctory, and the help of the coffee-houses, if it had materialized, would have been no more than that. It was the printer who actually controlled the distribution and publication of the paper, and he was given extensive assistance by the boys who delivered it on publishing days. These boys were obliged to do a great deal more than simply to carry the paper: they accepted advertisements,[134] took orders for books of guards,[135] sold title pages and indexes,[136] delivered and sold supplements,[137] collected questions from querists,[138] accepted subscription requests,[139] and delivered private answers to querists.[140] When the editors proposed doing away with the supplements to go on a thrice-weekly publication schedule, the boys were assigned the duty of collecting the opinions of subscribers in regard to the change.[141] These boys were the principal link between publisher and reader.

Next in importance to the boys' duty of delivering the regular issues of the *British Apollo* to subscribers was that of collecting quarteridges. Although at first these collections were made when the boys delivered the papers,[142] it later became necessary for them to collect on days when the paper was not published.[143] Very probably this practice was an added expense, for it was explained in the course of the first volume that the delivery of the monthly supplements on Mondays was "at double Charge" for delivery boys,[144] but prompt delivery was more important than such an added expense. When there were complaints that the papers were brought late, the only alternative was to increase the number of boys who served "Walks," or routes: by the fourteenth issue it was necessary to add more assistance. In August of the first year there was dissatisfaction "in the Walks from *Bishopsgate-*

street to the *Tower*, and in *Southwark*" because papers came late, and division of the walks was promised.[145]   For the same reason boys were to be added in July, 1709, "one already being fix'd to serve at *Wapping, Shadwell, Ratcliff Cross,* &c.";[146] within two months there were complaints again in "*St. James's, Westminster,* &c." that resulted in a promise that "when the Gentry . . . [were] more come to Town" there would be another division.[147] Similar causes effected a promise of final division of the walks at the end of Volume II.[148]

Generally the boys were trusted servants of the publisher. When, for example, a customer claimed that no papers had been left for him during a quarter, the editors explained that they had been assured by the boys that "*all in their Walks subscrib'd for*" had been left, and requested the address of the unhappy subscriber.[149]   We must grant, however, that it is the nature of delivery boys to be errant from time to time, and those employed to distribute this periodical were normal.   The first one who wandered had apparently run away:

Whereas, the Subscribers who were serv'd by the Boy in the Blew Livery were disapointed of their Papers on Wednesday, the reason was, that the said Boy run away from his Service the Day before . . . His going away being a great Loss to the Gentlemen of the Society, and which they could not help; 'tis hop'd the Subscribers will be so kind as not to charge the Default to their Account.[150]

Yet in a week this boy had returned.   His employers "having not found him unjust in his Accounts," his customers were requested to remit to him any unpaid quarteridges.[151]   The projectors remained firm when a self-appointed critic revealed the carelessness of this "*once absconding*" boy, and continued to support him by professing that they were "Inclin'd to use all Methods Mild" in correcting him,[152] methods probably ineffectual—as is suggested by this note published two weeks later: "Whereas we have found the Boy, who went the Eastern Part of the City, too Negligent in his Business; we shall suddenly fix one in his Room more careful in delivering the Papers, being forc'd at present to make use of one of our other Servants."[153]

It was more than a year later when another lad disappeared,

this time not to return.[154] Details of his misdemeanor are revealed in a published communication:

Q. Gentlemen, *Several of your Subscribers being inform'd that one of your Servants, who serv'd your Papers, not only proved a dishonest young Rascal, in cheating you of your Subscription-Money, but also neglected leaving Papers with Several of your Subscribers to your great Damage, notwithstanding his Friends, as I have been told, gave their words for his good Behaviour. . . . If they have not made you just Satisfaction, we think you are oblig'd to expose them to the World, that others may be aware how they have to do with such Dishonourable Persons.*

The employers of the boy, however, had already done as much as was recommended:

A. We have propos'd to his Friends a slight Satisfaction to be made us, in Proportion to the Damage we suffer'd by him, which if refus'd, we shall be free in their Characters, that others may not be impos'd upon by them. However we have taken such care about our present Servants, that none need doubt their being faithfully serv'd for the future.[155]

That they were faithfully served by the boys can perhaps be assumed from the small number of complaints published. The only other breach of trust indulged in by the boys was one alluded to in the paper at the time the disputed December quarteridge of 1708 was asked for.[156] "If any of our Servants," it was insisted, "give other than respectful Language, it is contrary to our positive Orders."[157]

It was probably only general doubt that persuaded the "proprietor"[158] of the paper during its third year of publication to have his own servant rather than the boys collect for the paper. The suspicion extended even to his single collector, for the subscriber was asked "to receive a Printed Receipt . . . Sign'd by J. *Mayo,* Printer of the . . . Paper."[159] It was later admitted that it was "too much Trouble" for one person to gather the quarteridges, and once again the boys made the next collection (giving receipts this time);[160] but on the subsequent and final quarter day one person— the owner's personal servant—received all the payments from subscribers.[161] It seems that the proprietor suspected pilfering at collection time; after the third volume was completed, purchasers paid cash.[162]

This essay has been an attempt to picture in bold outline the manner in which the business problems of an early eighteenth century periodical were met. Here are shown the specific sources of income open to the publisher as well as the actual prices he asked for what he produced, so that the financial basis of this paper comes in sight and, by implication, that of many of its contemporaries. So, too, are disclosed the duties of the distributing agents, carriers, hawkers, booksellers, and even the coffee-houses. The practices of this question-and-answer journal may not be reflected in entirety by other papers of the period, but the very fact that they were contemporary suggests that their general methods of operation may have been similar in many ways. The *British Apollo* with good purpose discovered to its public details of distribution and sale, and so gives the historian unusually abundant information on certain obscure procedures of livelihood which animated early English journalism.

NOTES

1. After a continuous run the *Athenian Mercury* ceased publication in 1696, but revived for a month in 1697.

2. John Dunton, *Life and Errors*, ed. John Nichols (London, 1818), I, 189-90.

3. Along with others, both Defoe and Swift wrote poems in praise of the Athenian Society (conductors of the *Athenian Mercury*). See *The Poems of Jonathan Swift*, ed. Harold Williams (Oxford, 1937), I, 14-25, and James Sutherland, *Defoe* (Philadelphia, 1938), p. 34.

4. These publications are the *Post-Angel* (1701-1702), a monthly periodical containing a department of questions from the files of the *Athenian Mercury*; the *Athenian Spy* (1704), a single volume "discovering the secret letters which were sent to the Athenian Society by several ingenious Ladies"; the *Athenæ Redivivæ* (1704), another monthly journal composed of questions previously passed over by the Athenian Society; and the *Athenian Oracle* (1703-1710), four volumes of selections from the *Athenian Mercury*.

5. See *Defoe's Review*, ed. Arthur Wellesley Secord (New York, 1938), Vol. I, No. 58.

6. *Ibid.*, Vol. II, No. 31.

7. *Ibid.*, *Little Review*, Nos. 6, 7, 9, 11, 12, 15, 16, 17, 22. These are a few of the numbers of the *Little Review* containing nonsensical, abusive, and impertinent letters. For evidence that Defoe was busy with political affairs, see Sutherland, *Defoe*, pp. 152-53.

8. In his *Athenian News* (1710), No. 6, John Dunton stated that his *Athenian Mercury* was "Printed without Subscriptions," as if any periodical worthy the name should be financially secure without depending upon such a method.

9. I, 1. References to the regular issues of the *British Apollo* will be made in this manner. The Roman numeral indicates the volume number, the Arabic numeral the number of the issue. The date of the issue will be given when significant. For this study I have used the original issues of the periodical.

The quarter days were Lady Day (March 25), Midsummer Day (June 24), Michaelmas Day (September 29), and Christmas Day. The *British Apollo* asked for payment, however, on St. Thomas's Day (December 21) rather than on Christmas Day (see II, 76).

10. I, 1, 2, 3. In each of the first three issues there is a note similar to this one from No. 1: "That where any of these shall be left, the Bearer will wait upon them the following Day after Publication for their Pleasure herein. . . ."

11. II, 12.

12. *Ibid.* This seems at odds with the note in I, 3, where it is said, as in I, 1 and 2, that "where any of these shall be left, the Bearer will wait upon them the following Day," but the repetition of this promise in the third issue was possibly only an oversight.

13. I, 2.

14. I, 31, *et passim.*

15. I, 39. After I, 85, the recommendation left out the innkeeper as an intermediary. Country subscribers were asked only that a friend in town take the paper for them.

16. I, 12, 101.

17. I, 55.

18. I, 43; II, 87, 100.

19. I, 50. See also I, 14, 52; II, 31, 50, 51, 116.

20. I, 52. See also II, 44, 98.

21. I, 11.

22. I, 37.

23. I, 68.

24. I, 40.

25. I, 89.

26. They seem to have been justified in their objection. See above, note 9.

27. I, 90.

28. I, 91.

29. I, 117; II, 26.

30. II, 76.

31. This was the conventional term of reference to the regular issues of the paper. See, for example, II, 33.

32. I, 7.

33. I, 14.

34. I, 14, 23, 31.

35. I, 38.

36. I, 40.

37. Not all of these supplements were advertised immediately before publication, although in every issue of the periodical in a set paragraph of advice to new subscribers their price and frequency were mentioned. Initial advertisements of them may be found in I, 10, 14, 23, 31, 40, 49, 59, 84, 103; II, 9, 20, 24, 36, 46, 64.

38. I, 63. It is perhaps indicative of the quandary of the editors that on this very day they found it necessary to note that

We receiv'd a Letter Sign'd by 4 Persons, demanding a speedy Answer to a Question on the Penalty of loosing their Subscriptions and Money due to us: To which we answer; we have above 100 Questions which came before yours, for which we have not Room yet. As to your Threats, you may leave us when you will, we have 5 times your Number in a Day to supply your Room: If we know not how to get our due, we must be content to loose it, but your Reputation must be very small, if the Forfeiture of *that*, be not a greater loss to you, than our Money to Us.

39. I, 69.

40. I, 80 (November 17, 1708).

41. I, 85.

42. I, 85-97.

43. I, Monthly Supplement 9 (December, 1708). The quarterly books were advertised in I, 81, 104; II, 13, 41, 70. The first quarterly book, published November 22, 1708, was out of print by August, 1709 (II, 44). The last one, published on November 25, 1709, was advertised until February 6, 1710 (II, 97).

44. II, 33. By this time sixteen monthly and three quarterly papers had been published.

45. II, Monthly Supplement 5, 37.

46. II, 41. In this connection can be cited the promotional precedent of the *General Remark on Trade* by the projectorial Charles Povey, "Undertaker of the Traders Exchange-House in Hatton-Garden"; see, e.g., No. 213 (July 7, 1707). The cut on the left of the title shows a boy holding the *Remark*, and the cut on the right is a picture of a substantial building. Beneath the boy is printed an appeal to promote the paper's sale; out of the profits twenty poor boys are clothed, kept to school, and allowed 2s. 6d. a week, and at the end of two years are given £5 to put them out as apprentices to trades. Under the building is a similar appeal for advertisements; from their income and other business at Hatton-Garden one hundred decayed men and women are to be allowed £10 per annum and a room rent-free in such a college as is represented by the figure. The *General Remark* at times included questions and answers, prose and verse, in its varied mercantile regimen.

47. Concert tickets apparently sold for five shillings. See a question and answer on a proposal in 1711 to have nightly concerts, IV, 7.

48. II, 42.

49. The problem offered by the rival issues of the *Female Tatler* is too complex to be entered upon here. What facts are known are best summarized in John Harrington Smith, "Thomas Baker and *The Female Tatler*," MP, XLIX (1952), 182-88.

50. No. 21 (August 24, 1709).

51. *British Apollo*, II, 45-61 (August 31-October 26, 1709) and *Female Tatler*, Nos. 21-45 (August 24-October 19, 1709).

52. August 25, 1709.

53. See II, Quarterly Supplement 3 (November 25, 1709), where all the parts of a simple song fill four folio pages.

54. II, Monthly Supplement 7.

55. II, Quarterly Supplement 3 (November 25, 1709).

56. II, 41, 42.

57. II, 67 (November 16, 1709).

58. II, 69.

59. No suggestion that several performances could have accommodated all of the subscribers appeared in the paper.

60. It seems reasonable to suspect that publication of Steele's *Tatler* on Tuesdays, Thursdays, and Saturdays, and the publication of the two *Female Tatlers* on Monday, Wednesday, and Friday, the *Apollo* days, had something to do with this new plan, especially when the *Tatler* admittedly took custom from the *British Apollo*. See above, pp. 89-90.

61. II, 63 (November 2, 1709).

62. II, 77.

63. II, 80.

64. I, 33. The first duty of this sort was performed in I, 19.

65. I, 106; II, 7.

66. An index was first advertised in I, 56.

67. II, 3.

68. II, 2.

69. II, 5.

70. II, 7. Apparently few of the owners of public houses went immediately to Mayo's to spend sixpence, for several months later the projectors planned to place "Indexes fix'd to Boards" in several coffee-houses, an intention that was apparently never carried out. See above, p. 92.

71. III, 15, 16.

72. IV, 12. This issue promised the index "this Week," but so did the last issue of the periodical (IV, 20).

73. I, 56, 57.

74. I, Monthly Supplement 9 (December, 1708).

75. III, 1. See above, p. 91.

76. I, 9.

77. See I, 26, 38, 91, 117, for examples.

78. I, 80.

79. II, 5.

80. II, 10, 12.

81. The last advertisement of sets of the first volume appears in II, 20 (July 8, 1709).

82. II, 86 (January 11, 1710).

83. III, 1, 154; IV, 1.

84. III, 154.

85. Earlier advertisements of sets of Volume II did not mention their price (see, for example, III, 1). Actually, subscribers had paid about the same for the second and third volumes as for the first.

86. Three stanzas on Bickerstaff's plan specifically refer to the announcement in *Tatler* No. 102 (December 3, 1709) of the pocket reprint in press.

87. The "Book" was the set of three volumes octavo.

88. II, 86 (January 11, 1710). Many such questions as this one, probably the majority of them, were simply a means the editors subtly availed themselves of in order to obtain what seemed to be public approval of their projects and policies.

89. II, 98.

90. III, 44.

91. III, 91, 103, 107, 123, 124, 128.

92. III, 91.

93. *The Penny Post: or, Tradesman's Select Pacquet*, No. 2 (March 15, 1717).

94. I, 1-4, 6-12.

95. In this periodical, for example, the most frequent advertiser of all was Roger Grant, who proclaimed his skill as an oculist in one hundred ninety-two issues.

96. I, 14.

97. II, 31.

98. II, Quarterly Supplement 3 (November, 1709).

99. III, 28.

100. Only the regular issues carried advertisements.

101. I, 1. Several months earlier Charles Povey's *General Remark on Trade* offered books full of guards at 1s. 6d. "to Past them on, so as to keep them Clean; each Book being capable of holding two entire Volumes" (No. 234, August 25, 1707).

102. I, 3.

103. II, 48. See also I, 33. At least one contemporary periodical writer accepted money for answering questions: see Defoe's *Review*, Vol. I, No. 95.

104. II, 109.

105. In 1704 Defoe's *Review* had an estimated circulation of only four hundred: James R. Sutherland, "The Circulation of Newspapers and Literary Periodicals, 1700-1730," *Library*, 4th ser., XV (1934), 111.

106. I, 1, 25, 117; II, 54. Similar directions appeared in every regular issue of the paper.

107. II, 54.

108. I, 1, 3, 25, 38, 117; II, 50; III, 1, 15, 28. As we have seen (above, p. 88), the editor insisted that the selection of advertisements was left to the printer.

109. III, 153.

110. I, 85; II, 70; III, 14, 54, 148, 153.

111. I, 6.

112. II, 24.

113. II, 69.

114. III, 1.

115. I, 53, 55, 56, 59. It is of small significance, but the colophon during the last twenty issues of the periodical—the half-sheet issues of Volume IV—included along with Mayo's name that of another printer, John Morphew.

116. Mayo's shop was in Fleet Street.

117. I, 1.

118. I, 26.

119. I, 1, 3, 25, 27, 37, 38.

120. I, 27.

121. I, 62. Bickerton advertised his shop in the *British Apollo*: "A Shop near the Pump in St. Paul's Churchyard to be Let: Enquire at Mr. Bickertons at the Flower-de-luce." See I, 52, 53, 55, 56, 57, 59.

122. *Ibid.* Quite probably Carter rented Bickerton's shop; both Bickerton's move and Carter's assistance were announced in this issue of the periodical, only twelve days after Bickerton had last offered a shop to be let.

123. *Ibid.*

124. I, 78-84. At this same time Aaron Hill was putting forward proposals for a book he later published as *The Present State of the Ottoman Empire*. He announced in the *British Apollo* that many who subscribed to Keble and Bickerton for his book were liable to be disappointed, "the said Booksellers not having given in their Names or Money" (I, 69). It may well have been that Keble was guilty, because Bickerton continued to serve as agent for the periodical.

125. III, 44.

126. III, 91.

127. IV, 9.

128. III, 154.

129. I, 85.

130. II, 47.

131. II, 7.

132. II, 25.

133. II, 51.

134. I, 1.

135. I, 3.

136. I, 65; II, 50; III, 15.

137. I, 14, 85; II, 15, 50.

138. I, 65.

139. I, 1, 2, 3, 40.

140. I, Quarterly Supplement 1, p. 9.

141. II, 63. These were written opinions which the boys were to deliver to the editors.

142. I, 12, 37, 65.

143. I, 91, 117.

144. I, 40.

145. I, 50.

146. II, 31.

147. II, 51.

148. II, 116. For a versified complaint about late delivery, see I, 101.

149. II, 98.

150. I, 43.

151. I, 45.

152. I, 51.

153. I, 55.

154. II, 87.

155. II, 100.

156. See above, p. 79.

157. I, 91.

158. By January, 1710, Marshal Smith had bought out the other seven men concerned in the project: see John Dunton, *Athenian News*, No. 6 (March 25, 1710).

159. III, 78.

160. III, 118.

161. III, 154.

162. *Ibid.*

THE *AUTHORSHIP OF THE* FREE-THINKER

THE FREE-THINKER

Nos. 1-350, March 24, 1718-July 28, 1721.

Folio half-sheet; double issue of sheet and a half.

Semi-weekly.

Editor: Ambrose Philips.

Colophon: "London, *Printed for* W. Wilkins, *at the* Post-House *under* Will's Coffee-house, Covent-Garden; *and Sold by* W. Graves, *at the* Black Spread Eagle *in* Pater-Noster-Row; and J. Graves *in St.* James's Street: *Where Letters and Advertisements are taken in.*"

THE AUTHORSHIP OF THE *Free-Thinker*

NICHOLAS JOOST

THE *Free-Thinker* was a leading literary periodical of the post-Addisonian years, yet little has been written about its authorship beyond frequent but casual mention of a few recurring names in histories of periodical literature. No one has answered in satisfying detail the pertinent questions relating to the authorship of this worthy follower of the *Tatler* and *Spectator*. What was its instigation? Who were its editor and contributors? What papers did they write? And what procedures did they follow in editing and writing this journal? Resolving these questions will add substantially to our knowledge of the *Free-Thinker* and, beyond that bound, to the history of early periodical publication and its relation to the Augustan political and social scene.

I

The fourth Monday in March, 1718, saw the appearance of a new periodical half-sheet entitled *The Free-Thinker*, published by the bookseller Wilkins, "To be continued every *Monday* and *Friday*," and priced at twopence.[1] The paper was started at the inspiration of the government, as explained by Thomas Burnet in one of his letters to George Duckett. "The Government," wrote Burnet of this "pretty well written" paper the *Free-Thinker*, "have sett the Author upon it." The government also knew, according to Burnet, that a "Club" of the editor's acquaintances was "assisting to him, so that a Paper now and then would be a kindness to me."[2]

Obviously the *Free-Thinker* was politically inspired; however, it never openly acknowledged the support of the government, which in 1718 was Earl Stanhope's Whig ministry. The reader of the periodical who is not aware of its submerged political direction accepts it as a loyal, comparatively impartial organ of free discus-

sion, whereas in reality the *Free-Thinker* was distinguished from
its more literary predecessors—the *Tatler* and the *Spectator*—by
its active support of the government and by the expression the
journal gave to such support.   Series of articles advocated methodi-
cally the Whig point of view in politics, the latitudinarian point of
view in religion, and Cartesian and Lockean epistemological
theories; the general tone of the *Free-Thinker* is relatively serious,
even philosophical, for such a genre as that of the essay periodical
of morals and manners.

The apt mouthpiece for these ideas is the eidolon of the journal,
Mr. Free-Thinker. He reflects not only the varied interests of the
Free-Thinker and its conscious policies; also, he is in a measure a
product of the personalities of the editor and contributors. The
eidolon of a freethinker was chosen by the editor precisely because
such a character-mask would allow a broad scope for comment by
the editor and his aides. Mr. Free-Thinker could and did write on
any topic that came within the compass of a reasonable man's
thoughts.

II

The editor of the *Free-Thinker* was Ambrose Philips. To aid
him in his publication, Philips had the assistance of a group of contributors of whom eight are fully identifiable. These men are
Hugh Boulter, later the Archbishop of Armagh; Gilbert Burnet
fils, Prebend of Salisbury Cathedral and Chaplain to George I;
Conrade De Gols; James Heywood; Zachary Pearce, later the
Bishop of Rochester; Henry Stephens, Rector of Malden, Surrey;
Leonard Welsted; and Richard West, later the Lord Chancellor
of Ireland. Sir John Fellows is represented by one letter, and
another is signed jointly by four ex-prisoners, George Brown,
Jacques Laurent, Mary Mason, and Rebecca Sherman. In addition,
George Stubbes, Rector of St. Lawrence Newlands, Essex; Thomas
Burnet, the brother to Gilbert; and George Duckett may have
been contributors, but no specific papers are ascribed to them. Sir
Richard Steele may have written for and certainly directly influenced the *Free-Thinker*.

There is no list of contributors or contributions, essay by essay,
in any edition of the *Free-Thinker*. Some editorial information

about authorship does, however, exist. The four collected editions of the *Free-Thinker* (1722-23, 1733, 1739, and 1742) contain Nos. 1-159, less than half of the issues. It is to the last two of these reprints that we turn for information about authorship. The title page for each volume in both editions lists the contributing writers as co-authors, and a short anonymous preface, which appeared in both the 1739 and the 1742 editions, gives additional details. Philips is named as author as well as editor, and the principal contributors are listed—West, Stephens, Gilbert Burnet, and Boulter. Since Nos. 160-350 of the *Free-Thinker* were never reprinted, we must proceed without the help that a preface to such an edition might give us on the authorship of these papers. In the later numbers, however, we find essays of the men named as authors of some of the earlier ones. Moreover, at intervals of six months throughout the life of the *Free-Thinker,* Philips printed recapitulatory essays that listed the various papers forming units of the several series that had run concurrently during the previous six months of publication. It is not illogical, then, to assume that the man whom Philips named as author of a series in the earlier numbers continued writing the same series for the entire life of the journal. Thus, by combining the information of the recapitulatory essays with that of the 1739 preface (repeated in the edition of 1742) and then by applying this combined information to all 350 papers of the *Free-Thinker*, we can ascertain the authorship of many numbers. Evidence of authorship for those contributors not mentioned in the preface to the 1739 edition is scattered. In only one case, that of Welsted, does the editor name a contributor in the issues of the *Free-Thinker* itself.

On the strength of internal and external evidence connecting them with the periodical, the contributors fall into three categories. The first consists of contributors who are known by name and by specific contribution. The second category consists of persons whose connection with the *Free-Thinker* can be established but whose identities outside their contributions remain unknown or, if their identities are known, whose specific contributions remain unknown. The final category consists of contributors who are known only by pseudonyms or initials.

III

As editor, Ambrose Philips wrote the greater part of his journal. The history of the *Free-Thinker* forms but a minor portion of his biography, however, even during the years from 1718 to 1721; for at this time he was also justice of the peace for Westminster and a commissioner of the lottery. In point of fact Philips' editorship occupies only one chapter in the long story of his continual hunt for political preferment. Still, that editorial position must have aided him beyond its duration, for when Hugh Boulter, one of his co-authors, became Archbishop of Armagh in 1724, Philips went to Ireland as the Lord Primate's secretary. As a minor officeholder he remained in Ireland, where one sees him presenting an edition of the *Free-Thinker* to such an influential member of the Irish gentry as General Richard St. George.[3]

Today most students of the Augustan age think of Philips as one of those worthies on whom Pope wasted his exquisitely vitriolic couplets in the *Dunciad*. Or perhaps an occasional scholar recalls him as the unfortunate target of Henry Carey's parody "Namby-Pamby," which satirized those verses written "*To Miss* Margaret Pulteney, *daughter of* Daniel Pulteney, *Esq; in the* Nursery," beginning "Dimply damsel, sweetly smiling." Fairly or unfairly, "Namby-Pamby" has damned Philips' name and memory for well over two centuries, and his verses remain the epitome of the infantine style. As an editor, essayist, and translator of some merit, he is by no means so well known.

The preface to the 1739 edition of the *Free-Thinker* speaks of "*Mr.* Philips, *the Author of some of these Papers, and Editor of them all*." Philips is also stated to be the "*Publisher and Conductor*," the "*Author of many of the Papers*"; however, the preface does not attribute to him a specific series of papers, such as it does to all the contributors whom it names. Philips' work in the *Free-Thinker* is consequently more difficult to identify. It falls in two categories, his work as editor and his contributions as author and translator.

To Philips in his editorial capacity should go the introductory essays, the semi-annual essays of a recapitulatory nature, and the prose of the final essay; for these pieces no other authorship has ever been proposed.[4] In general, the use of the editorial "I" when it occurs in prose that functions as editorial exposition becomes the assumptive norm for determining Philips' work as editor. On the basis of this tenable criterion we see that Philips wrote as the conductor of the *Free-Thinker* all the replies to letters and the remarks and comments on correspondence. James Heywood attributed the "Answers, and Remarks" to his letters in the *Free-Thinker* to the "Author," who was, of course, Philips.[5] Without stretching the argument too thin, one may plead that what held true for Heywood held true for the other correspondents. The editorial prose in twenty-six issues containing poetry we may also ascribe to Philips,[6] as well as the editorial introductions to essays and to prose fiction scattered throughout the issues of the journal.

As author and translator Philips contributed to the *Free-Thinker* both poetry and prose. Of the thirty-one issues in the journal that contain poetry, fifteen sets of verses in twelve issues are by Philips.[7] Several of his poems are printed for the first time in these papers. In her edition Miss Segar credits the *Free-Thinker* with publishing ten of Philips' poems, but has not given the *Free-Thinker* credit for first publishing the following verses by Philips: "George Came to the Crown" and Anacreon's "*Ode* 34," both in No. 107; "To the Memory of the Right Honorable the late Earl of HALIFAX," in No. 29; "Lying at her Feet," in No. 112; and in No. 217, the "*Third* ODE of ANACREON. On LOVE."[8]

Philips' non-editorial prose contributions to the *Free-Thinker* are less easily identifiable than is his poetry, as no comprehensive standard exists for determining the canon. Each body of prose of unknown authorship in the *Free-Thinker* we must, therefore, examine separately to determine the writer's identity.

The translations from Fénelon that appear throughout the periodical may be ascribed to Philips for several reasons.[9] Introductions to such papers are always written editorially, in the first person singular, and apologies for these tales are put forth in the first person, as in No. 80: "Having, from the Beginning, stiled my self a *Fairy-Philosopher*, my Readers may imagine, I shall, at my Leisure, consult the Records of the invisible, powerful People, with whom I hold some Correspondence." This intimate mingling of the editorial attitude and the pronoun of the first person singular with the introductory matter of the fables constitutes one kind of internal evidence for ascribing the translations from Fénelon's *Fables* and his *Dialogues des morts* to Philips. The use of these materials is, moreover, much more flexible and varied than the editor's use of contributions by such constant and important writers for the journal as West and Gilbert Burnet. A fable may be serialized, as in Nos. 109-110; it may be used as an exemplum in a hortatory essay, as in No. 253; or it may be used frankly to entertain, as in No. 92. External evidence further supports the evidence gathered from an examination of the techniques used in presenting these translations from Fénelon. Philips was already known as the translator of the *Contes persanes* and the adapter of Racine's *Andromaque* as *The Distrest Mother;* he had written one of the best known essays in the *Guardian,* No. 16, containing matter translated from the French; using French sources, he had written (or adapted) a biography of Mme. de Maintenon in *Guardian* Nos. 46-48; and in *Guardian* No. 81 Philips had already translated Fénelon into English. Finally, on purely negative evidence all the issues containing translations from Fénelon may be assigned to Philips, since the preface to the 1739 edition of the *Free-Thinker* does not assign them to any of the other known contributors, and at the time of the *Free-Thinker's* publication no other English translation of the *Fables*—published in Paris in 1718—was in print. Twenty-one fables and four dialogues of the dead, then, would seem to be translations by Philips from the French of Fénelon.

At least three papers are adaptations of Philips' earlier writings. *Free-Thinker* No. 267 prints the tale of the vizier Caversha, "out of the *Persian Tales,*" which Philips had translated from the French version of Pétis de la Croix in 1714.[10] No. 35 is in part verbally identical with No. 20 of the *Grumbler,* which Philips had contributed in 1715 to this journal edited by Thomas Burnet, and No. 46 is in part verbally identical with *Grumbler* Nos. 10 and 11, also written by Philips in 1715 for Burnet.[11]

The *Free-Thinker* papers dealing with aesthetic and literary topics are in all probability by Philips. The known abilities of his contributors lie in religion and politics rather than in aesthetics. Heywood and Welsted, who might otherwise be candidates for authorship of such a paper as No. 18 on the quarrel of the ancients and the moderns or No. 168 on prose style and its relation to rhetoric, are not to be considered. When Heywood printed his own contributions, neither of these was included; and Welsted's contributions were carefully acknowledged by the editor. By a process of elimination Philips may be assigned such essays, twelve in number.[12]

According to the preface to the 1739 edition, various light and facetious essays written *"in the Nature of the Spectators"* are by Philips. Almost certainly these include such feminist essays as Nos. 147, dealing with the need of women for philosophy, and No. 174, on "the Nature of Coquetterie," both of which evince the editor's attempts to attract a largely feminine reading public. Again, No. 248, a dialogue between a "Minion of Fortune and a Philosopher," adumbrates the translations from Fénelon's *Dialogues des morts* that later appeared in the *Free-Thinker*. No. 126, written by Philips at the behest of Steele in an attempt to heal the breach between the London physicians Woodward and Mead, has its sequel in No. 215, in which the editor voiced his soothing comments on the Bangorian controversy then current in the Establishment; indeed, a note in No. 215 refers the reader to No. 126 as an example of temperance in controversy. No. 201 follows Steele's practice of devoting an occasional paper entirely to answers to correspondents. No. 56 is pleasantly facetious upon the experience of beginning another six months of publication. No. 43 is more serious, less imitative, and more representative of Philips' original bent in the *Free-Thinker*, with its overt appeal for a royalty that will, in the editor's frame of reference, be freethinking. But in No. 8 we find Philips writing an anti-Jacobite polemic, a literary endeavor that, although met with often enough in his journal, seems to have been mostly the labor of some contributor such as West rather than the editor, who preferred ridicule's rapier to the polemical bludgeon.

Other issues may, for one reason or another, be tentatively assigned to the editor, but their provenance is doubtful on the basis of internal and external evidence. Of the 350 *Free-Thinker* issues, at least fifty-seven appear to be wholly by Philips and at least 109 in part by him.[13]

The variety of literary forms used by Philips is wide, within the formal limits of the essay journal: verse, usually light, lyric, short, and even when sober "Ever elegant in woe," like the mourning muses of Philips' elegy on Lord Halifax; short tales, such as his translations of Fénelon's *Fables;* the essay, of course; the letter, susceptible to many purposes; the dialogue; and the "character." Philips' subject matter was less varied, tending as it did to follow here the lead of the *Spectator*—with "improvements." Generally, Philips seems to have left to others such topics as religion, political and economic theory, and medical science. Occasionally he indulged in polemics, sectarian and factional. He did revise a paper on astronomy that had appeared previously in the *Grumbler.* Usually, however, he wrote on morals and manners and aesthetics in the respected tradition of Addison and Steele. His original contribution to the *materia* of the essay journal was not so much as a writer as it was as an editor. Philips forced within the framework of bourgeois belief a popularization of the rationale of the new science, adulterating and altering the thought of Descartes and Locke. He refused to recognize the heterodox implications of contemporary freethinking; he appropriated the name of "freethinker" and defined it anew in order thereby to teach what he conceived to be the lessons of philosophy. This philosophical improvement over earlier essay journals is consonant with the editor's desire to improve his readers—as Addison and Steele had desired, but with less barefaced systematic zeal than Philips, their friend and imitator.

IV

Despite Thomas Burnet's assertion that the *Free-Thinker* was written by a "Club," the contributors to the journal do not appear as a tightly knit group. Rather, some of them—a small number— seem to have been closely allied by ties of blood, of marriage, and, as we should expect, of ecclesiastical and political ambitions. The rest are scattered individuals who wrote purely for diversion or from motives that with the passage of time are effectively concealed. In Nos. 1-159 most of the contributors wrote on their particular fields of interest; the assumption is that they wrote consistently on those topics throughout the life of the periodical. Naturally, the most persistent research will not be rewarded with certainty in every case; yet a surprisingly large portion of the numbers of the *Free-Thinker* can be confidently assigned to some known person. Among these contributors Hugh Boulter stands out because of his ecclesiastical rank and his close relation to the editor. In 1718 as Archdeacon of Surrey he was not above journalism as a means of preferment. It is to Boulter's credit that when he went to Ireland as newly appointed Primate, he took his friend Philips with him and on arrival appointed his erstwhile editor as his secretary and afterwards procured him a seat in the Irish House of Commons. Pope's comment on the friendship was not kindly; he asked in the *Epistle to Dr. Arbuthnot,*

> Does not one Table *Bavius* still admit?
> Still to one Bishop *Philips* seem a Wit?

This reference to the bishop—in 1719 Boulter had been appointed chaplain to the King and in November of the same year consecrated Bishop of Bristol[14]—illuminates Philips' growing dependence on a man whom earlier he had been able to treat as an equal and, indeed, had been able to favor. These brilliant ecclesiastical preferments came, very likely, as rewards for party services rather than for theological distinction. Undoubtedly Dr. Boulter's *Free-Thinker* papers fall in the category of party services.

The preface to the 1739 edition of the *Free-Thinker* ascribes the series of essays on *"Education and Learning"* to Boulter. Another title given to these nine issues is the "Supplement to the Preliminary Lectures."[15] Boulter may have had a hand in other papers of a similar nature; it is difficult to believe that such a close friend of the editor and so constant a contributor for the first months would write no more papers after No. 146.[16]

Another contributor, the Reverend Gilbert Burnet, was the second son of Bishop Burnet, the historian. Gilbert Burnet the younger was appointed chaplain to the King in 1718, when he was aiding the government by writing for the *Free-Thinker.*[17] The preface to the 1739 edition states that Dr. Burnet wrote the religious lectures against *"Superstition and Enthusiasm"*—essays not pro-rationalist but anti-Catholic in purpose—comprising ten, possibly twelve, numbers of the *Free-Thinker.*[18]

Conrade De Gols was not mentioned by Philips or in the 1739 preface as a contributor to the *Free-Thinker,* but he appeared in the journal on three occasions. A personal advertisement in No. 255 (August 29, 1720) informed "T. C.," who had directed a letter dated August 20, 1720, to "a Nobleman," that "a Reward of Three

Hundred Pounds is lodged in the Hands of Mr. *De Gols,* of the Bank, as desired by the said *T. C.*" Two issues later another personal notice appeared: "The *Free-Thinker* thanks Mr. D. G. for his Letter." And No. 271 published a third personal note: "N. B. *In my next I shall begin to publish the Packet of my kind Correspondent,* D. G." The connection between Mr. D. G. and Mr. De Gols of the Bank may seem tenuous until we observe the nature of Mr. D. G.'s contributions and of Mr. De Gols's occupation. The "Packet" acknowledged in No. 271 duly appeared in Nos. 272, 274, and 278—a series in which D. G. analyzed the very questionable position of the South Sea Company's stocks. Indeed, in No. 272 D. G. contributed what proved to be one of the most popular papers in the entire run of the *Free-Thinker; "There being a Demand,"* it was reprinted, according to No. 274. This series, the major portion of which is given over to statistics, shows a closely detailed knowledge of the speculations in South Sea stocks. Obviously, then, D. G. must have had some close connection with the South Sea Company, as he had an insider's knowledge of the speculations then current on the Exchange. And this is precisely the kind of knowledge that Mr. De Gols would have had. For Mr. De Gols of the Bank was none other than the De Gols listed in an obituary notice of 1738 as *"Conrade de Gols,* Esq; late Cashire of the *South Sea Company."*[19] In 1733 he figured prominently in the investigation into the derelict South Sea Company's finances, conducted by the House of Lords.[20]

The evidence leading to the conclusion that Conrade De Gols wrote three issues of the *Free-Thinker* may be summed up as follows. The personal notice to D. G. and the correspondence signed D. G. concern an individual with initials corresponding to those of De Gols's name. D. G.'s technical knowledge of a complicated, not to say muddled, financial speculation is what would certainly be expected from a cashier of the South Sea Company. And the publication within a short time of a series of personal notices concerning D. G. and De Gols, followed by a sensational and apparently authoritative correspondence signed by D. G., strengthens the chain of coincidence. On the basis of this circumstantial evidence De Gols appears as one of the contributors to the *Free-Thinker.*

Another correspondent not named in the preface to the 1739 reprint has proudly asserted his authorship. James Heywood collected a small volume of *Letters and Poems on Several Subjects*, first published in 1722 and reissued with "Additions" in 1726. The title page of the second edition lists among *Letters and Poems on Several Subjects* "LETTERS to the Authors of the *Spectator, Free-Thinker, Censor, Journal, Plain-Dealer,* &c." and ."Their Answers and Remarks." Heywood's apology for the collection explains that as his letters to "several Authors, that have entertained the Town with their Speculations," have met with a "favourable Approbation from such ingenious Gentlemen as Sir *Richard Steel,* and Mr. *Philips,*" he has the "greater Hopes they will meet with a Kind Reception from every candid Reader." Heywood goes on to account for his anonymity in the *Free-Thinker* and other journals by explaining his use of *noms de plume.* "Several of those Letters I writ in a female Character, some of them I sign'd with the initial Letters of my Name, and others under fictitious Characters." By these means Heywood impersonated "a Maid, a Wife, a Batchelor, a marry'd Man, a School-Boy, a Bankrupt, &c." Although he may not have been aware that he was doing so, Heywood makes it clear that an apparent diversity of correspondents in any given essay journal does not necessarily indicate a great number of readers who wrote letters to the editor. Actually, in the *Free-Thinker* and in other essay journals, many letters presumably from different persons may have been composed by one indefatigable literary amateur, writing, like Heywood, "at Intervals, when . . . disengag'd from Business, purely for . . . Diversion."[21]

Heywood contributed to sixteen issues.[22] Seven of these form a distinct series written by Philips as Mr. Free-Thinker and by Heywood as Miranda, a young lady of independent means, and as Bob Smart, a young bachelor.[23] Though composed mostly of letters, the series does contain two poems. One, in *Free-Thinker* No. 140, entitled "To my Successful Rival," is by Heywood; "To Miranda," in No. 103, Miss Segar has assigned to Philips.[24] The Miranda series offers an insight into the more curious practices of Augustan journalism. Heywood's letter in *Free-Thinker* No. 95 (February 16, 1719), the first in the series, also appeared in Mist's *Weekly Journal* No. 12 the following Saturday (February 21,

1719). Although Mist carried out a parallel development of the Miranda series of letters, neither journal made any charges of plagiarism. For some reason Heywood did not choose to acknowledge the inclusion of his letters in Mist's paper. In the light of his published assertion Heywood is seen to be one of the more constant contributors to the *Free-Thinker*, overlooked though he was in the preface to the 1739 edition.

Like Heywood and De Gols, Zachary Pearce is not named in this preface as a contributor. An anonymous notice in the *Gentleman's Magazine* of one of Pearce's works is the primary source for the information that Pearce wrote for the *Free-Thinker*. Following a list of Pearce's writings, the reviewer writes that "To the above we beg leave to add, that No. 114 in the *Free-Thinker*, we are well assured, was also by Bishop Pearce, which, as the learned Editor seems not apprized of it, and the work that contains it is in few hands, our readers will not be displeased to see in some future Magazine."[25]

Philips' editorial introduction in No. 114 is pertinent. "I have been impatient," the paper begins, "for an Opportunity to return my Thanks to the ingenious Gentleman, who sent me the following serious Entertainment, which has lain by me ever since the Nineteenth of *February*." Then, after printing the contribution, Philips comments, "Thus far my unknown Correspondent pursues his Fiction upon the Thought of *Cicero*. . . ." There seems to be an inconsistency between the claims of the correspondent in the *Gentleman's Magazine* and the statement in the journal itself until one recalls that such a disclaimer of identity as that published in the latter may have been an editorial device intended to stimulate readers' curiosity.

A theme similar to that in No. 114 is the subject of No. 301; this issue, also by an unknown correspondent, contains a piece of allegorical fiction in the guise of a letter. The allegory belongs to that genre perhaps best exemplified by the famous Vision of Mirzah in the *Spectator*. No. 301 is a vision of man's progress through time and eternity; its general similarity in theme and point of view to No. 114 suggests a possibility that the same author wrote both numbers. The correspondent who wrote No. 301 also wrote a letter, published in No. 311, complaining about the editor's re-

jection of his poetry. His only other contribution, printed in No.
329, was a prose dialogue between Euphues and Sophronius on the
problem of the most suitable occupation. That Pearce may have
written Nos. 301, 311, and 329 remains a probability, but one
strengthened by their similarity in theme, point of view, and
literary technique to No. 114; by the allegedly anonymous authorship of all four; and by the Ciceronian overtones of Nos. 114 and
329, an outcome—in the former paper, at any rate—of Pearce's
labors as an editor of Cicero's dialogues on oratory.

Besides Boulter, Burnet, and Pearce, another clergyman whose
contributions can be identified wrote for the *Free-Thinker*. He
was Henry Stephens, of whom the preface to the 1739 edition
states that "N° 6. 106. 149. 157. *and* 158. *were written by the late
Mr.* Henry Stephens, *Rector of* Malden." Like Philips, Stephens
was obligated to Archbishop Boulter, his patron and friend of long
standing, for preferments. Whether Boulter was a means of
getting Stephens' essays—turgidly allegorical and as homiletic as
secular sermons—printed in the *Free-Thinker* or whether both
men knew Philips is uncertain. Why Stephens, whose obscurity
is not quite complete, should have been named in such comparatively distinguished company as that of Boulter, Philips, and West
as a writer for the *Free-Thinker* remains another of the journal's
mysteries.[26]

To nine numbers of the *Free-Thinker* the minor poet Leonard
Welsted contributed verses that in all cases save one Philips
identified.[27] Such a procedure in itself was not customary with the
editor, for he mentioned none of the other regular contributors
by name in the issues of the *Free-Thinker*. Initials or pseudonyms
were appended occasionally to letters, poems, or essays; otherwise
anonymity was the rule. Why Welsted alone should have been
singled out is an unsolved problem. Perhaps he allowed the
Free-Thinker to use his contributions after stipulating that his
name be signed to them. Possibly he was named because he had
been commended to Philips by Steele as the latter's protégé.
Again, Philips may have felt that some special recognition should
be given to this brother poet, who with Steele and Dennis had
puffed Philips' *Pastorals*. At any rate, Welsted contributed

substantially, and Philips apparently accepted his poems with enthusiasm and appreciation.

In the memoir of Welsted prefixed to the edition of his works, John Nichols stated that five poems that originally appeared in the *Free-Thinker*, among which a " 'Love-Tale' of Acon and Lavinia stands foremost in rank and merit," are particularly pointed out by Philips, "who tells us, his friend was then engaged in a translation of Tibullus, of which a specimen was printed in the Free-thinker." Nichols added that two more poems by Welsted originally appeared in the *Free-Thinker*, "a translation of Horace Book I. Ode XIX . . . and a Song," and that "Another Ode of Horace (Book IV. Ode II.) . . . I have ventured . . . to ascribe to him on conjecture."[28] Nichols failed to ascribe to the *Free-Thinker* the initial appearance of Welsted's "To Zelinda," which was printed in No. 241 and later included among the poet's collected works.

The last of the contributors to the *Free-Thinker* whose specific contributions are known on the basis of direct evidence, internal or external, is Richard West, who probably used the *Free-Thinker* as a means of political advancement. Along with Boulter, West went to Ireland; he became Lord Chancellor of Ireland in 1725 and one of three Lords Justices in Ireland (during the Lord Lieutenant's absence) in 1726. His early death at the age of thirty-seven—a death that gave occasion to a great deal of scandal—effectually prevented his becoming as generous a patron to his former editor as the Lord Primate proved to be. West, father of Thomas Gray's friend and husband to the sister of Thomas Burnet and the younger Gilbert Burnet, wrote the series of lectures on politics in the *Free-Thinker*, according to the preface to the 1739 edition: "*those* [papers] *on* Politicks [were written] *by the above late Lord Chancellor.*" The same writer remarks of West's contributions, "*there are indeed some of these* [papers] *written by the late Lord Chancellor of* Ireland, *Mr.* West, *upon the Excellency of our Laws and Constitution, which have nothing in that way equal to them in the Spectators; for a very plain Reason, viz. because no Lawyer equal to him was concerned in that Undertaking.*" The series of papers on politics comprises a total of fifteen issues,[29] of which only the first nine appeared in the 1739 edition. Apart from this series are seven papers with themes similar to those of the political essays by West; there is a possibility that West may have written entirely or may have collaborated in the writing of these numbers.[30]

To this rather heterogeneous group of contributors—Boulter, Gilbert Burnet, De Gols, Heywood, Pearce, Stephens, Welsted, and West—may be assigned at least forty-one entire issues and portions of twenty-seven other issues of the *Free-Thinker*. The variety of subjects on which these men wrote is, with two exceptions, in the tradition of the *Spectator*. One of the exceptions has been pointed out: West's series of essays *"upon the Excellency of our Laws and Constitution,"* which, the anonymous writer judged, *"have nothing in that way equal to them in the Spectators."* The *Spectator* also had nothing in the way equal to the papers on religion, at least as the *Free-Thinker* understood religion. Burnet, Stephens, and, occasionally, Philips wrote polemics that, purporting to be impartial and reasonable examinations of "Enthusiasm" and "Superstition"— those enemies of "true" religion—were actually unconcealed tirades against alleged Catholic practices. These two deviations from the relatively nonpartisan stand of the *Spectator* reveal, of course, the *raison d'être* of the *Free-Thinker*. Admittedly, the rest, which is to say the bulk, of the subjects dealt with in the journal are much too important to be denominated as mere window dressing. Morals and manners, fashion, education and learning, belles lettres, finance, literary criticism, and reflective and even philosophical matters were included in Mr. Free-Thinker's view of the world, by the writers whom we have noted. Comprehensive as their collective point of view was, nevertheless it had a political bias; all these men can be shown to have been Whigs, and some of them were active in the party's business. This latter group, the inner circle writing for the *Free-Thinker*, was composed of the two Burnets, Boulter, West, and Philips. Stephens, De Gols, Pearce, Heywood, and Welsted seem to have been friendly in varying degrees with the editor (though it is possible that Philips did not know Pearce) but not concerned in the party writing for which the government at least partially subsidized the *Free-Thinker* during its three and a half years of publication.

V

Ten other persons were associated with the *Free-Thinker* in various ways. Of this group, six people had letters in two issues of the journal. Besides the comments of Philips and a letter signed pseudonymously by Ignoramus, a single issue prints a joint letter in which four debtors just delivered from the Marshalsea prison—George Brown, Jacques Laurent, Mary Mason, and Rebecca Sherman—express their gratitude to Mr. Free-Thinker for his help in releasing them. A nobleman whose name is printed as "Lord ———" we know solely by his two letters to Sir John Fellows, "Sub-Governour" of the South Sea Company, whose brief note of reply is, apparently without permission, reprinted with Lord ———'s letters in one issue.[31] Other issues may have been contributed by four men—Thomas Burnet, George Duckett, Sir Richard Steele, and George Stubbes—whose connection with the *Free-Thinker* we can adduce with varying degrees of certainty, but whose contributions we cannot specifically designate.

Thomas Burnet was the author of several unspecified numbers of the *Free-Thinker*, to accept his word for the fact that he had written cooperatively or had helped revise various contributions. Early in the life of the journal Burnet told George Duckett, "I send you here six of my *Letters* to the *Freethinker*, which I was desired by a very considerable Man to write towards the Support of that Paper, which is written by Direction of the Government."[32] This statement refers to a pamphlet entitled *A Letter to the Free-Thinker* that Burnet as "Eubulus" had brought out in July of 1718. David Nichol Smith, the editor of Burnet's letters, explains that "The 'very considerable Man' at whose wish this pamphlet was written had intended it to promote the ineffectual design of university legislation."[33] Perhaps Boulter's series on education and learning was the result of this governmental direction, but Burnet does not appear to have written any comparable set of papers for the *Free-Thinker*. In another letter Burnet asserted that the *Free-Thinker* was written by an "Author," who must have been Philips, but that the essays were revised by a club—"every one before they go to the Press. And sometimes we quite work up a new Paper, when we do not like what is brought to us." Burnet also asked Duckett in this passage, "If any good whimsicall turn should come into your head, you may now and then work up a *Paper* and send it me. . . ."[34]   Obviously it is impossible to ascribe with certainty any specific papers to Burnet or to Duckett on the basis of such a letter; however, it is certain from this passage that Thomas Burnet collaborated with Philips on the *Free-Thinker*, and Burnet's friend Duckett well may have written several issues for the club to revise.

Burnet, like Boulter and West, received advancement after the *Free-Thinker* ceased publication.   He was made consul at Lisbon, and remained there for several years.   In none of the editions of the *Free-Thinker* is he mentioned, although he was living in London at least some part of the period 1722-1742.[35]   Just what the reasons were for the omission of his name and the publication of his brother's on the title page and in the preface of the 1739 edition of the *Free-Thinker* remains unknown.

George Duckett was an antiquarian and an amateur who tried his hand at satires and anti-Catholic tracts.   He collaborated with Burnet on the *Grumbler* and in the composition of several satires, the best known being the *Homerides*, directed against Pope, then translating Homer.   We have no direct proof that Duckett contributed to the *Free-Thinker*, but it is possible that one or more letters, or perhaps such essays as Nos. 120, 121, and 122—discussions of Roman manners with comparisons between ancient Roman and contemporary British manners—may have been sent to Philips from Duckett's country residence, Hartham.   Like his friend Thomas Burnet, Duckett was rewarded by the Whigs and became a commissioner of the excise in 1722, a position he held until his death in 1732.[36]

Sir Richard Steele also may have contributed to the *Free-Thinker*.   George Aitken in his biography of Steele first noted that Steele "probably wrote some papers for the *Free-Thinker*."   Among the Blenheim manuscripts Aitken found a fragment of a draft beginning: "When I open'd my Design in Writing this paper, and Explained the Character of a Freethinker, I declar'd that this name ought not to be given to those who transgresse the Bounds of Reason and Justice, but must be kept within proper regulations, and that the *Outlaw* of all men living had the least Pretence to be esteem'd a *Freethinker*."[37]

Over sixty years after Aitken's discovery of the fragmentary draft in the Blenheim manuscripts, John Loftis used the same evidence to connect Steele with Philips' essay journal. Loftis has found corroborating evidence for the connection by relating this short fragment, "obviously intended for *The Freethinker*," to another Blenheim fragment of Steele's work, a satirical essay answering the speech by the Jacobite Tory, James Shippen, on the King's German extraction and on his ignorance of the English language. The link between the two fragments—the paragraph and the essay on Shippen—is a verbal one, the repetition in the essay of an antithesis found in the shorter piece: "a Spy may betray the whole Army, but a Deserter brings only his single Force." This antithesis, asserts Loftis, is precisely that which Steele establishes between Shippen and the traitor James Shepheard in his unfinished essay. There is in the longstanding friendship of the two men and in the coincidence of their political views supporting evidence that Steele wrote the essay on Shippen about the time Philips began his new periodical; moreover, *Free-Thinker* No. 8 consists of an essay deploring the conduct of James Shepheard. No. 32, one of many papers fulminating against Catholics and Jacobites, refers to No. 8 and calls Shepheard the Jacobites' "Martyr," repeating an epithet from Steele's essay on Shippen.[38] In addition to these persuasive arguments, further investigation of the *Free-Thinker* makes clearer not only the mere fact of a relationship but, as well, the connotations of that fact.

The passage that Aitken found and that Loftis commented on does not, to be sure, occur in the *Free-Thinker*, although the thought is analogous to that of many passages in the journal. In the *Tatler, Spectator*, and *Guardian* both Addison and Steele had written against freethinkers and freethinking pretty consistently; that Steele modified his erstwhile forthright opposition to the extent of distinguishing between degrees of freethought that were acceptable and unacceptable is essential to an understanding of his connection with the *Free-Thinker*. For, while no direct, specific evidence of authorship links Steele to any of the essays in the *Free-Thinker*, this modification of his views very probably influenced Philips' conceptions of content and of editorial purpose.

Two examples will show the importance of Steele's influence in shaping his friend's efforts in journalism. Having known Philips and having publicized his work in the *Tatler* and *Spectator*, Steele may properly have felt that Philips in his turn ought to assist younger writers by publishing their work in the *Free-Thinker*. One writer whom Steele patronized and encouraged and used to recommend among his acquaintance was Leonard Welsted.[39] Welsted was the only poet appearing in the *Free-Thinker* whose name was there fixed to his work.

Steele's connection with the *Free-Thinker* through Welsted is conjectural, but his influence on the journal can be proved by direct evidence. Apparently he consulted with Philips and considered the *Free-Thinker* "a suitable periodical to make disinterested comment."[40] Steele desired Philips' aid in settling a serious quarrel between two London physicians, Woodward and Mead, and he wrote a pamphlet to the *Free-Thinker* entitled *The Antidote, in a Letter to the Free-Thinker*. Answering Steele's plea to settle the quarrel reasonably and quietly, Philips wrote *Free-Thinker* No. 126. Steele replied with a second pamphlet, *The Antidote*, No. II, in which he thanked Philips for his paper on the quarrels of the town but asked for another essay on the same subject. This, however, he did not get. These two pamphlets addressed to the *Free-Thinker* in flattering language are surprising documents by one who in the *Tatler*, *Spectator*, and *Guardian* had written so vigorously against the evils of freethinking.

Steele's attitudes on several controversial topics—the South Sea speculation, property, and private benevolence toward debtors—are echoed in the *Free-Thinker*. Like Steele, the *Free-Thinker* was merciless in denouncing the South Sea Bubble at the beginning of the decline in value of the stocks. And, like Steele, the journal later became moderate and even conciliatory in its criticism of the speculation, when the great debacle of the South Sea Company occurred.[41] Allied to Steele's view of the South Sea speculation was his view of property, published at the beginning of 1719 in a pamphlet, *The Crisis of Property*.[42] The complex arguments adduced by Steele to support his contention that the Bank of England and not the South Sea Company deal with the national debt—these need not concern us. That Steele prophesied a crisis in property as a result of the ministers' accepting the proposals of the South Sea

Company is the important fact here, for No. 299 of the *Free-Thinker* contained a statement that there loomed "a Controversy concerning *Property*." This controversy was the same as that prophesied by Steele in his pamphlet on the crisis of property. In their opposition to the government's support of the South Sea Company, both the *Free-Thinker* and Steele were ranged with Walpole against the ministers then in office, headed by Stanhope. Fortunately for Steele and the *Free-Thinker*, they were propagandizing for the ascendant political power.

Steele's cult of benevolence and sentiment may have influenced many papers in the *Free-Thinker*. Fourteen numbers belong wholly or partly to a series entitled by the editor the papers on "Charity and Compassion."[43] Instigated by an unsigned letter and continued chiefly through the efforts of this unknown correspondent, the series purposed to release from the Marshalsea those indigent debtors who languished indefinitely in prison for want of funds to gain their release. Steele's increasing difficulties in settling his debts may have resulted in this correspondence; for in 1719, during the run of part of this series, there were four actions for debt against Steele, brought up at Easter and Michaelmas terms.[44] Richard Savage has related that on one occasion when he, Steele, and Philips were emerging from a tavern in Gerard Street, Soho, they were warned by a tradesman that there were bailiffs on the watch, and all three rushed off in different directions panic-stricken.[45] That Steele's mounting financial troubles coincided with the appearance in the *Free-Thinker* of the "Charity and Compassion" papers; that the rhetoric and the sentiments of the unknown correspondent are not unlike Steele's—these facts cannot be offered as proof that Steele wrote letters to the *Free-Thinker*. Added, however, to other and more obvious circumstances surrounding Steele's connection with Philips and the *Free-Thinker*, the "Charity and Compassion" series becomes a link in the chain connecting Steele and the journal.

The conclusion seems justifiable that on the basis of internal evidence the *Free-Thinker* shows the influence of Steele on its policies and content. As for his influence on its form, the *Free-Thinker*, like many of its contemporaries, used the mold of the *Tatler* and *Spectator*. Finally, though concrete evidence is lacking, that Steele wrote for the *Free-Thinker* is strongly probable.

The tradition naming the Rev. George Stubbes as a contributor to the *Free-Thinker* is both late and garbled. In the *Annual Register* for 1776 John Straight praised Stubbes, "Rector of Gunville, in Dorsetshire," as a "worthy, honest, intelligent writer, though little known as such," and stated that he "wrote many of the best papers in the *Free Thinker*, 1718 (in conjunction with Ambrose Philips and others)."[46] Straight added that Stubbes was "intimately connected with Mr. Deputy Wilkins, the Whig printer in Little-Britain, by marrying his sister for his first wife, who, by the way, was taken in by the French Prophets."[47] This Wilkins was, of course, the printer of Philips' *Free-Thinker*, and if the account be accepted, Stubbes may have been connected with the *Free-Thinker* through Wilkins.

By the nineteenth century Straight's statements had been amplified. Nathan Drake, especially, commended Stubbes's contributions to the *Free-Thinker* but did not mention any specific essays that he wrote. Drake generalized that of the contributors Stubbes was "by far the most considerable," "many of the best papers in the collection being of his composition." Drake also changed Stubbes's domicile and parish to Granville in Dorsetshire.[48]

The account of Stubbes by the antiquary Richard Rawlinson differs from those of Straight and Drake in important respects, and as it consists of notes by a contemporary of Stubbes, it may well be more trustworthy than the later accounts. Rawlinson does not connect Stubbes with a parish in Dorset; rather, he was domestic chaplain of the Duke of Dorset and rector, at different times, of Pusey in Berkshire and St. Lawrence in Essex. In 1736 he married Mrs. King, "only daughter of the Revd Mr King . . . of Gunville in Essex"; Rawlinson does not mention a first marriage. Rawlinson lists the works ascribed to Stubbes by Straight and Drake and adds several homiletic and critical items, the most interesting being *Some Remarks on the Tragedy of Hamlet Prince of Denmark written by Mr. William Shakespeare*; however, he does not list Stubbes as a contributor to the *Free-Thinker*.[49] Undoubtedly the Stubbes of Straight's and Drake's notes and the Stubbes of Rawlinson's note are the same man, but the biographical and bibliographical lacunae and discrepancies in these accounts make it difficult to ascribe any *Free-Thinker* papers to Stubbes.

It is true that three important series in the *Free-Thinker* have no identified authors—the series on the plague scare of 1720, the one on the growth of British trade and commerce, and the epistemological essays entitled the "Porch of Knowledge." And it is possible that Stubbes was the author of any one of these. But his bent as a writer was, to judge by his known published work, belletristic and homiletic rather than scientific and philosophical. If he did write for the *Free-Thinker*, it is more probable that he contributed verses to the poetical miscellanies, or he may have written literary criticism or translations.

This problem of "lost" authors is ever recurrent, even in the literary history of our most recent past. The business of writing for periodicals was, in 1718, more informal, more casual, less highly organized and coordinated than is the corresponding occupation in the twentieth century. If in the hustle of party job-writing some of even Steele's later, and lesser, work was forgotten and lost, perhaps irretrievably, it is easy to understand how in the ephemeral field of the essay journal such very minor reputations as those of Thomas Burnet, Duckett, and Stubbes would wither so rapidly that no accurate or adequate record remains of their contributions to the *Free-Thinker*.

VI

The most difficult category of contributors is that of writers who succeeded in covering their identities with initials and pseudonyms, in the fashion of the day. The *Free-Thinker* contains its share of such disguised contributions: a single issue may have as many as three or four, and seventy-six issues enclose ninety-five contributions bearing eighty pseudonyms or sets of initials of writers unknown. In ten cases the same signature is employed more than once: Euphues, L. L., Philander, Philaretes, Reader, and Sylvia occur twice; P. S. thrice; E. W. four times; and A. B. six times.[50] Combinations of letters like P. S. and A. B. lent themselves with special readiness to use by more than one unimaginative person. There is no evidence of true identity and little hope of puzzling out the people behind most of these pen names and groups of initials: the same person may have repeated his fictitious signature, different people may have chosen the same signature, these many masks may have hidden a large number of authors, and they may have been assumed by a relatively few writers. In general, more-over, these essays and letters do not bear the obvious stamp of personality, in a word, the style that marks his work as the labor of a single writer.

In one instance we are told that three of the letters, though signed by different pseudonyms, were written by one person—Icenus in No. 45, Mnemonides in No. 72, and Philonous Icenus in No. 150. For in this last paper the editor makes his "most grateful Acknowledgments to a worthy Country-Correspondent" for these contributions, and then goes on to assure his readers that the method which he had "all along observed in sorting the Letters" sent to him enables him to inform the public that all three were written by "one and the same Latent Philosopher." We also know that Heywood wrote a series as Miranda and Bob Smart and two other papers as Belinda and James Philobiblos and that in eight issues he contributed as J. H.; and we know that the initials used by De Gols were his own.

The printer's name appearing on the colophon of the *Free-Thinker*, W. Wilkins, also appeared in No. 204 affixed to a burlesque letter purporting to have been written by "a Hero in Low Life; who, I dare say," explained the editor, "never lays out Two Pence in Print and Paper, unless it be for a Seditious Ballad." To understand "the Drift and Wit of this Letter," the reader must remember "the Vulgar Distinctions of *High* and *Low*, which have distracted the Nation." The correspondent "is a notable Prize-Fighter"; "he, and his Companions, upon a Conviction for Deer-stealing, were committed by the Justices to Prison for a Year; and not being able to pay the Penalty at the Expiration of the Term, they were ordered to stand in the Pillory, in the next Market-Town." The letter itself is a plea, addressed by "W. Wilkins" to "a Fox-hunting Justice," that the populace might not pelt him on the pillory. As an example of Augustan humor it is opposite, in its casually cruel condescension, to the fourteen papers on "Charity and Compassion" that Steele may have inspired. Both letter and introduction seem to have been a practical joke played on Wilkins, that "Whig printer," and we gather from this freedom that Philips and Wilkins must have been on intimate and friendly terms.

Aside from the modest, timorous, or frivolous resort to false initials and assumed names, anonymity was the habitual sign of authorship in the *Free-Thinker*, as it was in most essay journals. But this absence of signature does not, of course, mean that a large proportion of the *Free-Thinker* papers cannot be identified as the work of men of whom records exist, records such as obituaries, memoirs, reviews, prefaces, diaries, letters, and even Parliamentary proceedings. By means of such records at least 208 of the 350 numbers of the *Free-Thinker*, in whole or in part, we can now ascribe to Ambrose Philips, Hugh Boulter, Gilbert Burnet the younger, Conrade De Gols, James Heywood, Zachary Pearce, Henry Stephens, Leonard Welsted, and Richard West.[51] In one issue a letter is signed by four released debtors—George Brown, Jacques Laurent, Mary Mason, and Rebecca Sherman. In another there is a correspondence between an unknown nobleman and Sir John Fellows, subgovernor of the South Sea Company. Finally, we may assign to Thomas Burnet, George Duckett, Sir Richard Steele, and George Stubbes their not altogether definable parts in writing, or in influencing the writing of, Philips' journal. The problems of authorship in the *Free-Thinker* and the methods of their solution have a variety sufficient to illustrate those of many another early periodical, particularly among the essay journals.

VII

Leading as it does to a more detailed knowledge of these writers, a study of the authorship of the *Free-Thinker* enables us to evolve certain general conclusions regarding that journal's policies, techniques, and relation to the Augustan milieu.

Philips as an editor instituted no startling innovations in practice. He consistently adhered to the journalistic rule that an author ought to appear anonymously or ought to disguise himself by using a pseudonym or initials. The result of this convention has been the loss of the names of many writers that otherwise we should know today. The author of the preface to the edition of 1739— himself anonymous—stated that *"several of the Authors"* of the *Free-Thinker* and the *Spectator* *"were the same Persons, and have written in the same Spirit."* Under the circumstances, however, these persons, except for Philips and Pearce, do not emerge into the light.

But a study of the authorship of the *Free-Thinker* has its more positive aspects as well. First, we may surmise how the *Free-Thinker* was conducted. Customarily, the editor and the more important contributors wrote on subjects of which they had knowledge as specialists. At least once, and probably occasionally, the subject and the point of view to adopt toward it were handed to Philips and his colleagues by Whig politicians in the highest circles of government. Less politically important material often was volunteered by readers of the journal or was contributed by the more regular writers. With his material assembled, the editor arranged it in orderly sequence. He selected an appropriate motto for each issue and regularized the periodicity of the different series of papers. Holding to the accepted alternatives of authorial disguise or anonymity, the editor assembled poetry in miscellanies, divided the fiction into serialized numbers, spaced his contributors' efforts effectively in order to secure variety and attractiveness of appearance and contents of the *Free-Thinker*, and handed his manuscript over to the printer Wilkins.

Familiarity with the journal results in deprecation of Thomas Burnet's assertion that the papers were composed by a club of gentlemen who somewhat bibulously revised or cooperatively wrote the issues. On the basis of assertions in the essays themselves relating to their manner of composition, only No. 144 seems to be the product of cooperative endeavor. Excluding the poetry and correspondence, most of the numbers of the *Free-Thinker* seem to be the work of individuals rather than a group, however informal. "It is only by interpreting the word 'club' as a group of contributors to a joint enterprise that we can apply it to such collaborators as these. Although the plurality of authorship is common knowledge" in the case of the *Free-Thinker*, we have "no evidence that any organization bound the contributors together,"[52] beyond the Establishment and the Whig party.

This investigation of the contributors to the *Free-Thinker* reveals interesting additions to their canons. The antiquary Nichols has already uncovered most of Leonard Welsted's contributions to the *Free-Thinker*, but the several series written by Archbishop Boulter, Gilbert Burnet the younger, and Richard West the elder form substantial additions to their works. Principally the writing

of Ambrose Philips stands out; seen in their context, the flood of
Augustan journalistic hack work, these papers have more to distinguish them than mere competence, whether it be the urbane
humor of No. 1 or the dignity and temperance in controversy of No.
126. Philips' work as one of the most important translators of his
day appears in his excellent translation of Fénelon. He translated
four of the *Dialogues des morts* and twenty-one of the *Fables* of
Fénelon, but unfortunately these passed from notice even in their
own day. Both Ozell and Bellamy made their later translations of
the *Dialogues des morts* and of the *Fables* in ignorance of Philips'
first, if incomplete, translation.[53] Despite the opinion of posterity
Philips seems to have regarded with favor his own verse first
published in the *Free-Thinker*. In his case, however, as in the case
of every contributor except Welsted, the prose in the *Free-Thinker*
is more distinguished than the verse.

The 208 issues of the *Free-Thinker* that can be assigned, in
part or whole, to known authors include much verse and fiction,
many essays and letters. Besides belles lettres, the content of these
papers covers politics, educational theory, aesthetic criticism, sectarian controversy, and observations on morals and manners.
These categories of topics do not complete the list of subjects discussed in the *Free-Thinker*, and some of the representative groups
of papers are by authors still anonymous: much of the verse; the
series of essays on economics and trade; a serialized treatise, written
from the medical point of view, on the plague scare of 1720 (a
hitherto unnoted addition to the contemporary literature on that
subject); "lectures" on epistemology; and a lengthy correspondence
on the tribulations of the debtors at the Marshalsea.

In the light of what now is known about the writers for the
Free-Thinker its place in the Augustan scene becomes clearer. The
Free-Thinker had connections with political circles inside the Whig
ministry of Stanhope; also it had social and literary connections with
Steele; nevertheless, its principal relationships were with the prominent Burnet family and with Walpole's faction in the Whig party.
The famous Bishop Gilbert Burnet had recently died, in 1715, but
as the chief clerical apologist for the Protestant succession he re-
tained posthumously his position of authority for the partisans of
the principles of the Whig-inspired Revolution of 1688, commonly

called Revolution principles. In consequence, the *Free-Thinker* must have gained partisan prestige and favor from its connection with the Burnet family. Two of the late bishop's sons, Thomas and Gilbert, and a son-in-law, Richard West, wrote for the journal. A close family friend, Hugh Boulter, rose to eminence during the publication of the *Free-Thinker*. Their services to the Whigs in writing for the *Free-Thinker* apparently benefited not only Boulter but both the younger Burnets, West, Stephens, Duckett, and even Zachary Pearce, who became a King's chaplain at this time, 1720. As for Philips, he seems later to have been helped by his friendship with the Burnet group when Boulter took him to Ireland.

Influential to a degree this literary circle may have been; yet for all its political and religious distinction it did not glow with the corruscating brilliance of such coteries as those surrounding Addison and Pope. Neither the papers by Philips nor those by his contributors add to the major works of the Augustan Age; but surely their modest luster should not have faded to its current dimness. As Henry Fielding pointed out in his *Champion*, there is room for other papers to shine, as well as the *Tatler* and the *Spectator:* " 'tis an Affront to the Nation, to imagine its whole Stock of Genius depended on any two Lives whatever." Addison and Steele, "Those justly celebrated Gentlemen have, certainly," says Fielding, "a Claim to be plac'd at the Head of *this* Table of Fame, but the Door ought not to be shut on their Successors. And, among them, The *Free-Thinker* has a legitimate Title to be introduc'd the *Foremost.*"[54]

NOTES

1. The text of the *Free-Thinker* used in this study is that of the original half-sheet issues, Nos. 1-350. The use of matter from other editions is duly noted.

2. Sir Thomas Burnet, *The Letters of Thomas Burnet to George Duckett, 1712-1722*, ed. D. Nichol Smith (Oxford, 1914), p. 148.

3. *The Poems of Ambrose Philips*, ed. Mary G. Segar (Oxford, 1937), pp. xiii-liii, contains the recent standard biography of Philips; S. F. Fogle in "Notes on Ambrose Philips," *MLN*, LIV (1939), 354-59, supplements and corrects Miss Segar's memoir. General St. George's copy of the *Free-Thinker* is now in the Newberry Library.

4. Nos. 1, 2, 3, 55, 105, 159, 210, 264, 314, and 350.

5. James Heywood, *Letters and Poems on Several Subjects*, 2d ed. (London, 1726), title page.

6. Nos. 9, 23, 29, 41, 51, 63, 78, 98, 103, 107, 112, 116, 124, 133, 166, 184, 195, 217, 227, 239, 241, 305, 319, 337, 339, 350.

7. Nos. 9, 29, 51, 78, 103, 107, 112, 195, 217, 319, 339, and 350. Philips' poems in the *Free-Thinker*—or at least those he wished to preserve as his own—were reprinted in a collection, the publication of which he supervised in 1748, after his return from Ireland to England.

8. See her edition of Philips' poems, pp. 176, 177, 179, 183.

9. Nos. 76, 80, 84, 92, 109, 110, 128, 129, 177, 178, 179, 180, 191, 192, 205, 210, 221, 225, 236, 242, 247, 253, 263, and 314 contain translations of the *Fables;* Nos. 269, 273, 281, and 346 contain translations of the *Dialogues des morts.* A more detailed consideration of this series of translations can be found in my article, "The *Fables* of Fénelon and · Philips' *Free-Thinker*," *SP,* XLVII (1950), 51-61.

10. *The Thousand and One Days: Persian Tales,* 3 vols. (London, 1783), I, 42-43.

11. Nicholas Joost, "Burnet's *Grumbler* and Ambrose Philips," *N&Q,* CXCIII (August 7, 1948), 340-42.

12. Nos. 18, 168, 218, 252, and 258, and in part Nos. 70, 239, 249, 270, 291, 311, and 338.

13. Wholly by Philips are the introductory essays, Nos. 1, 2, 3; the recapitulatory essays, Nos. 55, 105, 159, 210, 264, 314; translations of the *Fables,* Nos. 80, 84, 92, 109, 110, 128, 129, 177, 178, 179, 180, 191, 192, 205, 210, 221, 225, 236, 247, 253, 263, 314; translations of the *Dialogues des morts,* Nos. 269, 273, 281, 346; adaptations of his earlier work, Nos. 35, 46, 267; aesthetic and literary papers, Nos. 18, 168, 218, 249, 252, 258, 291, 338; essays written in the tradition of the *Spectator,* Nos. 8, 56, 126, 147, 174, 201, 215, 248; and verse, Nos. 9, 51, 195, 217, 339. Partly by Philips are papers containing replies to letters and comments on correspondence, Nos. 7, 11, 13, 17, 21, 27, 33, 37, 40, 45, 49, 52, 57, 59, 61, 66, 72, 74, 76, 82, 86, 93, 95, 97, 108, 119, 123, 127, 130, 131, 134, 136, 137, 140, 143, 145, 150, 152, 153, 154, 161, 162, 163, 173, 182, 186, 188, 190, 193, 198, 200, 204, 206, 207, 214, 220, 223, 224, 229, 231, 233, 235, 237, 242, 244, 251, 254, 257, 259, 260, 268, 272, 274, 275, 278, 284, 285, 289, 303, 305, 307, 309, 313, 340, 345; issues with editorial comment on poetry, Nos. 23, 29, 41, 63, 78, 98, 103, 107, 112, 116, 124, 133, 166, 184, 227, 239, 241, 305, 319, 337, 350; translations of the *Fables,* Nos. 76, 242; aesthetic and literary papers, Nos. 70, 239, 270, 311; No. 43, with an essay in the tradition of the *Spectator;* and verse, Nos. 29, 78, 103, 107, 112, 319, 350, this last an issue consisting of verse and a recapitulatory essay. A caveat to the reader of this article: the total here is a total number of issues, not of contributions to various issues. Philips often contributed two or three brief works to an issue—a poem, a short essay, a comment on letters coming in to the editor.

14. *Remarks and Collections of Thomas Hearne* (Oxford, 1906), VII, 64, 70.

15. *Free-Thinker* Nos. 105 and 159 point out that this series consists of Nos. 85, 87, 89, 91, 111, 113, 115, and 117 (to which No. 146 is added as a supplement to Nos. 113 and 117).

16. He possibly wrote Nos. 167, 202, 203, 254, and 280.

17. Osmund Airy, "Gilbert Burnet (1643-1715)," *DNB,* III, 405.

18. Nos. 22, 34, 54, 62, 71, 77, 83, 96, 199, 216, and possibly 315 and 335.

19. "A List of Deaths for the Year 1738," *Gentleman's Magazine,* VIII, 490.

20. "Proceedings of the Parliament," *Gentleman's Magazine,* III (1733), 693-96.

21. Heywood, *Letters and Poems,* pp. 31-32; I have reversed italics in quoting these prefatory remarks.

22. Nos. 95, 103, 108, 123, 136, 140, 152, 169, 182, 190, 198, 207, 223, 251, 260, and 268. No. 140 contains a poem by him in a letter by Thyrsis; Nos. 190 and 260 both contain two letters by him; in No. 169 two letters by him are summarized; and in No. 207 one letter by him is summarized, one quoted in part,

and a third given in its entirety. All of these letters, save the one in No. 140, were reprinted by Heywood in his *Letters and Poems*, pp. 111-91. The poem in No. 140 was reprinted in *Letters and Poems*, pp. 208-10.

23. Nos. 95, 103, 108, 123, 136, 140, and 190. Heywood's letters in the Miranda series are signed Bob Smart in No. 103 and Miranda in the other papers, except No. 140. Heywood's poem in No. 140 is not signed but purports to be by Thyrsis, who wrote the letter enclosing the poem; however, Thyrsis' letter was not acknowledged by Heywood in his *Letters and Poems*. Heywood used his initials for letters printed or summarized in Nos. 152, 169, 182, 190 (as the husband of Miranda), 198, 207, 260, and 268.

24. Segar, *Poems of Philips*, p. 179.

25. *Gentleman's Magazine*, XLVII (1777), 183; Pearce's contribution to the *Free-Thinker* is printed on pp. 627-29. See Nicholas Joost, "Zachary Pearce," *N&Q*, CXCIII (January 24, 1948), 37.

26. Nicholas Joost, "Henry Stephens: A Bibliographical and Biographical Note," *N&Q*, CXCIV (September 3, 1949), 379-80.

27. Nos. 98, 99, 112, 124, 133, 166, 184, 241, and 337. Welsted's name did not appear in the last of these papers.

28. *The Works, in Verse and Prose, of Leonard Welsted, Esq.* (London, 1787), pp. xxiii-xxiv. Nichols did not explain the conjecture that led him to ascribe to Welsted the translation of Horace, Book IV, Ode ii, merely noting, p. 81: "This Ode is ascribed to Welsted (but with no great positiveness) on conjecture."

29. Nos. 58, 64, 69, 81, 100, 104, 132, 135, 151, 194, 211, 279, 282, 331, and 341.

30. Nos. 176, 255, 276, 299, 325, 327, and 333.

31. For the four prisoners, see No. 188, which forms a portion of the "Charity and Compassion" papers, referred to in this essay, page 124 and note 43. For the correspondence between Lord —— and Sir John Fellows, see No. 297. The editor vouches for the authenticity of this exchange of letters, but what is more convincing is the editor's evidently unauthorized appropriation of the privately written note by Sir John Fellows. That Lord —— sent Philips his own letters and the one by Sir John Fellows seems an obvious inference, as this maneuver was a part of the *Free-Thinker's* campaign, itself part of Walpole's larger effort, to discredit Stanhope's ministry by publicizing its disreputable connection with the South Sea Bubble. Note that Philips cites Sir John Fellows as "Sub-Governour" but that William Courthope, *Synopsis of the Extinct Baronetage* (London, 1835), lists him as "Fellows of Garshalton, co. Surrey. Cr. 20 Jan. 1718-19. / I Sir John Fellows, governor of the South Sea company, created as above, *d. s. p.* 26 July 1724, aet. 54, when the title became Ext."

32. Burnet, *Letters to Duckett*, p. 155.

33. *Ibid.*, p. 286.

34. *Ibid.*, p. 148.

35. J. A. Hamilton, "Sir Thomas Burnet," *DNB*, III, 410.

36. William Roberts, "George Duckett," *DNB*, VI, 90-91.

37. George A. Aitken, *The Life of Richard Steele* (London, 1889), II, 202, n. 1.

38. John Loftis, "The Blenheim Papers and Steele's Journalism, 1715-18," *PMLA*, LXVI (1951), 207-10. Loftis does not point out that when Steele, in his unfinished essay on Shippen, writes that he "has commissioned a group of young men to assist him in his supervision of Britain, one of whom is specifically charged with regulating the passions of London and Westminster," he is perhaps referring obliquely to Ambrose Philips. As editor Philips would have been charged with regulating the passions of London, and as Justice of the Peace

for Westminster he would have been charged with regulating the passions of Westminster.

39. Aitken, *Life of Steele*, II, 257-58.

40. Rae Blanchard, ed., *Tracts and Pamphlets by Richard Steele* (Baltimore, 1944), p. 501. The two tracts by Steele here mentioned are reprinted in Miss Blanchard's edition. For the occasion of *The Antidote, in a Letter to the Free-Thinker* (June, 1719) and *The Antidote*, No. II (June, 1719), as well as for the ascription of these two anonymous pamphlets to Steele, see Miss Blanchard's commentary, pp. 501-2.

41. Aitken, *Life of Steele*, II, 237-45, discusses Steele's change of views regarding the South Sea speculation. *Free-Thinker* Nos. 241, 262, 264, 265, 266, 267, 272, 274, 278, and 287 exemplify the change of attitude of the journal in this matter.

42. Blanchard, *Tracts and Pamphlets*, pp. 559-71, reprints this pamphlet.

43. Nos. 186, 188, 193, 200, 220, 223, 229, 231, 235, 242, 244, 249, 253, and 289.

44. Aitken, *Life of Steele*, II, 203-4.

45. *Johnsonian Miscellanies*, ed. George Birkbeck Hill (Oxford, 1897), II, 161-62.

46. XIX, 36. This article on both Stubbes and Straight was reprinted from the *Gentleman's Magazine*, XLVI (1776), 213-14, where no authority is stated.

47. *Ibid.*, p. 37.

48. *Essays, Biographical, Critical, and Historical, Illustrative of the Rambler, Adventurer, and Idler* (London, 1809), I, 36-37.

49. Bodleian MS. Rawl. J. 4° 3, fols. 401r-402r. See also *Alumni Oxonienses*, ed. Joseph Foster (Oxford, 1891), IV, 1439.

50. Euphues wrote in Nos. 53 and 163; L. L. in Nos. 11 and 21; Philander in Nos. 7 and 41; Philaretes in Nos. 29 and 239; Reader in Nos. 59 and 270; Sylvia in Nos. 57 and 63; P. S. in Nos. 153, 206, and 237; E. W. in Nos. 123, 130, 134, and 319; and A. B. in Nos. 73, 150, 162, 220, 275, and 280. In No. 294 the editor acknowledged receipt of a guinea from A. B. for charitable uses.

51. A recapitulation of the total attributions to these nine authors, by complete issues and by portions, is as follows: Philips, 57-109; Boulter, 9-0; G. Burnet, 10-0; De Gols, 0-3; Heywood, 0-16; Pearce, 1-0; Stephens, 5-0; Welsted, 1-8; West, 15-0; total, 98-136. The discrepancy between these 234 contributions and the 208 issues containing the contributions disappears when one recalls that on occasion Philips shared an issue with one or more contributors.

52. Robert J. Allen, *The Clubs of Augustan London* (Cambridge, Mass., 1933), p. 218.

53. J. Ozell, *Fables and Dialogues of the Dead. Written in France by the Late Archbishop of Cambray . . . Done into English from the Paris Edition of 1718. . . .* (London, 1722), and D. Bellamy, *Twenty-Seven Moral Tales and Fables, French and English. By the Late Celebrated Archbishop of Cambray. . . .* (London, 1729).

54. *Champion* No. 38 (February 9, 1740).

ESSAY FORMS IN THE PROMPTER

THE PROMPTER

Nos. 1-173, November 12, 1734-July 2, 1736.

Semi-weekly.

Folio half-sheet.

Editors: Aaron Hill and William Popple.

Colophon: "Printed for J. PEELE, at *Locke*'s *Head,* in *Amen-Corner, Paternoster Row*: Where LETTERS to the AUTHOR are taken in. [*Price Two-Pence.*]"

Essay Forms in the *Prompter*

W. O. S. SUTHERLAND, JR.

THE LEADING LITERARY form in the *Prompter* is the essay. This journal, like many other eighteenth century literary periodicals, carried numerous poems and letters, as well as dialogues and dramatic pieces. But the principal form, appearing in over half the issues, was the essay. In spite of the importance of the form in this journal as well as other serials, just what the periodical essay was is a question that has never been fully or satisfactorily answered. The chief obstacle to an answer is that the form is so flexible and is used in such divergent ways that it is difficult to find a basis upon which the essays can be compared and discussed. The purpose of this article is to find such a basis. The essays of the *Prompter* will be examined to see whether there is some sort of recurrence by which particular essays may be classified into groups. Though such a classification will be valid only for the *Prompter*, it may suggest a basis for examining other essay journals and for learning more about how eighteenth century periodical essays were constructed early in their historical development, before criticism began to rely strongly on the easy diagnostic tests of tone and topic.

The *Prompter* is a good subject for analysis. The essays are written on a variety of subjects. Aaron Hill and William Popple, the two authors, were quite different in temperament, experience, and age, and these differences are reflected in their papers. Popple, whose literary experience was at this time somewhat limited, wrote on traditional subjects and on matters which affected him personally. Hill, who was older and a veteran projector and essayist, often reached beyond traditional matter. Both men did have one common interest, the theater; so amid a variety of subjects one prominent, constant theme reappears. In the second place, both authors wrote traditional essays. By 1734 the writing of periodical essays was an art with a tradition, and both men were

content to use the form as they found it. Neither experimented.
Of course, since, they did write literary essays, they often show their
awareness of style and form, but they did not innovate. This conventional quality assures few aberrations from what might be called
the essay norm. Finally, the *Prompter* provides enough essays
for an analysis, enough essays to ensure that the results will have
meaning.

Since the term "essay" is often used loosely, some sort of
limitation should be made in deciding the papers here to be examined. As written by Hill and Popple, a normal essay is a single
unit of prose of about two thousand words, enough to fill both
sides of a folio half-sheet. Some of the essays have fewer words,
but sufficient to make both sides of the leaf look full. There may
be one or several subjects. Although these may vary widely from
one paper to another, they do conform generally to the subject
matter usually associated with the essay periodical of manners and
morals. With two exceptions essays are complete within a single
issue.[1] About papers of this kind there is no question.

But beyond these are papers which might or might not be
called essays. To such doubtful examples the following standards
are here applied. An essay should have a minimum length of
about a thousand words. It should be written for the material it
presents, not as a mere introduction or framework for a letter or a
poem, though both these forms may be integrated into an essay.
A poem or letter may follow, but should not be considered a part
of the essay. Quoted papers are excluded, as are papers made up
of writings obviously or apparently taken from a book or pamphlet.
Nor are any real or mock manifestoes, declarations, and similar
special forms considered essays. Such limitations on the term
"essay" will, of course, have some effect on the results of the
analysis which follows. That effect should be a desirable one,
for it means the elimination of papers which would cause abnormal
complications.

The pivotal decision in determining the kinds of essays in the
Prompter, or any other essay periodical, is the selection of a
criterion. There are many possible ways of classifying essays; the
most popular seem to be those which depend upon subject matter—
nature, critical, religious essays—and those which depend upon

tone and style—formal, informal, and light. Such classifications are useful for discussions of content and style, but here the criterion should be one that will help in an analysis of the form itself. The best criterion seems to be that of structure. How are the parts of the essay arranged? And why? This seems a logical standard. All essays have structures and these can be compared; yet structure is not arbitrary, for it is determined by the components of the essay, like content and approach, as well as by the idiosyncrasies of the author. Also, when the various kinds of structure are under analysis, the general form of the essay is being analyzed too; then the larger problem of what is the essay form is met rather than ignored, as it would be ignored if an arbitrary component like content were used. Of course, the use of structure as a criterion by no means eliminates the many difficulties encountered in classifying essays. The extreme flexibility of the form itself inevitably leads to some confusion, and a few essays seem to defy distinctions. The limitations of the author, digressions, elaborate introductions, long quotations, and extraneous material all make for difficulties. Each essay has its own peculiar problems, but through the exceptions, difficulties, and individual differences the basic structure can usually be made out.

Classification by structure shows the way the essays are put together and the essential variations in this process. Structure is defined here as the relation of the parts of the essay, the developed thoughts, to the main theme and to each other. These parts may appear as a sentence, several sentences, as a paragraph, or as several paragraphs. The relation between these ideas, the development of the essay, depends ultimately upon the content of each part, but for itself the content is not important to the present purpose. The important matter is relationship. Determining these different relationships will show what essay types the authors of the *Prompter* used.

On the basis of structure the essays in the *Prompter* tend to fall into five large classes, called here the *simple, integral, topical, commentary,* and *narrative*. Ideally each structure has at least one distinctive quality which separates it from the others. These forms, it should be emphasized, are deduced from the essays themselves and not from any intentions of the authors.

I

Simple Structure

This form, which includes thirteen essays,[2] is termed *simple* because the parts of the essay are built in an uncomplicated way upon one central subject; there is no independent development of any of the ideas that make up the whole. Essays of this type are coherent and unified, the subject being the unifying force. The author states his theme, always a restricted one, and the essay is devoted to restatement, illustration, expansion, and modification of this single idea. In the relationship of the parts there are two important variations. In one variation there is a tendency for each of the ideas to refer directly to the subject; the paragraphs are related more closely to the theme than to each other. In the second variety the subject is still central to the essay, but one paragraph seems to grow out of or be suggested by another. This second kind is usually not climactic in the *Prompter*. In both variations a single, rather restricted theme dominates, and no subordinate idea in the essay receives independent development.

The first variation, in which each part relates directly to the subject, can be seen in No. 165. The author of the paper remarks on a group of people whom he calls "*erased* Mortals," people who were formerly accomplished in some field, but are now completely ignorant of it. The essay is made up of examples of erased mathematicians, dancers, divines, housewives, and the like. By giving many examples of the same thing it achieves unity. No. 37 is a fairly clear example of the second, more popular variation, in which one idea suggests another. In this essay the author objects to the inordinate number of gifts and contributions made to the opera singer Farinelli. The recurrent notion in the essay is that such an unworthy, shameful custom ought to be discontinued. The paper begins by describing satirically the collection of money for the opera singer. Then there follows an estimate of the amount given to Farinelli. This estimate is compared to the amount paid to men who had spent their lives at the bar or in the service of the crown. Then comes the notation of a few selected presents given to the singer. Finally there is a statement of the conclusion to which the reader has been led: a clear expression of the disapproval already implied or directly stated throughout the paper. This essay is coherent and balanced, and makes a strong single impression.

The lack of complication in this form is often blurred by two tendencies of the authors. The tendency to digress causes some deviation. More important is the disposition to stop and develop one particular part of the essay. Such rudimentary reaching toward complexity, though treated here as simple, is evidence of the merging of this form with the more complex integral form. Both these tendencies detract from a singleness of impression, though such a detraction is not necessarily a weakness.

Since the simple structure would seem to be a useful one, it is perhaps surprising that the authors of the *Prompter* did not make more use of it. Both men, however, preferred more complex essays. Hill especially so; he wrote only half as many of these simple papers as did Popple. Of the three most important forms in the *Prompter*, this has the least number of essays—thirteen, compared to twenty-six for the topical and thirty-eight for the integral. The authors used this simple development for a variety of subjects. About half the essays in this group deal with morals or manners. Though there were papers on opera in this category, the simple form has less than its proportionate share of papers on the theater. The explanation probably is that this form is especially suited to a paper that argues one important point, and most theatrical papers are not so simple in content. Some of the specific subjects and themes that are treated are the duties of a Prompter, a plea for debtors, an attack on opera, and an attack on a rival journal.[3] There are several successful essays in this group; indeed such a compact, coherent structure should encourage a clear, unified, easily comprehendible paper. Further, the use of a simple development prevents much dispersion of effort. It should be said, however, that the papers as a group do not have the originality and vigor that can be seen in many of the topical and integral essays.

II

Integral Structure

Thirty-eight integral essays make this form the most popular in the periodical.[4] Two traits distinguish it. First, the parts relate to a common subject or theme. The subject of the essay is a restricted one, and the development is usually coherent and compact. This same kind of close relationship has already been seen in the simple structure. The second trait is that the parts themselves are given independent, individual development. A part does not consist of a single idea, but of several ideas worked together. Each part of the essay belongs to a larger unity, but it is itself a smaller unit containing its own structure. This independent development of parts, or of some parts, makes the integral a complex form. The kind of development within the parts does not in any way determine the classification of the essay. This depends upon the complexity of the parts and their relationship to the subject. Since the authors were not consciously following these forms, difficulties sometimes arise in determining how simple or complex a structure is as well as the exact relationship of one part to another. In spite of some occasional mergings of forms, however, the normal integral pattern is clear.

An example of the integral structure is No. 57 by Popple. The essay has one dominant purpose: to show how error has crept into the representation of characters on the stage. Polonius is the example used. The author divides the paper into two quite distinct sections. The first is an exposition of the character of Polonius as Shakespeare drew him. The second gives examples, with appropriate comment, of the misrepresentation of the character on the stage. The break between the two divisions is obvious; each develops its own subordinate subject independent of the other. Together the two discussions fulfill the main purpose of the paper.

Though No. 57 is cited as an example of this form it shows only one kind of relationship between the parts. An analysis of the integral form in the *Prompter* shows five variations within the general framework. (1) The largest of these variations, about half the integral papers, follows a progressive movement in which one part leads to the next. Card-playing women are monsters; they neglect their families; the government should do something about gambling.[5] Each part grows out of the one which precedes it; one part suggests another, though all relate to the main theme. (2) In another popular variation some particular assertion is the subject of the paper, and each part is designed as support for that assertion. Popple's defense of one of his own plays is an example. The

Double Deceit is a good play—the fable is good, the characters are good, the conduct of the piece is good, and the sentiments expressed in the play are worthy ones.[6] Counterparts of both these variations have already been noted among papers using the simple structure. (3) Seven papers exemplify the somewhat more involuted arrangement of a general statement followed by a detailed discussion or example of the statement. The first part of No. 16 maintains in general terms that the patriotism of historians leads them to misrepresent some incidents involving their own country. The second part takes a particular example of this misrepresentation from the *British Empire in America*, a contemporary pamphlet. This relation is not the same as the variation in which each part supports the assertion, for in this more involved relationship one of the parts is the assertion. (4) Another useful variation is based upon contrast or antithesis. No. 57 on Polonius, already cited, is an example of contrast. (5) The smallest subgroup consists of those which divide a subject into its component parts. In No. 85 love is divided into the gross, cleanly, and elevated, though exigencies of space caused the highest type to be omitted. Of course, the connection among parts is not so clear in some essays as in others. That is to be expected. The unexpected is that these essays fall into such a limited number of variations as clearly as they do. Probably an important fact in explaining this sharp definition is that fairly short essays usually have very few independently developed parts, therefore not enough to cause an extremely complicated relationship within the essay.

This form was used frequently for critical papers and for papers on the theater. In short criticisms both authors liked to make several points and develop them. The points often constitute a unified paper, an integral essay. The same sort of approach is characteristic of the theatrical papers. No. 54 discusses the Playhouse Bill. One section explains the defects of the proposed bill; the other, ways of improving it. Papers of this sort combine to some extent the advantages of variety and concentration.

Many of the best papers in the *Prompter* follow the integral form. The structure encourages coherence, at the same time allowing the introduction of ideas and material not directly concerned with the main subject or theme. It allows, as the simple structure often does not, a developed, satisfying discussion of points raised in the paper. It was the form usually employed for papers which carried detailed arguments. In addition to papers on the theater and criticism, this essay type was often used for papers on morals and manners. The number on other subjects is negligible. The form was very popular with both authors: Popple wrote eighteen, Hill seventeen. The authorship of three papers has not been determined.

III

Topical Structure

The topical form ranks next to the integral in popularity. A third of the essay papers, twenty-six, fall into this category.[7] This essay form is complex, but not unified, since the main parts of a topical essay have little or no connection with each other. The main topics are joined together loosely, casually, with no single unifying subject or theme running through the whole paper. The topics may remain within a broad field, though the link between them is often only tenuous. In the normal pattern each part receives independent development, though occasionally a part will be random comments rather than a well defined unit. This essay form depends for its effect on diversity and discursiveness rather than upon a single impression from the total essay.

No. 100 demonstrates the topical development. The first part of the essay is an elaboration by Hill of the complaint that the theaters present the same plays again and again. The complaint together with an explanation of the motives behind such repetitions makes up about a fourth of the paper. A transitional paragraph points out *Hamlet* as the play that can be seen most often without tiring the spectator. The rest of the paper is an explanation of how *Hamlet* had been and should be acted. The connection between the two topics is only general—that *Hamlet* was one of the frequently repeated plays and that the actors did not exploit the character Hamlet fully. The second topic is suggested by the first, but the two are not divisions of a single unified subject.

The authors of the *Prompter* took advantage of the great latitude this form allows. The close association that the parts of an essay might have has already been seen in No. 100. Other essays show a more tenuous relationship. For example, No. 105 contains two dramatic reviews, of the *Double Dealer* and the *Rival Queens*. The connection is associative. Both plays were being performed, and both were objectionable because of their immorality. But no attempt was made to integrate the two reviews, to subsume the two parts to a single purpose. At the opposite extreme from No. 100 is No. 123, in which there is no connection at all between the parts. The recto of the half-sheet is given over to an attack on the *Grub-street Journal*. The verso is a discussion of theatrical matters. Between the parts of most topical essays there is a fairly obvious connection, but there are enough essays with little or no connection to establish that No. 123 is not an exception. Apparently Hill and Popple felt few restrictions when using this form.

The tendency to blend with another form, a tendency already noted for both the simple and integral essays, is apparent here too. In this case it is toward a simpler structure, a collection of random remarks and one developed discussion. In No. 4 even the single, developed part is rather discursive. This whole essay very nearly becomes a stream of random comments. It suggests, though it does not realize, a new structure corresponding to the simple as the topical corresponds to the integral.

The concept of this form is quite different from those already discussed. Here unity is not virtue. Here the phrase "single essay" may be a mere physical description. The result, of course, is to allow a great deal of freedom to the writer. Since the authors wrote some twenty-six topical essays, certainly they valued this form and the freedom it gave. The simple and integral structures provide a unity which the topical essay can never achieve. But unified patterns were clearly not the only ones upon which the essays of the *Prompter* were built. Looseness, diversity was also an ideal. Some essays, for example No. 82, are poorly written and fall into this category because they were poorly conceived or poorly executed. Such essays are, however, exceptions to the usual topical paper. Hill and Popple were equally fond of this structure, and both wrote many pleasing topical essays.

Though such a large number of the *Prompter* papers lack coherence and unity, it is not proper to say that all these essays ramble. The writing of many of them is obviously controlled.

Nevertheless, it is somewhat surprising to find that a third of the single essays do not have a single subject. These topical essays demonstrate clearly that in this periodical at least singleness of purpose was an ideal for only some essays. Just as important was the essay which moved from one topic to another without particular care for coherence or balance. Discursiveness is often associated with the essay, but not to this extent. Of course, this is but one kind of miscellaneousness in the periodical. Other papers show it too; often several letters, several poems, or heterogeneous material are used to make up issues.

A fact which this analysis emphasizes is that most of the *Prompter* essays are of the complex form. Of the seventy-seven essays so far discussed, thirteen are simple and sixty-four complex. Independent development of the parts of so many of the essays is striking. This complexity arises partly from the fact that many of the essays make several points and the authors felt the need of expatiating upon each. It may also be traced in part to the authors' apparent lack of a restricted concept of form for their essays. Certainly a simple development leading to a climax might be valuable, but it is not often used in the *Prompter*. The popularity of a complex structure was probably an encouragement to the use of the topical form, in which the essay moves not from one phase of a subject to another but to another subject altogether.

IV

Commentary Structure

The commentary form consists primarily of a detailed exposition of particular passages.[8] In the *Prompter* its purpose is argumentative. A few lines, usually from an opponent, are quoted, and these lines are themselves the subject of discussion and analysis. Commentary essays should be differentiated from those in which quotations are used as illustrations. For example, No. 28 quotes frequently from James Thomson's *Liberty*, but the quotations are used to support or illustrate some point made in the text; the quotations themselves are not discussed.

No. 118, which contains a short prayer called the Philosopher's Prayer, illustrates the use of the commentary essay in the *Prompter*. The general intent of the essay is to show the injustice of criticisms made of the prayer in the *Grub-street Journal*. Quotations are taken from the prayer, and each is followed by a comment on these lines. The discussion includes a refutation of criticisms made by the rival journal. There is little or no unity between the parts of the paper. Each part is concerned with itself. There is, however, a unity of the whole. It comes from the use of an introduction and conclusion, from the fact that all quotations .are from the same source, and from the intention which pervades the essay.

The faults of the commentary essay are obvious. Possibly the general reader might not understand the details which are its subjects. Nor is there much chance of original subject matter or method. In addition, the form lacks structural unity, but fails to compensate with discursive charm. Nevertheless, it offers important advantages. Journalistic arguments in the eighteenth century were often lengthy and detailed, and the commentary structure allowed support or refutation of particulars. The form also made it possible for an author to emphasize and expatiate upon specific rather than general matters. Further, argumentative papers would attract readers already interested in the argument. There are five of these papers in the *Prompter*, all by Popple and all concerned in some way with his feud with the *Grub-street Journal*. The tone of most of the commentary essays indicates that whatever other advantages there may have been in using this form, Popple himself got a great deal of personal satisfaction out of refuting the arguments of his enemies.

v

Narrative Structure

There is only one example of a narrative essay in the *Prompter*.[9] It is, nonetheless, a distinctive structural form which warrants a separate classification. The essay, No. 121, is an account of one incident, which comprises several occurrences. The relationship of one part of the essay to another is chronological. There are other relationships but this is the essential one. No. 121 recounts the story of a basket maker and a vain gentleman, a fictional narrative. Hill, the author, points out the moral as the story progresses and sums it up briefly at the conclusion.

This single narrative essay is not an accurate indication of the importance of this form in the *Prompter*, for the narrative structure occurs many times within the framework of some more complex form. No. 23, for example, describes an incident and then comments on it; the first part of the paper follows a narrative structure, though the whole essay does not. No. 82 has a very long account in narrative form, but a digression at the close throws the essay into the topical category. In addition, little stories about the supposed author and his activities were a staple of this periodical just as they were of many others. Although brief narratives were popular, the authors of the *Prompter* found little use for the narrative structure through a whole essay.

From this analysis of eighty-three essays in the *Prompter* five structures emerge: simple, integral, topical, commentary, and narrative. Individual essays may at times diverge, but these normal patterns are clear. Any divergence is not so much toward formlessness as toward blending with another form.

This disposition toward overlapping among the three most popular forms—the simple, integral, and topical—is caused by the fact that the three are very closely related. They are, indeed, corresponding parts of a larger unity. Two characteristics divide the three. First, it should be determined whether or not there is a specific subject for the whole essay, one that binds it together into a unity. If all the parts relate to the same theme or to each other, the essay form is either simple or integral. If there is no single subject, the form is topical. Second, it should be determined whether the development of the parts is simple or complex. If there is independent development within the parts of the essay, the paper is classed as one of the complex forms, integral or topical. If there is no independent development the structure is simple. This double division means that each of these three forms is related in some essential respect to at least one of the other two.

The narrative and commentary structures, though not so easily schematized, are still related to the other forms. The narrative development closely resembles the simple. The chronological relationship is, however, a special sort different from either of the variations discussed under the simple form. The commentary form corresponds to the integral structure. Each separate comment is self-contained, but each contributes to a unified impression. The commentary structure is not, however, coherent, a fact which differentiates it from the integral. Each of the five essay structures is distinctive, but is related to one, at least, of the other forms.

Although Hill and Popple were often conscious of the literary qualities of their essays, they were not consciously molding them into set categories. They were, apparently, just writing papers for the *Prompter*. Yet it is also clear that their essays do fall into a rather limited number of structural patterns. Of course, other components were necessary for an essay, but these patterns are the basic structures. Their existence demonstrates that though the essay was flexible, it adhered to a few recurring forms, the general outlines of which are fairly rigid in spite of variations.

The patterns which have been deduced from the essays of the *Prompter* cannot certainly be applied as they stand to other periodicals. Different authors, different conditions should logically lead to some changes in the patterns in the essays of other journals. But these forms with changes and modifications may help to suggest a basis of comparison and means of analysis for periodical essays beyond those of the *Prompter*.

NOTES

1. Nos. 101-2 and 140-41.
2. Essays of simple structure are Nos. 1, 5, 14, 36, 37, 47, 97, 106, 107, 146, 147, 165, and 167. The general outlines of the simple and integral forms have been described by George R. Cerveny, *Facts and Judgments* (New York, 1946), pp. 117 and 125f.
3. Nos. 1, 36, 106, and 107.
4. Essays of integral structure are Nos. 3, 7, 9, 11, 12, 13, 15, 16, 21, 23, 28, 29, 30, 38, 41, 42, 54, 57, 63, 64, 66, 68, 75, 85, 92, 93, 99, 103, 109, 115, 118, 128, 136, 140, 141, 142, 145, 151.
5. No. 75.
6. Nos. 140-41.
7. Essays of topical structure are Nos. 2, 4, 10, 27, 31, 34, 35, 51, 53, 56, 62, 72, 82, 95, 100, 104, 105, 113, 117, 123, 124, 133, 144, 153, 156, 161.
8. Essays of commentary structure are Nos. 98, 101, 102, 112, 119.
9. No. 28 is arranged chronologically, but the essential relationship of the parts places it with the integral form.

THE FEMALE SPECTATOR, *A COURTESY*
PERIODICAL

THE FEMALE SPECTATOR

Nos. 1-24, April, 1744-May, 1746 (numbers for two months omitted, in July, August, or September of 1744 and in March of 1746).

Monthly.

Quarto.

Editor: Mrs. Eliza Haywood.

Colophon: "*LONDON*: Printed and published by T. Gardner, at *Cowley*'s *Head*, opposite St. *Clement*'s Church, in the *Strand*, 1744."

The *Female Spectator*, a Courtesy Periodical

JAMES HODGES

FOR TWO YEARS in the seventeen forties the ladies of England were honored with monthly numbers of a periodical designed entirely for them and edited by a member of their own sex. Mrs. Eliza Haywood—sometime dramatist, novelist, and journalist—was the first woman on the English journalistic scene to undertake the publication of a periodical directed toward women and filled with page after page of reading substance that few women could possibly resist. The *Female Spectator* courted feminine attention and served the ladies by entertaining and instructing them on such ever interesting subjects as love and marriage, parent-child relationships, female education, moral and social decorum, and other miscellaneous themes. Using the essay as her basic literary form, the editor of this new periodical for women also included some fiction, a host of letters, and other types, such as poetry, character sketches, a dialogue, and even a little drama. In diverse literary manner there is matter sufficiently varied in the *Female Spectator* to please any taste and to supply answers to the feminine problems of the mid-eighteenth century.

The advice Mrs. Haywood offers the ladies of her age is strikingly similar to the counsel given by the various writers on conduct who preceded, and were contemporaneous with, her. Although courtesy writers before 1744 had for the most part been concerned with the behavior of men, a few had devoted their attention to women—for example, Vives' *Instruction of a Christian Woman* in the sixteenth century, Brathwait's *English Gentlewoman* in the seventeenth, and Wetenhall Wilkes's *Letter of Genteel and Moral Advice To a Young Lady* in the eighteenth. But whether directed toward man or woman, courtesy books gave advice on a variety of topics, concerning themselves with human conduct as a matter of practicality rather than as a subject for mere speculation.

In religion, a favorite subject, the demand is for the most part standard in character: to love and honor God, to pray, to read the Bible, to attend church and behave respectfully there. Domestic problems are regarded as a matter of great importance. The attitude of the courtesy writers toward sexual morality is on the whole a conventional one, with frequent admonitions to young people of both sexes against evil company which may lead to debauchery. Women in particular are told to avoid anything which may undermine their morals and endanger their chastity. Marriage is considered in both its social and its personal aspects. A wife is to be chosen for eminently practical reasons: virtue, suitability of age, temperament, and upbringing are the main considerations, beauty being of secondary importance. Parents are reminded of their duty in caring for their offspring, and are urged to provide for them liberally and to allow them some freedom in their choice of a profession and of a mate. In return, children are told to honor parents and to defer to their wishes. Education is a topic in which, from Elyot to Chesterfield, writers on courtesy are greatly interested. Details of personal behavior are minutely considered, and recreations suitable for ladies and gentlemen are described at length in courtesy books before 1744.[1]

The *Female Spectator*, like these courtesy books, offers advice which is entirely practical in character and is based not upon any academic theorizing about life but upon a real appreciation of its actual difficulties and problems. Mrs. Haywood, of course, is not here the writer of sexy, luscious romances, but is rather concerned with many of the same phases of feminine experience that her predecessors had been in offering advice to the women of their respective eras, and because she was reaching her readers through the medium of a periodical she conformed to the journalistic taste of the time by altering the usual long essay of standard courtesy-book pattern. Defoe gave some advice to women in his *Review*, and since the time of Addison and Steele writers of periodicals had composed informal essays on special phases of moral and social life in the manner of the *Tatler* and *Spectator*. Beginning thirteen years after Cave's *Gentleman's Magazine* and a dozen years after the *London Magazine* first reached the public, the *Female Spectator* satisfied the mid-century demand for a miscellany. Indeed, the essay-miscellany character of the *Female Spectator* demonstrates the transition in periodicals from the single compact essay to the pure miscellany, which by the close of the century usurped the popularity enjoyed by the essay periodical in the reigns of Anne and the first George.

Speaking through the medium of a titular eidolon, Mrs. Haywood shapes each number of her journal into an omnibus essay in which a diversity of matter is set forth in a variety of literary forms. In her journalistic catchall Mrs. Haywood gives her readers conventional essays both admonitory and editorial; and to sweeten her *utile* she sprinkles it copiously with pieces of prose fiction, letters, bits of poetry, and other lively literary types. In each issue she kneads all together so skillfully as to leave the illusion of a single, uninterrupted essay.

Although the fiction, the letters, and the other forms employed in the *Female Spectator* are designed only as illustration of, or points of departure for, the essays, Mrs. Haywood devotes slightly more than half the total space in the periodical to them. But despite their comparative brevity the essays are the true center of emphasis in each issue. The editorial essays, employed for the discussion of eidolon, club, and policy, appear infrequently; the didactic admonitory essays are used generously, sometimes ponderously. But despite heaviness and frequent vagueness the *Female Spectator* never seems less than genuinely sincere in her desire to effect a reformation of the indiscretions, small and large, she sees about her. As an active career woman Mrs. Haywood knew, however, that her periodical must entertain as well as instruct if it were to continue in existence. So in her twenty-four issues she offers heartfelt admonitions with sufficiently racy illustrative examples to her female readers, and she seems as sincerely interested in their moral and social success as any of her admonitory predecessors who wrote courtesy literature in conventional form.

Courtesy books appearing in England before 1744 were more concerned with the relationship between man and woman after marriage than before; yet a few devoted some space to the problems of unmarried women, generally warning them against the wiles of omnipresent seducers. As early as Castiglione the tone was set: ". . . for certainly the urgence of lovers, the arts they use, the snares they spread, are so many and so continual that it is but too great a wonder that a tender girl can escape. . . ."[2]   Richard Hyrde in his 1540 translation of Vives' *Instruction of a Christian Woman* had admonished the ladies in the same vein:

Give none ear unto the lover, no more than thou wouldst do unto an enchanter or a sorcerer. For he cometh pleasantly and flattering, first praising the maid, showing her how he is taken with the love of her beauty, and that he must be dead for her love, for these lovers know well enough the vain-glorious minds of many, which have a great delight in their own praises, wherewith they be caught like as the birder beguileth the birds.[3]

The young ladies of 1673 received similar warnings against the insidious wiles of the seducer: "The best way therefore to countermine those Stratagems of men, is for women to be suspiciously vigilant even of the first approaches. He that means to defend a Fort, must not abandon the Outworks, and she that will secure her Chastity, must never let it come to too close a siege, but repass the very first and most remote insinuations of a Temter."[4] In the eighteenth century the same sort of advice was given to the ladies. In 1722 young women were warned against yielding too readily to the passion of love by John Essex in his *Young Ladies Conduct*,[5] and in 1744 they were admonished against the addresses of unscrupulous men and told how to distinguish a pure and genuine passion from an unworthy one by Wetenhall Wilkes in a *Letter of Genteel and Moral Advice To a Young Lady*.

Thousands of your Sex have been gradually betray'd from innocent Freedoms to Ruin and Infamy; and Thousands of our Sex have begun with Flatteries, Protestations, and Endearments, but ended with Reproaches, Perjury, and Perfidiousness. She that considers this will shun like Death, such baits of Guilt and Misery, and be very cautious to whom she listens. When a man talks of honourable Love, you may with an honest Pleasure hear his Story; but, if he flies into Raptures, calls you an Angel or a Goddess, vows to stab himelf like a Hero, or to die at your Feet like a Slave, he no more than dissembles; or, if you cannot help believing him, only recollect the old Phrase, *Violent Things can never last.*[6]

When Eliza Haywood undertook to offer counsel to the young

ladies of her day on their affairs of love, she warned them against the many trickeries and subtleties of betrayers, and offered solutions for various other problems resulting from the relationships of men and women in love. In the *Female Spectator*, as in English courtesy books, the whole question of sex is regarded from a practical rather than from a romantic point of view. Through the words of her eidolon Mrs. Haywood, herself experienced in love's tribulations, strives conscientiously to account for inexplicable attractions in love. Of two persons of equal merit we may like one better while he may be least inclined to like us at all. Three woeful tales are related to illustrate such a lamentable fate.[7] Lovers, more than any other people, complain of ingratitude and with least reason, the Female Spectator feels. When two people are in love and one breaks away, this person is called ungrateful; but Mrs. Haywood believes that, since love is not an action of the will, if one changes it is not from ingratitude but from weakness and instability. Lovers betray and abandon each other because they did not well consult their hearts before making the "first overture," an occasion demanding serious consideration.[8]

To the Female Spectator fickleness in love is a detestable trait in men and women alike. Such light-heartedness was shown by Amaranthus, a brave young military officer who promised to marry Aminta on his return from battle in Germany. Each was admittedly consumed with a great passion. After becoming a hero at Dettingen, however, Amaranthus returned only to spurn Aminta by saying that he was then devoted to his king and country and consequently no woman could deserve his attention. Aminta, deserted and remorseful, lives in isolation in the country trying to forget her beloved, who was savage, not heroic, in treating her in such a heartless manner.[9]

Mrs. Haywood condemns still another type of ingratitude in love affairs. If a person is loved by one for whom he has neither inclination nor aversion, but only indifference, and yet affects love in order to advance his social standing or fortune, this person is carrying on a pretence that is both ungrateful and sordid. The readers of the *Female Spectator* are presented, as an admonition against bargainers in love, the closely averted tragedy of the young Celemena, who was victimized by a maliciously greedy fortune hunter. The warning is clear: love does not deserve to be called love when it is not accompanied by friendship based upon esteem. He who is found worthy of admiration is suitable to be loved if no disparity of age, birth, or habit forbids the "soft Impulse."[10]

Shrewdly conscious of the power of love, Mrs. Haywood often informs her readers that a lady may do what she pleases with her lover if she handles him properly. To illustrate this point a story is told of a woman who converted her lover from a state of barbarism to one of elegance and wit. A country gentleman had a son so sullen, rough, and intractable that education seemed wasted on him. He avoided all gentle conversation and all attempts to make him similar to others of his rank and fortune. Then an orphan beauty to whom his father was guardian came to visit his family. She was affable, good-natured, cheerful, interested in learning, and free from pride, foppery, and affectation. The son soon lost all inclination for his former way of living and turned to reading, music, and dancing because she loved them so. In a few weeks there was accomplished what years had failed to do, and love alone had wrought this miracle. The son and the orphan were married with the approval of all. As this Mr. Sullen tried to make himself worthy of this woman of sensibility, he became the master of all accomplishments required for social success. This is true of all who really love; they try to be what will be most engaging to the object of their affections.[11]

I therefore maintain, that every beautiful Woman ought to answer for all the Follies of her Admirers, provided that she continues them in her Train; and that it may not be said that I lay too great a Stress on the Influence of my own Sex, I would also have every Man of Sense condemned for the Impertinencies committed by the Woman he makes his serious Addresses to.—As the mutual Desire of pleasing each other in both Sexes is natural and laudable, each would doubtless be reform'd when they found it the only way to answer that great End.[12]

Exhorting the men among her readers that they, too, should conduct themselves properly in affairs of the heart, the Female Spectator publishes a story contributed by a female correspondent in which a lady takes justifiable revenge on a man who has caused her many heartaches. The story, entitled "The Lady's Revenge," encourages the ladies to rely upon their wit and ingenuity when dealing with villainous lovers. Ziphranes, a modishly fickle rake, astonished all the town by concentrating all his attention on Barsina, an agreeable lady of fortune. After plans were made for the marriage, Ziphranes avoided Barsina completely. In a short time Ziphranes wrote her that he was accepting another proposal of marriage more to his advantage. Justifiably, Barsina came to hate Ziphranes and to plan her revenge. One day in the park she met him and through dissimulation persuaded him to come to her house for one last farewell. She received him for breakfast with the greatest civility. After the meal Barsina ordered a bottle of cypress wine, some of which they drank. Then Barsina informed Ziphranes that the wine had been poisoned and that they would die together. Like a man distracted he ran home and got three physicians to administer powerful drugs, which almost brought Ziphranes to his death. In the meantime he heard that Barsina was dead and had been buried. While in the country for his health he saw an eerie figure all in white which reminded him of Barsina; this experience nearly killed him. It was Barsina herself whom he was seeing, since the wine had not been poisoned at all and her funeral had taken place only in mock form. Having satisfied her resentment, Barsina returned to town with all her former serenity and good humor. Her acquaintance approved her method of punishing Ziphranes for his inconstancy, and even his friends complimented her. Elismonda, the contributing correspondent, concluded that more women should show such spirit when abandoned and betrayed by men rather than give way to fruitless grief. The Female Spectator congratulates Barsina for bringing about an event which answered all her purposes and at the same time secured her reputation from censure. Her spirit should be emulated by all spurned ladies, and the men are warned to remember the fate of Ziphranes before they are so quick to betray.[13]

Why did Mrs. Haywood pay more attention to the relationships between men and women before marriage than did the writers of courtesy books? The most likely reason is the difference of medium. Long before 1744 the journalistic patron had been accustomed to sprightly discussions on love, especially through the observations of Richard Steele in the *Tatler, Spectator, Guardian,* and *Lover*. Also, to appeal to a wide audience Mrs. Haywood needed to ensnare the attention not only of the mothers but of the young ladies as well, who, if this new periodical failed to please, could readily turn to romances and plays. Richardson, Fielding, Lillo, and Steele made for strong competition.

Although frequent warnings against the predatory male and occasional bits of advice on other love problems were given by courtesy writers, commentators before 1744 were much more concerned with marital problems than with those facing the young maiden in love. From Richard Hyrde's translation in 1540 of Juan Luis Vives' *Instruction of a Christian Woman* to the appearance of the *Female Spectator* the ideal established by courtesy books was at best wedded happiness, with the wife hardly more than an appurtenance to her husband's dignity, or, at worst, a cynical avoidance of what is believed to be inevitable wedded misery. Hyrde, in a section completely devoted to wives, took up the nature of wedlock, choice of a mate, and behavior in the married condition, which should be pervaded by a spirit of sweet concord.[14] In the seventeenth century ladies were sufficiently advised on the problems connected with marriage. In 1631 Richard Brathwait in his *English Gentlewoman* assured the ladies that a wise woman understands her husband's nature before marriage and is prepared to adapt herself to it.[15] In 1688 Halifax in his *Advice to a Daughter* suggested that a wise wife will study her husband's temperament and turn his faults to her own advantage; Halifax admitted that the woman works under unavoidable handicaps, but if she is sufficiently adroit, if she is mistress of artifice, if she knows the tricks of the game, she may emerge from the conflict substantially victorious.[16] In the eighteenth century, before the days of the *Female Spectator*, the ladies had been informed on marriage: for example, in Steele's *Ladies Library* a woman was advised to submit to her marriage state with a meek and quiet spirit,[17] and in Wilkes's *Letter of Genteel and Moral Advice To a Young Lady* the young woman considering marriage was urged to be faithful to her husband in all conditions of fortune and to be mild and good-natured, for only thus could she combat an irregular husband.[18]

Like some of the courtesy writers before her, Mrs. Haywood devotes a great deal of her attention to problems connected with marriage. Her advice to her patrons follows the conventional attitude of those writers who preceded her in offering sympathetic counsel to women. Early in her periodical she stresses the extreme importance of a proper marriage both to the individual and to society; also she realistically refers to the unhappinesses that result from marital irregularities:

. . . a Subject which never can be too much attended to, and the too great Neglect of which is the Source of almost all the Evils we either feel, or are Witness of in private Life.

I believe I shall easily be understood to mean *Marriage*, since there is no one Thing on which the Happiness of Mankind so much depends; it is indeed the Fountain-Head of all the Comforts we can enjoy ourselves, and of those we transmit to our Posterity:—It is the Band which unites not only two Persons, but whole Families in one common inseparable Interest:—It is that which prevents those numberless Irregularities and Confusions, that would else overthrow all Order, and destroy Society; but then not to pervert the Intention of so necessary and glorious an Institution, and rob it of every Blessing it is full of, lies only in ourselves. No violated Vows before pledg'd to another,—no clandestine Agreements made up by hasty and ungovern'd passion,— no sordid Bargains where Wealth, not Merit is the chief Inducement, —no notorious Disparity of Years, of Family, or Humours, can ever be productive of a lasting Concord, either between the Principals themselves, or those in Alliance with them. *Dirges*, rather than *Epithalamiums*, should be sung at Nuptials such as these, and their Friends pity, not congratulate their Lot.[19]

After so introducing her numerous discussions on marriage, the Female Spectator continues throughout the course of the periodical to present advice with sufficient examples of the ways marriage should, and especially should not, be conducted. Marriage is a thing of too serious a nature to be entered into inconsiderately or wantonly. Clandestine marriages are hazardous, and those who rashly take the sacred bonds upon them are in very great danger of soon growing weary of them. There should be love on both sides, or the marriage will be a failure.[20] A man and a woman who are considering marriage should know each other longer than a day, a week, or a month; and they should make every effort to learn each other thoroughly—their likes, dislikes, habits, manners, and

beliefs. Many marriages have been dismal failures simply because the participants did not really know the true nature of the
marriage partner.[21]

A type of marriage that is especially to be deplored, according
to the Female Spectator, is the marriage in which there is too great
a difference in age. The story is told of old Pompilius and young
Lady Bloometta, who are congratulated to their faces but sneered
at behind their backs, for such an unequal match. With a discrepancy in age a conflict on the part of the younger one as to
sincerity and duty is certain to arise—"there are no Words to
express the Miseries of a loath'd Embrace. . . ."[22] The Female
Spectator informs her readers that this condition of unreturned
love is usually found in cases of forced marriages, for which the
parents are generally to blame.[23]

Warning her female readers against the common desire to
make the men in their lives completely submissive to their wills,
Mrs. Haywood tells the pathetic history of Amasina, the fairest
of all the beauties of her day. Amasina wished to make certain
that she had complete reign over her Palamon's emotions, and so
she became the perfect coquette, intending to render him more
assiduous and to maintain her independence after marriage. But,
at last, Amasina, deserted by an exasperated Palamon, was left to
suffer in secret repinings and unavailing repentance. The Female
Spectator stresses that the history of the unfortunate Amasina
should warn young ladies how dangerous it is to sport with the
affections of a man of sense. The fop or fool may think that
little artifices to enflame lovers are pretty amusements, but a man
who loves sincerely sees them as idle stratagems and can only resent
and despise them.[24]

A woman troubled with an unfaithful husband is counseled by
Mrs. Haywood to remain tender and amiable if she hopes to be
successful in regaining his affections. As a model for all wives in
their time of trial with false husbands the Female Spectator tells the
story of the patient Alithea, who lived through two years of her
husband's infidelity with the voluptuous, designing Melissa. None
of Dorimon's ill-natured complaints could force Alithea to lose
her calm patience and love for him. So much did she love her
husband that she secretly took the child of Melissa and Dorimon,

which Melissa had discarded. When Dorimon found out that his wife had done this in full knowledge of his past irregularities, he loved her more tenderly than ever, renounced Melissa, and begged forgiveness of Alithea, who was only too happy to grant it. The Female Spectator admonishes her audience that for her own sake a wife should be wary, even when most provoked, not to show in her behavior anything resembling the "Wretches of the Town." For it is not by force that women can hope to maintain influence over men. The most infallible maxim for women to follow is that they must seem to yield whenever they would truly conquer.[25]

Suggestions to women on how to reclaim wandering husbands and on how to maintain control over them while seeming only to submit in every respect had been a favorite theme in courtesy books for women. Wives were frequently advised to practice wise dissimulation as a means of reforming their husbands; but since such instructions generally came from men, a captious reader might wonder if they were the result of experience or of special pleading. For example, among Mrs. Haywood's not too distant predecessors, Lord Halifax in 1688 offered the suggestion: ". . . remember, that next to the danger of committing the fault yourself, the greatest is that of seeing it in your husband. Do not seem to look or hear that way; if he is a man of sense he will reclaim himself; the folly of it is of itself sufficient to cure him."[26] In 1722 John Essex concluded: "A Wife that knows her Husband takes Liberties with other Women, shall sooner reclaim him by a prudent Silence, disguising of the Matter, or taking notice of it calmly to him, than by Rage and Contention; Patience in this Case is as much her Interest as it is her Duty."[27] And in 1744 Wetenhall Wilkes advised his "favourite Niece in her Sixteenth Year" in much the same way:

In the Occurrences of matrimonial Life it is a Rule proper to be observ'd —to preserve always a Disposition to be pleas'd. An ill-managing Man is often brought to see his Errors, and to reclaim by the mild Advices of his Wife, and her obliging Condescensions to humour him. By her Gentleness and sweet Temper he is prevail'd on to inspect into himself, and to remove every Imperfection that is displeasing to her. . . . Meekness and Complacency are the only Weapons wherewith to combat an irregular Husband.[28]

Although she insists that all differences between husband and wife occasioned by any cause whatsoever should be reconciled whenever possible, the Female Spectator counsels separation if only unhappiness results from a continuance of the marriage state.[29] But she stresses that a woman should strive in every way to be a successful wife. To qualify for the position she should be the repository of her husband's "dearest Secrets, the Moderator of his fiercer Passions, the Softner of his most anxious Cares, and the constantly chearful and entertaining Companion of his more unbended Moments. To be all this she must be endued with a consummate Prudence, a perfect Eveness of Temper, an unshaken Fortitude, a gentle affable Behaviour, and a sprightly Wit. . . ."[30] Mrs. Haywood sets high standards indeed for the ladies of her time to emulate.

Among writers of courtesy books appearing before the *Female Spectator* the consensus of doctrine on parent-child relationships was that the child owes reverence, respect, love, and obedience to her parents. After generalizing on these obligations, many a writer went on to the all-important question of just how obedient a child should be to her parents' commands in the choice of a husband. The common answer was that the child has as much right to object as the parent has to direct. The selection of a mate should be a matter of agreement between parent and child. For example, in 1673 Richard Allestree stated: "But as a Daughter is neither to anticipate, nor contradict the will of her Parent, so (to hand the ballance even) I must say she is not obliged to force her own, by marrying where she cannot love; for a negative voice in the case is sure as much the Childs right as the Parents."[31] And in 1714, in the section of the *Ladies Library* devoted to the responsibilities of a parent, the author said: "Something has been observ'd of the Use of the Power of *Parents* over their *Children*, that it should be with *Equity* and *Moderation*. . . . As far as this Rule relates to the Marriage of their Children, I cannot forbear saying, that many, who have been otherwise good *Parents*, have in this been exceedingly to blame."[32]

Courtesy writers agree that above all other qualities parents most desire their children to acquire goodness; and since this is so, the parents themselves are warned to establish the model for their children to emulate. In no other way can they be assured of having children good and true. Prior to the time of the *Female Spectator* two such admonitions were: "*Parents* then, above all other, have one argument to be good themselves, for the sake of their *Children*: If you desire to have them good, the best way to make them so, is to give them the Example of it in being good your selves. For this Reason *Parents* should take care to do nothing but what is worthy of Imitation";[33] and "The Mother who passes her time in gaming, at plays, and in indiscreet conversations, very gravely complains that she cannot find a governess capable of bringing up her children; but what good can the best of education confer on children, with the example of such a mother before them?"[34]

Mrs. Haywood, in instructing parents of the 1740's, follows courtesy-book conventions by emphasizing parent-child cooperation in the choice of a mate and the training of children to excel in virtue. In the first number of her periodical she begins her advice to parents by assuring them that indiscreet marriages often occur among young people because the parents themselves have been too harsh.[35] She warns that parents are wrong to think that the convenient marriages they make for their children will necessarily be desirable ones. A child should be consulted and not forced into marriage, oftentimes with someone never seen before.[36]

Mrs. Haywood insists that parents should never be neglectful of teaching the young the importance of family life and of instilling in them sound principles of virtue.[37] Careless parents should be censured for not cultivating the genius they find in their children; they should also be constantly aware of their children's inabilities. A romantically inclined girl who is accustomed to talk of love and lovers will become an easy prey to the first offer. It is the business of parents to keep the mind of a girl of this type employed on other things and never to let her hear any discourse or read any book which might rouse the vanity of making conquests which is inherent in her.[38] Young ladies scarcely out of the nursery should not have the right to act as they please, choose their own company, or have their secrets; nothing is to their advantage or interest that cannot be told to their parents.[39] Neither should girls be completely isolated from a modest society and its pleasures.

... the Country-bred Ladies, who are never suffered to come to Town for fear their Faces should be spoiled by the Small-Pox, or their Reputations ruined by the Beaux, become an easier Prey to the Artifices of Mankind, than those who have had an Education more at large: As they rarely stir beyond their Father's Pales, except to Church, the Parson, if he be a forward Man, and has Courage to throw a Love Song, or Copy of Verses to Miss over the Wall, or slip it into her Hand in a Visit he pays the Family, has a rare Opportunity of making his Fortune; and it is well when it happens no worse; many a 'Squire's Daughter has clambered over Hedge and Style, to give a rampant Jump into the Arms of a young jolly Haymaker or Ploughman.

Our *London* Ladies are indeed very rarely laid under such Restrictions; but whenever it happens to be the Case, as Nature is the same in all, the Consequence will be so too.—Would Miss *Eagaretta* have ever condescended to marry the greasy Footman that run before her Chair, had he not been the only Man her over-careful Father permitted her to speak to?—Or would *Armonia* have found any charms in a *Mousetrap* or *Leathern Apron,* had she been indulged the Conversation of a *White Staff*?[40]

A tragic story of the betrayed and ruined Seomanthe is told as a warning of how an inexperienced girl can be tricked by a seducer who is inevitably only too aware of her ignorance.[41]

Although parents should devote sufficient time to the training of their children, Mrs. Haywood directs them not to deny themselves the necessities or even the pleasures of life just for their charges.[42] However, she can see no excuse for a "gadding Matron" who ought to have the care of her house and family at heart. "How odd a Figure does the Mother of five or six Children make at one of these nocturnal Rambles. . . ."[43]

The Female Spectator regrets that too few children allow their parents the respect due them, and illustrates the ultimate in filial esteem by telling the story of a young man who gave his father much more consideration than the miserly parent deserved.[44] Mrs. Haywood sums up her opinions on parent-child relationships as follows:

Obedience to Parents is an indispensible Duty.—No one, how great soever, ought to think himself exempt from paying it. Decency and Good Manners require it. Natural Affection obliges to it. The Laws of Man enjoin it, and the Law of God not only commands it, but annexes to the fulfilling it a Promise of long Life in the Land which he shall please to give us.

Yet, notwithstanding this, when a Parent through Avarice, Caprice, or Partiality, would force his Child to marry utterly against Inclination, I cannot think Disobedience a Crime, because we are not to obey our Parents in Things which are in themselves unlawful; and certainly there is nothing more opposite to the Laws of God, and more contradictory to the Institution, and even to the very Words of Marriage, than to vow an everlasting Love to a Person for whom one has a fixed Aversion.

But tho' we are not always bound to marry according to the Direction of our Parents, we ought not, however, to think ourselves at Liberty to chuse for ourselves.—If we cannot bring our Hearts to correspond with their Desires, we must not be so wholly guided by our own, as to bring into their Family a Person whom they do not approve of.[45]

Even though she does not in every point agree with her predecessors, Mrs. Haywood's advice on parent-child relationships is mainly conventional; and certainly in her great concern for the proper understanding between parents and their children she is in the tradition of those courtesy writers who offered advice to parents and children alike.

Education has always been one of the chief topics discussed by courtesy writers. And although the books of conduct before 1744 were disproportionately concerned with the education of men, many devoted some space to women and a few were designed for them alone. From the Renaissance to the appearance of the *Female Spectator* there was some divergency of opinion on the subjects worthy of a woman's attention, but among the various commentators there was almost complete agreement that the purpose of female education was to produce virtuous daughters, wives, and mothers. The girls are by no means encouraged to take places in a world of men, but rather they are admonished to make of themselves graceful and good companions for the men in their lives. Through education a girl can learn to deal with people and affairs which confront her daily.

Since the Queen was herself an admirable linguist, it was but natural that the praise of feminine learning should extend through the reign of Elizabeth. Richard Mulcaster's *Positions* of 1581 is a fairly typical example of educational advice that was given to women in the sixteenth century: "And is not a young gentlewoman, thinke you, thoroughly furnished, which can reade plainly and distinctly, write faire and swiftly, sing cleare and sweetely, play wel and finely, vnderstand and speake the learned languages, and those tongues also which the time most embraseth, with some *Logicall* helpe to chop, and some *Rhetoricke* to braue."[46]

With the death of Elizabeth the favor accorded learned women came somewhat abruptly to an end. In the first half of the seventeenth century there was a widespread contempt of learning as an appropriate pursuit for women. But in 1659, when Clement Barksdale translated as the *Learned Maid* a volume on the education of women originally written in Latin by Anna Maria van Schurman of Utrecht, the ladies of England were presented with an influential book which advocated a large and liberal curriculum for women. The author argues that many women are capable of profiting by a thorough education. Even though they do not engage in men's occupations, they have a right to the benefits of liberal studies, and parents should see that their daughters receive instruction in grammar, rhetoric, logic, physics, metaphysics, history, languages, mathematics, poetry, and fine arts.[47]

Early in the eighteenth century the *Ladies Library* admonished women to devote themselves to reading, writing, arithmetic, law, moral philosophy, accounts of voyages and travels, and Greek and Roman histories in translation. "I do not see the Necessity of a Woman's learning the *ancient* Tongues, but there are so many polite Authors in *French* and *Italian*, that it is pity the Ladies should not have the *Profit* and *Pleasure* of them."[48] Since "gallant Writers" lead the "Heart to Love," the ladies were warned to touch them warily: "Too much of this will be found among the Works of *Poetry* and *Eloquence*, with which none but Ladies of good Taste and solid Judgment should be trusted. The like Cautions are necessary with respect to *Musick* and *Painting*; the Fancy is often too quick in them, and the Soul too much affected by the Senses."[49]

Fénelon's treatise *De l'Education des filles*, first translated into English in 1721, had considerable influence on the education

of women in the eighteenth century.[50]   The author admonished
parents to be careful that a daughter be neither an ignoramus nor
a learned lady who indulges in exercises and studies fit only for
men.   Untrained women, for want of solid nourishment, are
corrupted by the artificial life and sentiments of popular romances,
and even set themselves up as critics of religion.   To prevent such
conditions, a girl's education should be directed with the greatest
care, following a program outlined thus:

Teach a girl to read and write correctly. . . .
A girl should know the grammar of her own language. . . .
Females should also be instructed in the first four rules of arithmetic. . . .
It will be prudent also to give them a knowledge of the principal rules
of justice. . . .
These instructions having been attended to, I think it may not be
improper to allow young women, according to their leisure and capacity,
the perusal of profane or classical writers, provided there be nothing in
them to inflame or mislead the passions. . . .   Put into their hands . . .
the Greek and Roman histories . . . let them be acquainted likewise with
the history of their *own country*. . . .   It is generally thought a necessary
part of a good education for a young Lady of rank to be taught the
Italian and Spanish languages: for my part I see no use in these
acquirements . . . besides these two languages often lead to books that
are dangerous. . . .   Latin should be taught to young women of good
judgment and discreet conduct only; who will set no greater value on
this study than it deserves; who will renounce all vain curiosity, and
have no other view than their own edification.
I would allow also, but with great care, the perusal of works of
eloquence and poetry, if I saw they had a taste for them, and solidity of
judgment enough to confine themselves to their real use: but fearful of
agitating too much their lively imaginations, I would have the utmost
caution observed in this respect: every thing that may awaken the
sentiments of love, seems to me the more dangerous in proportion as it
is softened and disguised.
Music and Painting require the same precautions. . . .[51]

When Mrs. Haywood decided to devote some space in her
journal to discussions on female education, she was following a long
established tradition among works on feminine behavior.   And as

was her usual practice, she took the *via media* in giving educational advice. Although she does not advocate the more advanced opinions of her near-predecessors, she believes in the efficacy of a somewhat liberalized education. All women are recommended to perfect themselves in certain subjects in order to meet life gracefully and to make of themselves good and faithful daughters, wives, and mothers. She is sympathetic toward the members of her own sex because their education has not been given adequate attention; thus "Vanity, Affectation, and all Errors of that Nature are infinitely less excuseable in the Men than in the Woman, as they have so much greater Opportunities than we have of knowing better."[52] If time were taken to instruct women in rules of wisdom, they could inspire their husbands with a reverence which would not permit them to treat women with lightness and contempt, "which, tho' some of us may justly enough incur, often drives not only such, but the most innocent of us, to Extravagancies that render ourselves, and those concern'd with us equally miserable."[53]

The Female Spectator insists that men who think women should learn only family management, cooking, caring for children, and handling of servants are guilty of gross injustice. Education does not make a woman scornful of household affairs; in fact, it makes her more sensible of her duties, more industrious, and more careful not to give any excuse for reproaches.[54] But "a Lady of Condition should learn just as much of Cookery and of Work, as to know when she is imposed upon by those she employs." To pass too much of her time with either may give her the reputation of a fine housewife but not of a woman of fine taste, nor will it qualify her for polite conversation or for entertaining herself when alone.[55]

To the ladies Mrs. Haywood offers philosophy as the most practical subject for their consideration. Philosophy is a "great resource" when a woman is struggling with hardships, and through it she can recognize her own indiscretions and equip herself with new resolutions for the future.[56] Next to philosophy Mrs. Haywood recommends history as suitable for feminine study. She does not wish women to become deeply learned but just to have a general understanding of the affairs of the world from the creation to their own time, "to the End they may be enabled to make an agreeable Part in Conversation, be qualified to judge for themselves, and divested of all Partiality and Prejudice as to their own Conduct, as well as that of others."[57]   Also, she gives her sanction to the study of "Natural Philosophy."[58]   Mrs. Haywood admits that "Music, Dancing, and the reading of Poetry and Novels may sometimes come in by way of Relaxation, but ought not to be too much indulg'd."[59]   Reading brings innumerable pleasures which relax and instruct, but two or three hours a day are sufficient time to devote to it.   No one should neglect friends and family for books.[60]

As an appendage to their formal discussions on education courtesy writers were concerned too with the moral and social demeanor of gentlemen and gentlewomen, pointing out certain discrepancies in morals and manners and offering counsel on the avoidance of these ills.   In 1631 Richard Brathwait advised his readers on their appearance and behavior in society in the following way:

And such are you, whose *generous* descent, as it claims precedence of others, so should your vertuous demeanour in these foure distinct subiects, Gate, Looke, Speech, Habit, improue your esteeme aboue others. In *Gate*, by walking humbly: in *Looke*, by disposing it demurely; in *Speech*, by deliuering it moderately; in *Habit* by attiring your selues modestly: all which, like foure choyce borders, perfumed with sweetest odours, will beautifie those louely lodges of your soules with all *Decency*.[61]

At the end of the seventeenth century Mary Astell commented: "There is a sort of Bravery and Greatness of Soul, which does more truly ennoble us than the highest Title, and it consists in the living up to the dignity of our Natures, scorning to do a mean unbecoming thing; in passing differently thro' Good and Evil Fortune, without being corrupted by the one or deprest by the other."[62]   In like manner John Essex, in 1722, concluded:

Let me then prevail upon you, Ladies, not to idle or sleep away your Time; not to prattle with one another for Hours together, and turn every Day into Gossiping; but be Diligent and Industrious to receive Instructions, and perform your Exercises with Chearfulness, and a real Intention to improve your selues; in order to which, *Temperance* and *Moderation* are the best Duties I can recommend to your Care and Observance, as the surest Methods to preserve your *Modesty* and *Chastity*. . . .[63]

Thus when Eliza Haywood chose to include rather abundant advice on moral and social decorum, she was following an old convention. Thanks to her concern the ladies of the period 1744-46 were warned against the moral flaws of jealousy, ingratitude, affectation, vanity, lying, gossip, and raillery. As to social indiscretions, Mrs. Haywood especially condemns attendance at public masquerades, excessive participation in gaming, over-indulgence in the use of tea and snuff, and affectation in the choice of dress. She regrets that the ladies of her age waste so much of their time in trifles and suggests that they can solve many of their problems through due attention to contemplation and reflection.

The Female Spectator assures her readers that there is nothing admirable about the passion of jealousy: ". . . it can only be of a base and degenerate Inclination, not of that pure and refined Passion which is alone worthy of the Name of Love." In love, and in other matters as well, vanity and arrogance are the co-workers of jealousy; they make a person hate to see the least civility paid to anyone but himself.[64] Ingratitude is an insidious sin—a vice detestable both to God and man. "One may be guilty of it even without knowing we are so; and innocent without the Direction of Principle.—There are indeed no established Rules for it, and the Definition is no less a Mystery than the Philosopher's Stone."[65] Mrs. Haywood warns her audience how foolish it is for a woman of age to affect the mode of a young girl in her dress, mannerisms, and activities. "How vain also is the Attempt!—*December's* Frost might as easily assume the Livery of gaudy *May*, as Fifty look like Fifteen. . . ."[66] Too, the Female Spectator admonishes women against vanity, which she feels usually results from the "ridiculous Flatteries" of men. "The Small-Pox is not half so great an Enemy to the Face, as Flattery is to the Mind of a young Virgin.—It empoisons all the noble Propensities, turns everything to Vanity," and causes her to consider only herself worthy of praise.[67] Lying is most contemptible: "nothing more demonstrates a Person to be dead to all good Sentiments, than to be hardened in this detestable Vice."[68] Another moral discrepancy is the love of gossip. "Nothing more plainly shews a weak and degenerate Mind, than taking a Delight in whispering about every idle Story we are told, to the Prejudice of our Neighbours."[69] And, finally, Mrs.

Haywood advises the avoidance of an improper use of raillery. "There is nothing requires a greater Delicacy of Sentiment and Expression, than what we call *Raillery;* and a Person must be very polite indeed, who knows how to practise it, so as not to give Offence."[70]

In turning to particular social errors Mrs. Haywood condemns attendance at public masquerades, for "in these mercenary Entertainments, the most abandon'd Rake, or low-bred Fellow, who has wherewithal to purchase a Ticket, may take the Liberty of uttering the grossest Things in the chastest Ear."[71] She warns the ladies that an excessive indulgence in gaming ruins many fortunes, occasions innumerable quarrels, perplexes the mind, and benumbs the body.[72] Championing tea taken in moderation as a harmless and agreeable beverage, she considers its excessive use as a social lapse.[73] She admonishes against intemperance in the use of the "Snuff-Box" and the "Smelling-Bottle" as well.[74] And, with genuine concern, she advises her patrons to observe principles of modesty and decorum in choosing their dress, since "even in such a trivial Thing as Dress, a *good* or *bad Taste* may be discerned."[75]

In addition to pointing out certain moral and social ills and advising the ladies against them, Mrs. Haywood suggests to her readers that they can acquire contentment and happiness through a proper exercise of contemplation. She readily admits that an agreeable society furnishes pleasures that are elegant, but she warns that even the best company grows insipid and tiresome to a woman if she is forever in it. All regulation and management require at least some small reflection and recess from company. A woman with an aversion to solitude flies in all companies indiscriminately, often later repenting the acquaintances she has made. Many women consider "those who preach up the Happiness of a more retired Life, as phlegmatic and vapourish"; such women owe their ruin to the unfortunate propensity among them of loving to be always in company. Mrs. Haywood by no means recommends a total avoidance of society, but she stresses the importance of a proper love of solitude for thought and meditation.[76]

On morals and manners the Female Spectator offers her readers the usual fare—quite like that presented by advisers on conduct writing in traditional form. And like them Mrs. Haywood devotes some little attention to religion, medicine, and the theater. Many writers on conduct were concerned with religion, and for the most part their advice was quite standard in character. In the seventeenth century Halifax stressed religion as a foremost consideration for his daughter:

The first thing to be considered is *Religion*. It must be the chief object of your thoughts, since it would be a vain thing to direct your behaviour in the world, and forget that which you are to have towards Him who made it. In a strict sense, it is the only thing necessary; you must take it into your mind, and thence throw it into your heart, where you are to embrace it so close as never to lose the possession of it.[77]

In like manner Mrs. Haywood recommends religion to be the chief concern of a lady's life, and she specifies for her readers the Established Church, since the "Clergy of the Church of *England* are infinitely less austere, than those of the Sects which take, as it seems to me, indeed a kind of Pride in dissenting from them."[78]

As early as 1540 the ladies had been counseled as to what share they should have in the medical care of their families: "I would she should know medicines and salves for such diseases as be common and reign almost daily, and have those medicines ever prepared ready in some closet. . . ."[79] In 1671 the author of *An Academy or Colledge* recommended that the ladies of his era be trained in the "making of some sort of Physical and Chyrurgical Medecins and Salves for the Poor, &c."[80] And in 1744 Wetenhall Wilkes suggested that the money generally laid out on cosmetics would be "expended to better Advantage in Balsams, Unguents, Plaisters, and Medicines for the Poor and Diseased."[81] The Female Spectator, too, suggests to her audience that they can help themselves, their families, and their neighbors by acquiring a certain skill in the use of medicinal herbs and plants.[82]

Before 1744 certain writers had grappled with the risky problem of whether attendance at the theater is proper for ladies and gentlemen. In 1688 Halifax, in his *Advice to a Daughter*, recommended the theater as appropriate recreation for ladies, but warned that no pleasure should be indulged to excess.[83] And in 1744 Wilkes commented: "If the Stage were under proper Regulations, it might be made an useful Entertainment, and a Source of pure Delight; but, as it now labours under certain Corruptions (such as ridiculing Religion and her Ministers, and frequently introducing dissolute and immodest Scenes) I advise you always to be acquainted with the Innocence of the Play before you see it acted."[84] Eliza Haywood, former actress and playwright, expresses the opinion in the *Female Spectator* that of all public places of entertainment the theater is the one at which a lady is least likely to meet undesirable characters. Thus she feels that no valid objections can be made to a woman's frequenting the theater since it is the seemliest place of amusement for her. The theater, Mrs. Haywood believes, can serve, too, as a moral force in the lives of the spectators. She tells her readers that she has known many people who, after seeing their own types of sin portrayed on the stage, have gone home from the theater and reformed to live admirable lives thereafter. Mrs. Haywood warns the ladies that no beneficial results can be had from the theater unless strict attention is paid to the drama. She regrets that too many people attend the theater because they are interested in being seen, in being heard, or in observing the actors and their habits rather than because they have a sincere concern with character portrayal or moral instruction. Mrs. Haywood advises the ladies to support the theater by giving proper attention to performances and by patronizing the plays of certain great dramatists of the past and the "living Geniuses" of the day.[85] Among early critics of the theater, some strenuously disapproved of it, some half-heartedly approved of it, and some approved of it if moderation were used in attendance. But it seems that no adviser of women before 1744 gave such complete sanction to the theater as did the Female Spectator.

In the period 1744-46 Eliza Haywood was presenting to the ladies of London through the medium of her monthly journal practical advice on their multifarious problems and difficulties. In offering admonitions to the women of her era, Mrs. Haywood was concerned with many of the same phases of feminine life as were courtesy writers who wrote in conventional form from the sixteenth century to the eighteenth, and in most details her counsel is similar. Although periodicals since the time of the *Tatler* and *Spectator* had contained informal essays on special phases of moral and social life, the *Female Spectator* devoted most of its attention to love, marriage, parent-child relationships, education, and morals and manners, with a comparatively brief treatment of religion, medicine, and the theater. The sizable success of the paper among its readers has been followed by a journalistic vogue that continues even into the women's magazines and "Advice" columns of the present century. Because of its commendable literary quality it holds a position of prominence in an age which produced the best essay journals. It has a large historical importance as the first periodical designed solely for female patronage. But, in the end, the greatest value of the *Female Spectator* rests on its effectiveness as a medium of courtesy counsel for the proper behavior of ladies and would-be ladies of mid-eighteenth century England.

NOTES

1. Along with the courtesy books themselves, the following works are basic in a study of courtesy literature: John E. Mason, *Gentlefolk in the Making: Studies in the History of English Courtesy Literature and Related Topics from 1531 to 1774* (Philadelphia, 1935); Myra Reynolds, *The Learned Lady in England, 1650-1760* (New York, 1920); Virgil Barney Heltzel, "Chesterfield and the Tradition of the Ideal Gentleman" (Ph. D. dissertation, University of Chicago, 1925); and Elbert N. S. Thompson, "Books of Courtesy," *Literary Bypaths of the Renaissance* (New Haven, 1924), pp. 127-71.

2. *The Book of the Courtier*, trans. Leonard Eckstein Opdycke (New York, 1903), pp. 216-17.

3. Ed. Foster Watson (New York, 1912), p. 105.

4. *The Ladies Calling in Two Parts* (Oxford, 1673), p. 16.

5. *The Young Ladies Conduct: or, Rules for Education, Under several Heads; with Instructions upon Dress, both before and after Marriage. And Advice to Young Wives* (London, 1722), pp. 23-24.

6. *A Letter of Genteel and Moral Advice To a Young Lady: In a new and familiar Method; Being A System of Rules and Instructions, to qualify the Fair Sex to be useful and happy in every State* (London, 1744), p. 83.

7. Mrs. Eliza Haywood, *The Female Spectator* (London, 1744-46), vii, 4-18, 29-34; xxi, 136-60. The first edition of this periodical has been used in this study; Roman numerals indicate the issue and Arabic the page.

8. *Ibid.*, vii, 53-55. Cf. *The Ladies Library. Written by a Lady. Published by Mr. Steele* (London, 1714), I, 154-77, where a discussion is given on what constitutes ingratitude in love. For the authorship of this compendium see George A. Aitken, *The Life of Richard Steele* (London, 1889), II, 39-41.

9. *Ibid.*, ii, 108-17. Cf. Du Boscq, *The Compleat Woman* (London, 1639), II, 13, where a complaint is made against fickleness in love: "After we have spoken of inconstancy, we must combat with perfidiousness, which is ordinarily inseparable from it."

10. *Ibid.*, vii, 55-67. Two other stories of this type are told in viii, 105-16, and in xiv, 65-102. Cf. Mary Astell, *Reflections Upon Marriage* (London, 1706),

p. 9, "He who does not make Friendship the chief inducement to his Choice, and prefer it before any other consideration, does not deserve a good Wife, and therefore should not complain if he goes without one"; and Jonathan Swift, "Letter to a Young Lady, on her Marriage," *Prose Works*, ed. Herbert Davis (Oxford, 1948), IX, 85-94, in which Swift stresses that marriage should be based on friendship and esteem.

11. *Ibid.*, xii, 360-72. For another story of this type see the same number, pp. 377-84.

12. *Ibid.*, xii, 371-72.

13. *Ibid.*, xiv, 103-24. Two other stories of this type are told in xx, 112-22, and in xxiv, 351-60. Cf. *Female Policy Detected: or, The Arts of a designing Woman Laid Open* (London, n. d.), p. 16: "Deal with a Revengeful Woman as with a Hand-Granado, which you cast from you as soon as the Fuse is lighted, lest it *burst* to the *prejudice* of him that fir'd it. . . . Trespass not on the Affections of a Woman who loves you to Excess; for Women (like Ale) if sweet will turn sour the sooner"; and Wilkes, *Letter of Genteel and Moral Advice*, pp. 81-83, where ladies are warned against the addresses of unscrupulous men and advised to show some ingenuity in defending themselves.

14. *Instruction of a Christian Woman*, ed. Watson, pp. 75-125.

15. *The English Gentlewoman, drawne out to the full Body: Expressing, What Habilliments doe best attire her, What Ornaments doe best adorne her, What Complements doe best accomplish her* (London, 1631), p. 105.

16. *The Life and Letters of Sir George Savile, Bart. First Marquis of Halifax &c. With a New Edition of His Works Now for the First Time Collected and Revised*, ed. H. C. Foxcroft (London, 1898), II, 393-402.

17. *Ladies Library*, II, 58-133.

18. *Letter of Genteel and Moral Advice*, p. 88.

19. *Female Spectator*, ii, 74-75. Cf. Halifax, "Advice to a Daughter," *Life and Letters*, ed. Foxcroft, II, 395-401. Halifax suggests to his daughter how she may control, or take advantage of, her husband's potential irregularities, which are discussed in detail. Cf. also Astell, *Reflections Upon Marriage*, p. 80, where the author concludes a lengthy discussion on proper decorum in marriage: "To wind up this matter, if a Woman were duly Principled and Taught to know the World, especially the true Sentiments that Men have of her, and the Traps they lay for her under so many gilded Compliments, and such a seemingly great Respect, that disgrace wou'd be prevented which is brought upon too many Families, Women would Marry more discreetly, and demean themselves better in a Married State than some People say they do."

20. *Ibid.*, iv, 227-29; xiv, 99-100; xxii, 251-52. Cf. John Essex, *The Young Ladies Conduct: or, Rules for Education, Under several Heads; with Instructions upon Dress, both before and after Marriage. And Advice to Young Wives* (London, 1722), pp. 95-96: "Marriage is an Affair of that Consequence in Life, that it is great Imprudence in a young *Lady* to venture on it, without good Consideration; great Ingratitude to do it, without Advice of Parents, Friends·&c. And lastly, great Folly to enter into it without your own free Choice and good Liking."

21. *Ibid.*, ii, 89-94; v, 301-2; vii, 52-54; xvi, 239-58; xvii, 269-70; xxi, 136-60. Cf. Essex, *Young Ladies Conduct*, p. 97: "You are to be intreated, I say, to consult your parents or Guardians, and be inform'd from them, that in so nice a Conjuncture, in order to a happy Marriage, Man and Wife should have but one and the same Interest; and to make up this, there must be a suitable Agreement and Harmony in Age, Humour, Education and Religion; nay, even in Families and Fortunes; and when all these concur, we may expect an equal Satisfaction, as the natural result of an equal Match."

22. *Ibid.*, ii, 73-77. Another story of this type is told in x, 221-29. Cf.

Ladies Calling, p. 85, "When a young Woman marries an old man, there are commonly jealousies on the one part and loathings on the other. . . ."

23. *Ibid.*, ii, 77-86, 124-32. Cf. *Female Policy Detected*, p. 100: "But on the other hand consider, when a wrinkled, toothless Woman, shall marry a beardless Boy, there can be no Love between such a couple, but continual Strife and Debate. The same may be said, when Matches are made by the Parents, and the Portion paid before the young Couple have any Knowledge of it, and so many times are forc'd against their Wills, fearing the Rigour and Displeasure of their Parents, and often Promise with their Mouths, but Refuse with their Hearts."

24. *Ibid.*, v, 302-17. See also ii, 86-89, 122-24; x, 196-99. Cf. Astell, *Reflections Upon Marriage*, p. 56, "She then who Marrys ought to lay it down for an indisputable Maxim, that her Husband must govern absolutely and intirely, and that she has nothing else to do but to Please and Obey."

25. *Ibid.*, vi, 356-83. Three other stories of this type are told in vi, 351-56, and in xiii, 16-28, 28-41.

26. "Advice to a Daughter," *Life and Letters*, ed. Foxcroft, II, 395.

27. *Young Ladies Conduct*, p. 105.

28. *Letter of Genteel and Moral Advice*, p. 88.

29. *Female Spectator*, xvii, 259-61.

30. *Ibid.*, x, 234.

31. *Ladies Calling*, pp. 19-20.

32. *Ladies Library*, II, 167.

33. *Ibid.*, pp. 246-47.

34. François Fénelon, *A Treatise on the Education of Daughters*, trans. T. F. Dibdin (Boston, 1821), pp. 211-12.

35. *Female Spectator*, i, 14-25. Cf. Halifax, "Advice to a Daughter," *Life and Letters*, ed. Foxcroft, II, 405, where the author recommends to his daughter that she not use too much restraint in dealing with her children: "The kind and severe parts must have their several turns seasonable applied, but your indulgence is to have the broader mixture, that love, rather than fear, may be the root of their obedience."

36. *Ibid.*, i, 39-47; iii, 136-44, 179-89; xx, 98-112. Cf. *Ladies Library*, II, 21: "And since it is impossible for any one to Love with another's Affections, but with their own, the *Parents* must consider this, especially how they engage their *Children* to Marry, where at least a hopeful prospect of this *Love* does not appear, least while they are endeavouring to make their *Children* Happy, they make them of all Creatures the most Miserable, and that irremediably so."

37. *Ibid.*, v, 300-1; xii, 341-42; xxiii, 321. Cf. Brathwait, *English Gentlewoman*, p. 202: "To be a *Lady of honour* is more than *titular*. She is onely eminent, who makes every action of her life a vertuous *president*. *Goodnesse* must be infused in her *blood*, that *descent* may partake of *desert*."

38. *Ibid.*, xxiii, 305-6; xxiv, 371-73. Cf. *Ladies Library*, I, 438-41: "Whereas Women, were they rightly educated, had they obtain'd a well-inform'd and discerning Mind, they wou'd be Proof against all those Batteries, see through and scorn those little silly Artifices which are us'd to ensnare and deceive them. . . Thus Ignorance, and a narrow Education, lay the Foundation of Vice, and Imitation and Custom rear it up. . . ."

39. *Ibid.*, iii, 193-98; xxiii, 284-307. Cf. Mary Astell, *A Serious Proposal To the Ladies, For the Advancement of their true and greatest Interest* (London, 1694), p. 25: "The cause therefore of the defects we labour under, is, if not wholly, yet at least in the first place, to be ascribed to the mistakes of our Education; which like an Error in the first Concoction, spreads its ill Influence thro' all our Lives."

40. *Ibid.*, i, 25-26.

41. *Ibid.*, i, 26-32. Three other stories of this type are told in iii, 193-98, and in v, 261-71, 271-92. Cf. Halifax, "Advice to a Daughter," *Life and Letters*, ed. Foxcroft, II, 405, where the author recommends the use of disguised parental force: "You must deny them as seldom as you can, and when there is no avoiding it, you must do it gently, you must flatter away their ill-humours, and take the next opportunity of pleasing them in some other things before they either ask or look for it; this will strengthen your authority by making it soft to them, and confirm their obedience by making it their interest."

42. *Ibid.*, iii, 151; xvi, 206-7; xxii, 191-250. Cf. Halifax, "Advice to a Daughter," *Life and Letters*, ed. Foxcroft, II, 404, where the author recommends moderation in dealing with children: "You may love your children without living in the nursery, and you may have a competent and discreet care of them without letting it break out upon the company or exposing yourself by turning your discourse that way, which is a kind of laying children to the parish, and it can hardly be done anywhere that those who hear it will be so forgiving as not to think they are overcharged with them."

43. *Ibid.*, iv, 204-5. See also v, 301; xxi, 127-60.

44. *Ibid.*, xxi, 177-86. Cf. Wilkes, *Letter of Genteel and Moral Advice*, p. 64, "Let your Obedience to your Mother be therefore your Delight and Exercise."

45. *Ibid.*, xxiii, 316-17.

46. *Positions Wherin Those Primitive Circvmstances Be Examined, Which Are Necessarie for the Training vp of Children, either for skill in their booke, or health in their bodie*, ed. R. H. Quick (London, 1887), p. 181.

47. *The Learned Maid, or, Whether a Maid may be a Scholar?* (London, 1659), pp. 4-5.

48. *Ladies Library*, I, 23.

49. *Ibid.*, I, 25.

50. Reynolds, *Learned Lady in England*, pp. 291-92.

51. *Treatise on the Education of Daughters*, trans. Dibdin, pp. 189-96.

52. *Female Spectator*, xv, 183. See also xvi, 223-35. Cf. Robert Burton, *Female Excellency: or, The Ladies Glory. Illustrated In the worthy Lives and memorable Actions of Nine famous Women, who have been Renowned either for Virtue or Valour, in several Ages of the World* (London, 1728), p. 5:
Though Women from the injurious estimates of the World, have been commonly reckoned uncapable of noble Undertakings, from which God and Nature have no more excluded the Feminine than the Masculine part of Mankind, yet it will be a little hard to pronounce that they really are so, if we consider how many outward Advantages Men are allowed above them, having their Parts improved by Education, Learning, and Arts, and so seem by Industry and Husbandry to become different from what they naturally would appear; and if Women had the same Helps, I dare not say but they would make as good Returns, of which there have been many famous Instances in former Ages.

53. *Ibid.*, x, 236-37. See also xii, 341-48.

54. *Ibid.*, x, 244-46.

55. *Ibid.*, xv, 177-78. Cf. Du Boscq, *Compleat Woman*, p. 26, "Though we blame it not, yet we must confess, that Musick, History, Philosophy, and other such like exercises are more accommodate to our purpose, then those of huswivery."

56. *Ibid.*, iv, 210-11, 229-30; x, 237-39; xxi, 130-63; xxiv, 373-75. From *Vives' Instruction of a Christian Woman* of 1540 to the *Female Spectator* the study of philosophy was usually recommended by courtesy writers; for example, in the *Letter of Genteel and Moral Advice*, p. 75, "It will likewise be of very great Service towards the ripening of your Judgment, to read the Morals and Reasonings of the ancient Philosophers. . . ."

57. *Ibid.*, xv, 168. See also x, 243; xv, 166-68, 170-73; xx, 124-26. History

is another subject commonly recommended by courtesy writers as being appropriate for women; for example, in the *Ladies Library*, I, 20-21, ". . . young Ladies should be encourag'd to read the *Greek* and *Roman* Histories. . . . Neither should they be ignorant of the History of *Britain*. . . ."

58. *Ibid.*, xv, 141-58; xvii, 291-307; xix, 40-64; xxiii, 269-83. The earliest courtesy books for women are silent on the matter of "natural philosophy," except for recommendations for women to study plants and herbs of medicinal value. But the eighteenth century adviser was concerned; for example, in the *Letter of Genteel and Moral Advice*, p. 78, "If you are studiously inclin'd, there are many rational Experiments and Operations in *Natural Philosophy*, that are convenient and necessary to be known, and that will abundantly reward the Pains of the curious with Delight and Advantage."

59. *Ibid.*, x, 243-44. See also iv, 210-11; xiv, 94; xv, 169. Cf. *Ladies Library*, I, 28, 63, "All these Arts, Poetry, Musick and Painting, are proper Entertainments only for Women of Quality; not for such as the Duties of their Families, and what they owe to Heaven, would wholly enjoy," and *"Dancing* is not of itself a Fault, but all that shou'd be aim'd at in learning it, is how to move gracefully; all beyond it may be call'd excelling in a Mistake." Cf. also Astell, *Serious Proposal To the Ladies*, p. 83, "A woman may study Plays and Romances all her days, & be a great deal more knowing, but never a jot the wiser."

60. *Ibid.*, v, 323-24; vii, 44-46; xv, 158-59. Courtesy writers in general recommend a moderate indulgence in reading; for example, Du Boscq, *Compleat Woman*, p. 7, "It is not necessary then to read many bookes, but to *read* the best, and especially never to be curious of such whereby we come not to be learned without danger to become vicious."

61. *English Gentlewoman*, p. 94.

62. *Serious Proposal To the Ladies*, p. 168.

63. *Young Ladies Conduct*, p. 32.

64. *Female Spectator*, x, 193-215. See also vi, 345-46; x, 218-21. Cf. Essex, *Young Ladies Conduct*, p. 104, "As to Jealousy, it is a Passion, which above all others, is most destructive to this State of Life, and most assuredly dissolves this sacred Tye of Marriage. . . ."

65. *Ibid.*, vii, 3. See also vii, 18-29, 39-44, 50-52. Cf. Sir Thomas Elyot, *The Boke Named the Governour*, ed. Foster Watson (New York, 1907), p. 186, "The moste damnable vice and moste agayns iustice, in myne oppinion, is ingratitude, commonly called unkyndnesse." From 1531, date of publication of the *Governour*, to 1744 courtesy writers for men and women alike condemned ingratitude as a base trait.

66. *Ibid.*, xvii, 285. See also xvi, 208-23; xvii, 271-90. Cf. Halifax, "Advice to a Daughter," *Life and Letters*, ed. Foxcroft, II, 413:

I will add one advice to conclude this head, which is, that you will let every seven years make some alteration in you towards the graver side, and not be like the girls of fifty, who resolve to be always young, whatever Time with his iron teeth hath determined to the contrary. Unnatural things carry a deformity in them never to be disguised; the liveliness of youth in a riper age, looketh like a new patch upon an old gown; so that a gay matron, a cheerful old fool, may be reasonably put into the list of the tamer kind of monsters.

67. *Ibid.*, xxiii, 319-20. See also iii, 167-79; xxiv, 361-77. Cf. Essex, *Young Ladies Conduct*, p. 11: "The Moment you cherish in your Breast any immoderate or irregular Desires, as Pride, Vanity, Anger, and the like; at the same time you will feel Storms and Tempests rising in your Soul, and discomposing all your Faculties, while Modesty, Humility, and Content, will bring you into a Calm; for Peace of Mind is never to be had by gratifying our Appetites, but by obeying of our Reason."

68. *Ibid.*, xviii, 377-78. See also xviii, 323-33, 371, 378-80. Cf. Elizabeth Jocelin, *The Mothers Legacie, To her Unborne Childe* (London, 1624), p. 57, "To conclude, let thy tongue and thy heart goe together, hate dissimulation and lying, and God will loue thee, which I humbly beg of him."

69. *Ibid.*, xiii, 3. See also xiii, 4-9, 13-54, 64. Cf. Du Boscq, *Compleat Woman*, p. 41, "Curiosity often agrees not well with silence, such women as desire much to learn newes, are not resolved to silence them, and slander infallibly makes distribution of that which imprudence gathers."

70. *Ibid.*, xxi, 163. See also xxi, 163-77. Cf. Wilkes, *Letter of Genteel and Moral Advice*, pp. 48-49, "Nothing more betrays the Narrowness of the Soul, and an evil Disposition of Mind, than Tatling and Backbiting; nothing can be more destructive of Society, than those two spit-fire Vices. . . ."

71. *Ibid.*, i, 34. See also i, 34-57; v, 292-97. Cf. Wilkes, *Letter of Genteel and Moral Advice*, p. 94, "Such Sallies of short-liv'd Mirth as proceed from Farces, Operas, Masquerades, Balls, and many other Diversions, are generally of so violent a Nature, that, like a Blaze of Thorns, they suddenly consume themselves, and never fail to leave a sullen Heaviness, a Fatigue and Dejection of Spirits behind them. . . ."

72. *Ibid.*, iii, 144-49; v, 317-18; xi, 309-10; xii, 325-40; xv, 133-34; xix, 3-26. Cf. Essex, *Young Ladies Conduct*, pp. 122-23:

Avoid *Gaming*, Ladies; for it disturbs the Passions, and excites to Anger; could you see your selves in that Condition, you would hate the Cause that ruffled your Temper so far, that you are not able to bear your own Faces in the Glass; then consider what an Injury the loss of Money at Play is to a Family, that after you have given your selves up to Gaming, you must bid adieu to good Housewifry, and good Humour; and twenty to one but by exposing your self to the just Resentment of your Husband, he bids farewel to you.

73. *Ibid.*, viii, 95-104. Cf. James Bland, *An Essay in Praise of Women: or, a Looking-glass for Ladies To see their Perfections in* (London, 1733), pp. 193-94: "The *Tea-Table*, simply consider'd, is altogether harmless, and the right Managing it is a becoming Qualification for a young Lady; and as the Theory of other Domestick Virtues are enough for her tender Years, it is requisite she should be skill'd in the Practice of this."

74. *Ibid.*, viii, 104-5. Cf. Wilkes, *Letter of Genteel and Moral Advice*, p. 94: "Snuff is taken by so many Ladies of refin'd Taste and unexceptionable good Qualities, that I have nothing to offer in Prejudice of its moderate Use; but, where it is taken to Excess, its Effects are injurious to the Complexion, Voice, Stomach, and Understanding."

75. *Ibid.*, xv, 187. See also ii, 104-8; iii, 151-52; xv, 179-86; xvii, 271-84; xx, 76. Condemnation of immodesty in dress has always been a favorite subject with courtesy writers; for example, Jocelin, *Mothers Legacie*, pp. 35-36: ". . . for I giue you leaue to follow modest fashions, but not to be a beginner of fashions: nor would I haue you follow it till it be generall; so that in not doing as others doe, you might appeare more singular than wise: but in one word, this is all I desire, that you will not set your heart on such fooleries, and you shall see that this modest carriage will win you reputation and loue with the wise and vertuous sort."

76. *Ibid.*, iv, 199-234, 239-55; vi, 334-46, 383-92; xiii, 56-59; xv, 131-32. Cf. Astell, *Serious Proposal To the Ladies*, p. 153, "A devout Retirement will not only strengthen and confirm our Souls, that they be not infected by the worlds Corruptions, but likewise so purify and refine them, that they will become Antidotes to expel the Poyson in others, and spread a salutary Air round about them."

77. "Advice to a Daughter," *Life and Letters*, ed. Foxcroft, II, 389.

78. *Female Spectator*, xxiv, 344-46. See also vi, 327-29, 348-50; xi, 256-306, 313-23; xiii, 44-56; xvi, 246-47; xvii, 306-7; xviii, 376-79; xx, 77-94; xxiii, 260-69, 317-19; xxiv, 324-32, 343-44. Cf. Astell, *Serious Proposal To the Ladies*, pp. 77-78, "And thoroughly to understand Christianity as profess'd by the *Church* of *England*, will be sufficient to confirm her in the truth, tho she have not a Catalogue of those particular errors which oppose it."

79. Hyrde, *Instruction of a Christian Woman*, ed. Watson, p. 120.

80. *An Academy or Colledge: Wherein Young Ladies and Gentlewomen May at a very moderate Expence be duly instructed in the true Protestant Religion, and in all Vertuous Qualities that may adorn that Sex* (London, 1671), p. 6.

81. *Letter of Genteel and Moral Advice*, p. 49.

82. *Female Spectator*, vi, 341-48; xiv, 114-21; xvii, 299-317; xix, 32-64.

83. *Life and Letters*, ed. Foxcroft, II, 422-23.

84. *Letter of Genteel and Moral Advice*, p. 93.

85. *Female Spectator*, iv, 257-59; v, 318-23; viii, 69-95; xii, 349-58; xix, 14-17; xxi, 136.

THE PRINTING HISTORY OF THE WORLD

THE WORLD

Nos. 1-209, January 4, 1753-December 30, 1756, and one undated
World Extraordinary.

Weekly.

Folio sheet and a half.

Editor: Edward Moore.

Colophon: *"LONDON*: Printed for R. DODSLEY in Pall-Mall,
(where letters to the author are taken in) and sold by M. COOPER
at the Globe in Pater-Noster-Row."

The Printing History of the *World*

George P. Winship, Jr.

THE BIBLIOGRAPHER "is an universal Scholar, so far as the
Title-Page of all Authors. . . . He has a greater Esteem for
Aldus and *Elzevir*, than for *Virgil* and *Horace*. . . . He thinks he
gives you an Account of an Author, when he tells you the Subject
he treats of, the Name of the Editor, and the Year in which it was
printed. Or if you draw him into further Particulars, he cries up
the Goodness of the Paper, extols the Diligence of the Corrector,
and is transported with the Beauty of the Letter. This he looks
upon to be sound Learning and substantial Criticism." His name is
Tom Folio, and Addison calls him "this learned Idiot."[1]

The work of the technical bibliographer, or learned idiot, is
with a commodity that is produced and sold for profit in response
to a demand, not with an expression or an art. By relating the
activity of production to the buying habits of consumers, bibliography helps to keep literary study in contact with what actually
took place. Although it is not the foundation of substantial criticism, it waterproofs the foundation.

The first thing a bibliographer observes about the weekly issues
of the *World* is the attractive appearance: six pages, with large type
well leaded in a single column and with lavish margins.[2] The
masthead is so set as not to economize but to consume space; the
last page in many issues is nearly blank. Save for a few appeals
to charity, there are no advertisements; and there is no news. The
contrast to the more crowded *Tatler* and *Spectator* is striking.
Equally significant is the difference in format from such a paper
as Fielding's *Covent-Garden Journal*, which had appeared in 1752.
The *Journal* was of four pages, each about twice the size of one in
the *World*, printed in three columns; less than half was devoted to
Fielding's essay, the rest to news and advertisements. Any contemporary reader picking it up in a coffee-house would regard it as

a newspaper. The *World*, however, would remind him of the *Rambler*, which had completed its run less than a year before the *World* began, and the current *Adventurer*. The format was in fact regarded as "the manner of the *Rambler*," as is shown by the publisher's agreement with the editor.[3] The literary historian should bear in mind that for several decades the periodical essay had been undergoing absorption into the newspaper. Physically, the *Covent-Garden Journal* was normal in the 1750's; the *Rambler* and a few others were exceptional.[4] We may observe in these handsome pot folios an attempt to reestablish the independent essay journal. A few years later, however, "The Idler" and "The Citizen of the World" appeared in newspapers.

A typical set of the folio *World* is bound in two volumes, with four annual title pages and an index. Any such run appears to be the first edition. But comparison of even a few copies reveals that the masthead of most issues contains a vignette of a writer in his study, gazing over his shoulder at a terrestrial globe—obviously a cut especially made for this publication. Other copies of some of the same issues have in the heading several rows of printers' ornaments, or "flowers." Are all variants of the folio *World* to be regarded as belonging to the first edition, published on the date indicated in the heading?

From the examination of three sets, the biographer of Edward Moore concluded that they were. Citing the discovery that the *Tatler* was sometimes printed simultaneously on different presses because of some last-minute rush,[5] John Homer Caskey suggested that this procedure was followed week after week for the *World* and that "numbers were handed out to subscribers indiscriminately." He believed that the issues with flowers were composed from proofs of those with vignettes. The hypothesis was tenable, though surprising. "Eighteenth century printing, even of the simplest sort (a folio sheet)," remarks Caskey, "may have been a slower process than we have supposed."[6]

Examination of a larger number of runs soon suggests a different conclusion. The variant with printers' flowers is fairly common in the first six issues; none after No. 6 has come to my attention. Usually the vignettes and flowers are not mixed.[7] The Harvard and Princeton runs, with flowers in the early issues, are incomplete and not in mint condition; a few of the Harvard issues may have passed through the mails. Runs with the vignette are usually fresher in appearance. Such superficial observation easily suggests the alternative hypothesis that the flowers on Nos. 1-6 indicate the true first edition and that copies with the vignette are reprints. William B. Todd, by painstaking comparison of the texts in these variant issues with the quotation of them in contemporary magazines, has now conclusively shown this to be the case.[8]

The priority of the variants with flowers suggests that when he launched the journal Dodsley did not risk an investment in a special cut but that during the first six weeks there was evidence the venture would succeed. Confirmation is found in a letter by Moore to Joseph Warton, two days after the publication of No. 7 (with vignette): "I need not tell you how the *World* goes. I suppose you have heard from Dodsley that he prints 2500 weekly."[9] The student will ask himself whether this information contributes to the literary history of this journal. The first five issues were written by Moore himself, but No. 6 was by Horace Walpole, the first of three dozen contributors, who included Chesterfield, two other earls, Richard Owen Cambridge, Soame Jenyns, and other members and hangers-on of the world of wit and fashion. Chesterfield wrote no fewer than twenty-three essays for the *World*, and Cambridge twenty-one. It appears that the *cacoethes scribendi* was endemic among Dodsley's fashionable customers, who could indulge in journalism on the acceptable pretext of helping the needy, deserving Edward Moore. In fact, the editor had to produce only sixty-two of the whole run of two hundred and ten numbers. Bibliography confirms, so far, the impression that the success of the journal depended upon its fashionable contributors.

From this evidence one may assume a small initial printing and a single increase to 2500 when the *World* had attracted the attention of contributors and customers. It would then be necessary to print up back numbers to take care of late subscribers and possibly to provide a stock of complete runs for sale as folio volumes. Such a situation would explain the cleaner condition of most vignette copies of the early issues. But more thorough investigation reveals a fuller picture. For each of the first two numbers five variants have been identified, and for some there is evidence of date. For example, the Huntington Library copy of No. 1, for January 4, carries the heading, "THURSDAY, *January* the 11th, 1753." The flowers in the heading indicate that it was reprinted early, probably only a week late, when the compositor would automatically set the date of the current Thursday. On the other hand, the run in the Berg Collection at the New York Public Library was assembled late. In June the vignette was broken across the middle, and the grateful bibliographer hopes that no apprentice or devil was severely punished for his carelessness. For the Berg copies of Nos. 1, 2, 9, 10, 11, and 18 have the vignette in its broken state. These are clearly seen to have been reprinted as late as June, but before the following January, when the cut suffered further damage that does not appear on these issues.

Are the variants confined to the early issues? Those recorded by Dr. Todd and myself total five each for Nos. 1 and 2, three each for Nos. 3 and 4, and two each through No. 11 and in No. 18. Neither of us has found later variants, and the progressive deterioration of the cut would make later reprints fairly easy to detect. The paper accounted for so large a part of the cost of producing any publication in the eighteenth century that small reissues of a literary periodical were preferred to overprinting; and "we may surmise," says Todd, "the earlier the number, or the more favorable its reception, the more frequent the resetting."[10] Each improvement in the circulation means an additional market for back issues; if several such improvements cause reprinting, there will of course be more variants of the earlier than of the later issues.

The hypothesis of a relatively steady circulation, after an early increase by several demonstrated steps, may be compared with two statements in the paper itself. Both are in a facetious context in papers by Lord Chesterfield. In No. 49 (December 6, 1753) the eidolon Fitz-Adam complains that notwithstanding "the utility of my weekly labours . . . the ungrateful public does not take above three thousand of them a week." In No. 111 (February 13, 1755) he has "the pleasure, of finding that two thousand of my papers are circulated weekly. This number exceeds the largest that was ever printed even of the Spectators, which in no other respect do I pretend to equal." The later essay, with the smaller claim, asserts that the paper appears "pretty generally" at the breakfast table of "every well-bred family in town," after it has been taken in by the sleepy porter between ten and eleven, as well as in the "city" and in "families of an inferior class." Although Chesterfield was writing in a humorous vein, his interest in Moore's affairs was genuine.[11] He may well have made inquiries about the success of the journal, and we need not assume that he would lie.

The circulation, if these figures are taken to be accurate, early reached 2500, continued to climb to nearly 3000 by the end of the first year, and then dropped somewhat to a figure which was nonetheless regarded as saturating the *World's* natural market. A leveling off is to be expected after the novelty of a paper written by persons of fashion had been exploited. Actually a change occurred also in the authorship. Moore, who had progressively less to do, was never deserted by his eminent friends, but "unknowns" increased. Essays not assigned in the publisher's list are presumably the contributions of the general public, dropped in the box at Tully's Head in response to the invitation in the weekly colophon.[12] In the first year there were only two; in the second, seven; in the third, twelve; and in the last, twenty. These figures may be taken as at least a corroboration of what Chesterfield said about widening public acceptance.

In various ways this investigation of the printing history of the *World* illuminates literary history. It makes clear that a literary periodical was not what it was so often called, an ephemeris, but that there was an active market for back issues in the original format. Although this study is concerned with trivial textual variants and with broken equipment in a way that would have shocked Samuel Johnson—who was contemptuous of counting the streaks of a tulip—it adds detailed knowledge of how that active demand was satisfied.

Furthermore, it helps us to understand Dr. Johnson at one of his best known moments of Olympian pique. It was in the *World* that Chesterfield published the two essays on the *Dictionary* that provoked the famous letter on patronage. This letter has been frequently discussed in terms of who was more at fault. A significant point, rather, is that in a prevailingly frivolous journal Chesterfield gave generous and indeed valuable recognition to the product of years of learned drudgery. This journal had copied the distinctive format of Johnson's own *Rambler*—circulation about five hundred[13]—but had enjoyed a commercial success some five times as great. Johnson was surely close enough to the bookselling trade to be well aware of that fact. If these circumstances are borne in mind, it is easier to comprehend Johnson's outburst with full sympathy for both men.

An essay journal of this period, notwithstanding the market for folio runs, was the preliminary edition and publicity campaign for a book.[14] The plan was to end the *World* when enough essays for a saleable collection had been produced; and accordingly No. 209, for the last Thursday in 1756, is devoted to Fitz-Adam's fatal accident. On his deathbed he announces the general index to the folio volumes, to be given out gratis at the publishers'. Unfortunately, not all of the contributors were aware of the plan, and the neatness of the series is disturbed by a "World Extraordinary," a letter from Walpole that came in late but could not be refused.

The further history of the *World* covers a full century. Already, early in 1755, the issues for the years 1753 and 1754 had been reprinted in three duodecimo volumes. In 1757 the whole was reprinted in six volumes, including another reprint of the first three. There were very few corrections and changes in the text. Meanwhile Faulkner, in Dublin, had been producing a duodecimo collection of each of the four years. He also pirated the full series in six volumes, calling it the third edition.[15] Dodsley referred to his own edition of 1761 as the third, although (counting the folio) it was his fourth of the issues for 1753-54. There were in all, independent of collections of "British Essayists" (to be discussed presently), at least eight London editions of the *World*, two published in Dublin, and four in Edinburgh.[16] Most of these are neat duodecimos.[17]

> London: Dodsley, 1755, 3 v. (for the years 1753-54)
> London: Dodsley, 1757, 6 v.
> Dublin: Faulkner, 1754-57, 4 v.
> Dublin: Faulkner, 1756-57, 6 v.
> London: Dodsley, 1761, 4 v.
> London: 1763, 4 v.
> London: 1767, 4 v.
> Edinburgh: Martin and Wotherspoon, 1770, 3 v.

London: Dodsley, 1772, 4 v.

Edinburgh: Alexander Donaldson, 1774, 3 v.

London: Long and Pridden, 1774, 4 v.

Edinburgh: at the Apollo Press, by the Martins, 1776, 4 v.

(London: Dodsley, 1782, 4 v.)

London: 1789, 4 v.

Edinburgh: 1793, 4 v.

(London: 1794, 4 v.)

The *World* is now and for a long time has been most easily accessible in one or another of the collections of British Essayists, which were for some generations a part of the typical private library. The canon ordinarily included at least the *Tatler*, *Spectator*, *Guardian*, *Rambler*, *Adventurer*, *World*, *Connoisseur*, *Idler*, and *Mirror*. These collections are discouraging both to the literary historian and to the bibliographer. From the frequency with which they were put on the market the historian can tell little about the purchaser's real regard for separate essayists and even less about whether any of the essays were read. The rows of little duodecimos are "bookcase furniture" for interior decorators, and perhaps many sets were used in no other way. And, like subscription sets and other ornamental books in our own century, these collections are sometimes difficult to describe. One discovers inconsistent numbering of volumes, inconsistent dates on engraved and printed title pages, and, in the widely owned American set of 1803-4, imprints scattered from Newburyport, Massachusetts, to Petersburg and Norfolk, Virginia. I list here those that I have come upon that contain the *World*, with such other information as may contribute to the history of this phase of publishing.

Harrison's British Classicks, London: Harrison and Co., 1786 (engraved title, 1787), 8 v., 8vo. This is a cheap and crowded edition, in which the *World* is bound into one volume with Lyttelton's *Dialogues of the Dead*.

Harrison, London: J. Walker, 1793, 8vo.

Parsons's Select British Classics, London: J. Parsons, 1793-94, 36 v., 12mo. The *World* occupies four volumes in the small format usually found in independent editions. This set includes the *Citizen of the World* and other essays by Goldsmith and Shenstone's *Men and Manners*. There are several biographical introductions.

Harrison, London: 1796.

Alexander Chalmers, ed., *The British Essayists*, London: J. Johnson and others, 1802-3, 53 v., 12mo. Included are the *Lounger* and the *Observer*, as well as the basic canon, but not Goldsmith and Shenstone. The biographical and critical introductions are long and valuable.

("Davies & Morgan's Edition of Select British Classics," before 1803. This inscription is found on engravings in the *Citizen of the World* volumes in the American set next cited. I have not found Davies and Morgan, but it may be a collection of the same nature as others in this list.)

Select British Classics, Newburyport: Angier March; Philadelphia: Samuel Bradford; Philadelphia: Conrad; etc., 1803-4. This is a piracy of Parsons.

Chalmers, London: 1807-8.

Chalmers, London: Nichols and Son, 1817, 45 v., 12mo.

James Ferguson, ed., *The British Essayists*, London: G. Offer and others, 1819, 45 v. This includes, additionally, the *Lounger*, the *Observer*, Goldsmith, Vicesimus Knox, and Bacon.

Chalmers, London: C. and J. Rivington, 1823, 38 v., 12mo. By this time Chalmers had included the *Looker-On*.

Ferguson, 2nd ed., London: J. Richardson, 1823, 40 v., 12 mo.

(L. T. Berguer, ed., *The British Essayists*, 1823. Dobson refers to this as a set of forty or fifty volumes: *Eighteenth Century Essays* [New York, 1896], p. xi. William Prideaux Courtney and David Nichol Smith list it as containing the *Rambler: Bibliography of Samuel Johnson* [Oxford, 1915], p. 35.)

Jones's University Editions of Select British Classics, London: Jones and Co., 1825. This is a cheap edition, less attractive than Harrison's, and the *World* is ordinarily bound with another work.

Robert Lynam, ed., *The British Essayists*, London: J. F. Dove, 1827, 30 v., 12 mo. This includes the *Lounger*, *Observer*, Goldsmith, Knox, the *Microcosm*, and *Olla Podrida*.

Jones, 1829, advertised five "elegant volumes" to contain approximately the same material as in Lynam's collection.

Chalmers, Boston: Little, Brown and Co., 1856, 38 v., 12mo.

The last large collection of eighteenth century essayists that I have discovered is the Boston edition, printed more than a quarter century after the London booksellers had killed the goose that laid the golden egg. In these standard sets the *World* entered far more homes than in earlier forms; to speculate on how often it was read is beyond bibliography. The *World* was accepted among the English prose classics, and significant for its reputation is its long ride on the tail of Addison's kite.

If Addison himself were not sufficiently dismayed by the concern of learned idiots with the circulation, popularity, and reputation of a periodical, I should like to know how he would regard another problem. Surviving sheets of the folio *World* ordinarily have small holes punched before binding at about the middle of the outer margin. These puzzled me for some time before I noticed a possible explanation in No. 29 of the *Connoisseur*.

With what raptures [says Mr. Town, Critic and Censor-General] have I traced the progress of my fame, while I have contemplated my numbers in the public coffee-houses strung upon a file, and swelling gradually into a little volume! By the appearance which they make, when thus collected, I have often judged of the reception they have singly met with from their readers: I have considered every speck of dirt as a mark of reputation, and have assumed to myself applause from the spilling of coffee or the print of a greasy thumb.

The spike file, certainly, explains the curious little holes in the margin; but where are the coffee stains on the *World?* Some of the cleanest copies show these perforations; and in general the dirty ones seem to me to have gone through the mails, not through greasy hands. Perhaps the *World* was not so great a favorite that coffee-house patrons grabbed it before they finished their coffee and wiped their fingers. Perhaps dog-eared and greasy sets were thrown away as not worth binding. But a whole new field of literary research is here thrown open—the examination of old books for crumbs, butter, and jam on the pages, with promise of monographs upon the menu of an eighteenth century coffee-house.

Such is the learning of Tom Folio.

NOTES

1. *Tatler* No. 158.

2. The usual type page is about 4 by 9 inches, varying in length and type face according to the length of the essay. An untrimmed page is about 7¾ by 12½ inches—pot folio size. A few issues of the *World* required eight pages for essays considerably longer than the usual 1600 words.

3. Ralph Straus, *Robert Dodsley* (London, 1910), pp. 186-87.

MEMORANDUM

That it is agred this 23^d day of February 1753, between Mr. Edward Moore of Hampton Court Gent. on the one part, & Mr Robert Dodsley of Pall mall Bookseller on the other part, as follows: viz: the s^d Mr Moore doth agree to write or cause to be written a Paper call'd the *World*, containing one Sheet & a half printed in the manner of the *Rambler*, and the s^d Mr Dodsley doth agree to give the s^d Mr Moore three Guineas for each of the Papers, so long as they shall both agree to publish them under that title: and whenever the s^d Mr Moore shall chuse to discontinue them, the s^d Mr Dodsley shall be at liberty to carry them on under that Title with any other Author; and if the s^d Mr Dodsley shall chuse to discontinue them, the s^d Mr Moore shall be at liberty to carry them on with any other Bookseller. And it is further agreed by the s^d Parties, that whenever the s^d Paper shall be collected & printed in smaller Volumes, that then one Moiety of ye Property of the Copy, & of the profits arising from printing any such Editions shall be the s^d Mr Moore's, his heirs Executors Administrators or Assigns; and the other Moiety shall be the s^d Mr. Dodsley's, his Executors Administrators or Assigns. In Witness whereof we have set our hands and seal the day above written

In presence of

JOHN HINXMAN.   EDW^d MOORE.

WILLIAM RANDALL.   RDODSLEY.

4. I have no knowledge that the format in question was used before J. Payne printed the *Rambler* and the *Adventurer*. It was later used for the *Connoisseur* and a few other journals, including the political *Test* and *Con-Test*.

5. F. W. Bateson, "The *Errata* in *The Tatler*," RES, V (1929), 155-66.

6. "The Two Issues of *The World*," MLN, XLV (1930), 30.

7. Of twenty runs, ten have the vignette: those of the American Antiquarian Society, the American Philosophical Society, the British Museum (two), the University of Cincinnati, the Library of Congress, the New York Public Library (two), Yale University, and my own copy. Flowers on early issues are found in a third British Museum set, and in those of Duke, Harvard, Illinois, Princeton, the Huntington and Newberry Libraries, and Mr. Sidney F. Barham, Jr., of Roanoke, Virginia. Dr. Richmond P. Bond's copy has flowers on only the first issue.

My examination of thirteen of these sets is supplemented by information supplied by Dr. William B. Todd in "The Printing of Eighteenth-Century Periodicals: with Notes on the *Examiner* and the *World*," *Library*, 5th ser., X (1955), 53; and "The First Edition of *The World*," *Library*, 5th ser., XI (1956), 283-84.

8. "Bibliography and the Editorial Problem in the Eighteenth Century," *Studies in Bibliography*, IV (1951-52), 52-55.

9. Alexander Chalmers, *The British Essayists, with Prefaces, Historical and Biographical* (London, 1802), XXVI, xv, xlvii.

10. "The Printing of Eighteenth-Century Periodicals," p. 50.

11. Chesterfield educated Moore's son after the latter's death. See John

Homer Caskey, *The Life and Works of Edward Moore*, Yale Studies in English, LXXV (New Haven, 1927), 164.

12. The list of authors was printed in the collected editions of 1761 and later. In the weekly issues all essays appear as the work of "Fitz-Adam" or of pseudonymous correspondents, but the authorship of some essays, such as Chesterfield's, was rather widely known when they appeared. See, for example, *A Series of Letters between Mrs. Elizabeth Carter and Miss Catherine Talbot . . .* (London, 1809), II, 132, 173, 177.

13. Murphy's *Johnson*, cited by G. B. Hill, Boswell's *Life of Johnson*, ed. L. F. Powell (Oxford, 1934-50), I, 208, n. 3.

14. Compare this passage from the concluding essay in the *Adventurer*:
When this work was first planned, it was determined, that, whatever might be the success, it should not be continued as a paper, till it became unweildy as a book: for no immediate advantage would have induced the ADVENTURER to write what, like a news paper, was designed but for a day . . . the work, therefore, was limited to four volumes, and four volumes are now compleated.

15. A bookseller's catalog (Colin Richardson, London, No. 93) lists "Third Edition. Dublin, G. Faulkner, 1756, 4 vols. 12mo." This may be identical with the annual volumes, of which the Library of Congress has II, 1755, and III, 1756.

16. Except as here noted, these have been examined by Dr. Bond or myself. The 1770 Edinburgh edition is in the catalogue of the Bibliothèque Nationale. Two entries in parentheses may be "ghosts." One, a London edition of 1782 in the old British Museum catalogue, is there treated as a "duplicate" of the edition of 1772 and is apparently no longer dated 1782 at the British Museum. The London edition of 1794 is, I believe, a part of Parsons' collected set of that year.

17. Octavo editions were produced in Edinburgh, 1776 and 1793.

INDEX

Index